Close Encounters in Nine Dragons Country and Venture into the Red Dragon's Den

Eric Hague

By the same author:

Close Encounters of the Fourth Kind
New Millennium (1996)

In the Shadow of Nine Dragons
The Highway Press (1958)

Brother Juniper
The Highway Press (1957)

God at Work
in Vanity Fair
One section of *The Phoenix Rises*
Edited by Leslie Lyall (O.M.F.)

Close Encounters in Nine Dragons Country

and

Venture into the Red Dragon's Den

by

Eric Hague

NEW MILLENNIUM
292 Kennington Road, London SE11 4LD

British Library Cataloguing in Publication Data.
A catalogue record for this book is available
from the British Library.

Printed by Roadkings Ltd. Ruskin Road, Southall, Middx.
Issued by New Millennium*
ISBN 1 85845 198 1
*An imprint of The Professional Authors' & Publishers' Association

Acknowledgements

To my loving and beloved wife Greta and my closest fellow-missionary in China and elsewhere. She encouraged me to continue my account of our spiritual adventures in Communist China, and painstakingly, again took the heavy load of the final proof-reading; and what a heavy load it has been.

We also thank our three sons and their families for their encouragement in times of difficulty, lovingly allowing us the Holy Spirit's directing, when we might have spent more time with them in their homes and livelihoods, and our six grandchildren.

But above all, we dedicate this double book to Jesus the Christ, Word of God, Hound of Heaven and Saviour of mankind. Also to our Heavenly Father, who has guided and led us in all our difficulties as well as our joys.

Thank you to Miss Fan Pu, our friend in China, for the Gospel paper-cuts.

We also thank God for our many Christian friends who have encouraged us by buying these books about the Close Encounters of the Fourth Kind and urging others to do the same.

We also thank our many Chinese friends who, in spite of their problems, have written to us in the beautiful name of Jesus, to encourage us in our separations in Body but not in Spirit.

Finally we thank our Cambridge friend, David Stubbings, who taught me how to master and conquer my obstinate computer.

Part One
Contents

Part One illustrations

Page

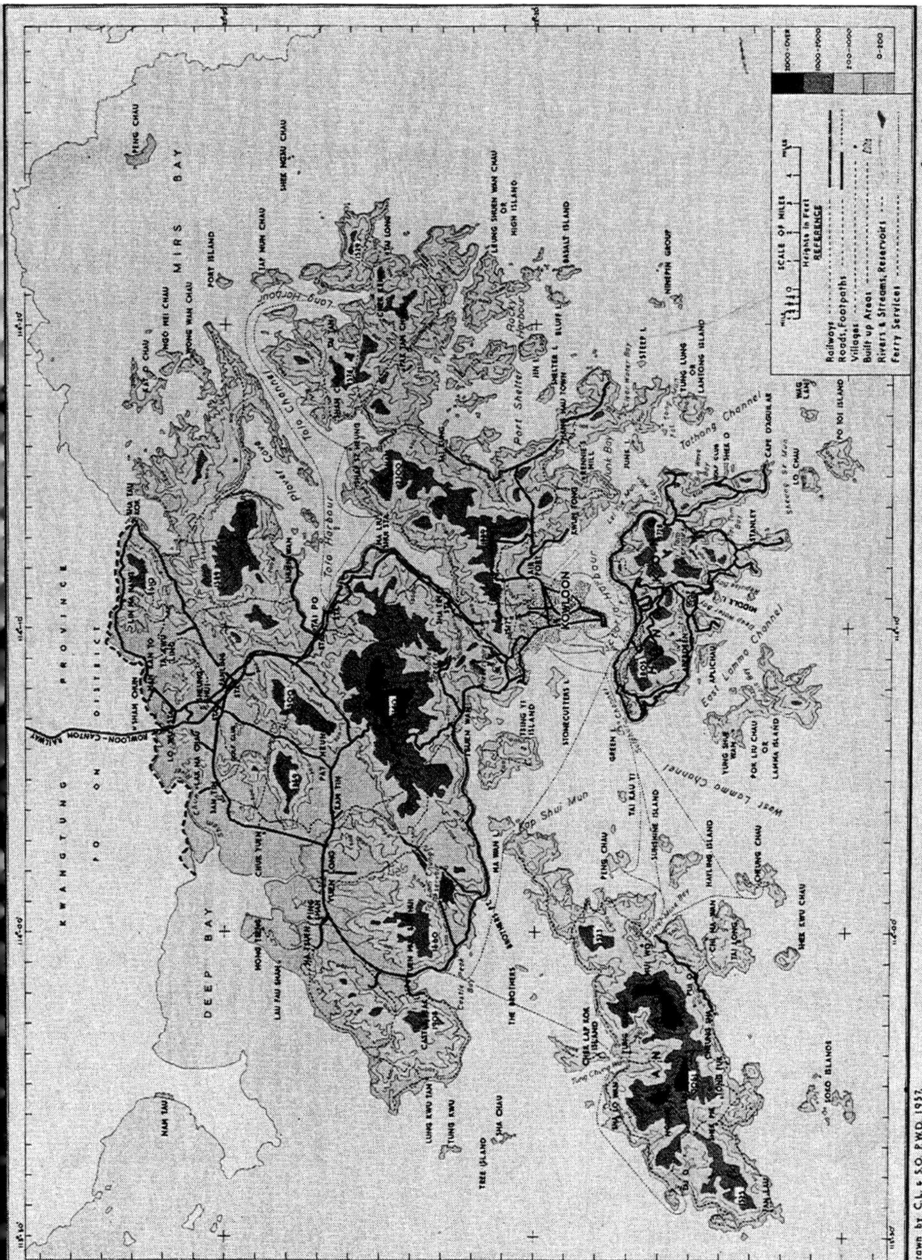
KWANGTUNG PROVINCE
PO ON DISTRICT
DEEP BAY
MIRS BAY
KOWLOON
Tolo Harbour
Port Shelter
East Lamma Channel
West Lamma Channel
KOWLOON-CANTON RAILWAY
SCALE OF MILES
Heights in Feet
REFERENCE
Railways
Roads, Footpaths
Villages
Built up Areas
Rivers & Streams, Reservoirs
Ferry Services
2000-OVER
1000-2000
200-1000
0-200
Drawn by C.L. & S.O. P.W.D. 1957.
Crown Copyright Reserved

Foreword

This book has two parts. Part 1 is entitled *Close Encounters in Nine Dragons Country* (Kowloon means 'nine dragons').

Part 2 is entitled *Venture into the Red Dragon's Den*, which is the new Chinese People's Republic, with Mao Zedong rapturously acclaimed as the Chairman when he announced: 'The Chinese People have stood up and broken the shackles of foreign nations at last'.

I was ordained in Liverpool Cathedral in 1939, as Hitler declared war on Great Britain I was three and a half years as curate of St. Cyprian's Church, Edge Lane, Liverpool. In 1943 I attended the CMS annual meeting and answered a call by the Bishop of Rangoon to offer myself for missionary service.

Six months later CMS accepted my offer and duly appointed me to the Chinese Diocese of GuangXi-Hunan and to the beautiful city of Guilin.

I sailed out in a Naval convoy via Capetown and Durban. I then crossed India by train to Calcutta, from where I flew over the Himalayas to Kunming, and then travelled by F.A.U. truck to Guilin. I arrived there on All Saints Day, November 1st. 1943.

Six months later the Japanese attacked Guilin, and the Chinese Nationalists announced a complete evacuation. Foreigners were evacuated by special train and the people by trucks and trains. Probably 100,000 refugees headed for Guiyang. The Japanese then headed for that city and the Chinese government commissioned eighty trucks for a second evacuation to Kunming, Yunnan Province. This truck convoy travelled through snow-covered mountains. Eight days later we reached Kunming to be welcomed joyously.

Most foreigners were forced to travel on to India but my English Bishop and I were granted permission to wait for any of our Christian families. I was now allowed to fly out to Chengdu, Szechwan and join some of our diocesan students at Chengdu university, where I remained until the allies dropped the atom bombs on Hiroshima and Nagasaki. The Japanese surrendered immediately and vacated China. The refugees then began to return to their distant homes. The US troops helped me to return to Guilin by plane and trucks.

When I arrived in Guilin I, as the only white foreigner, was asked to take charge of a large refugee camp. UNRRA offered financial help, food and travelling expenses, to thousands of refugees. I was also asked to help in the restoration of damaged churches, hospitals and homes damaged by the Japanese scorched earth policy. I remained there for six months until my English Bishop asked me to return to his home in Lingling, Hunan, the diocesan centre.

In due time the two Bishops called a Diocesan Conference to which all clergy and all other members came to recount the dangers they had faced in the war. It was a deeply moving spiritual experience.

At the conference I met all the delegates and amongst them our new missionary recruit. This was Dr. Greta Thompson. At once I became deeply attracted to her and, on a private walk, I said, "Greta I love you. Will you marry me?" She burst into tears and replied, "I came to China to be a missionary doctor, not to be a missionary wife!"

"May I then write to you?" I asked. She replied, hesitatingly, "Certainly. Why not?"

From that day I wrote daily and she responded likewise. In that way, over six months, we grew to know one another. The following Easter, feeling weary of incessant work, I asked the Bishop if I could have a holiday in Guilin. He agreed. I added, "I am going to Guilin to ask Greta to marry me". Surprised he replied, "You don't stand a chance!" and laughed loudly. Then added, "But send me a telegram – just one word; 'Yes' or 'No'."

The telegram said 'YES' and we were married in Hong Kong cathedral the following August. Her father and mother were due to travel to China at the time, and brought with them the wedding dress, the wedding cake and various sundries. Their ship's captain gave them permission to store things in the ship's refrigerator. It was a missionary crowded service and wedding feast, after which her parents had to catch their plane to west China, whilst we went for our honeymoon to St. Stephen's College (the Eton of the Far East) and duly returned to Guilin for our dual ministry.

One year later our first son was born and, at the same time, we received a letter from CMS HQ in London, saying that because of the growing seriousness of the China situation we MUST return to take my first and two year furlough. I also should finish off my Honours Degree in Chinese at SOAS, London University, to prepare ourselves for our second term in China, or rather in Hong Kong's British Colony, working amongst their Chinese students in the English and the Chinese universities. We eventually sailed out in 1952 for a five-year period. In 1957, to deal with our three boys' education, we duly returned to the UK.

The Bamboo Curtain was now preventing missionaries from returning, and it was not until 1982 that China reopened her doors to the outside world, and freed the Chinese Christian Church. Greta and I were led to go out to China that year. That is another story, and part 2 of this foreword.

The title of Part 2 is – *Venture into the Red Dragon's Den*, which is the present day 'Communist People's Republic of China'. This describes some startling encounters with the amazing growth of the Chinese Christian Church in spite of Communist rule.

Preface 1

Dr. Amy Wong Yi-ming
Guy's Hospital, London.
March 1994

Dr. Greta & Mr. Hague.
Oakington, Cambridge

Dear Dr. Greta and Rev. Hague,

The information I have found out about Dragons is as follows: The Dragon, to Chinese people, is considered a supernatural animal. The body of the Dragon comes from 5 different animals; the mouth is from the horse, the ears from the deer, the body from the snake, the skin from the fish, and the feet from the eagle.

Since it is from five animals, which live on land, in water or in the air, the dragon is considered a symbol of power. It is also considered lucky, but it is usually male, whereas the counterpart symbol of the female is the Phoenix.

I hope the above information will be of use to you.

I am fine and praying for God's guidance and help at all times.

I hope to come to see you as soon as I can.

Love,

Amy.

Preface 2

From another Chinese friend

It is said that, once upon a time, the Chinese Emperor visited Hong Kong, the Pearl of the Orient, and Kowloon on the mainland side of the Colony. On seeing the Dragon Mountains encircling Kowloon, near the China border, the Emperor said to his companion:

"We must call this place Eight Dragons."

"Sire" replied his companion, "The name is Nine Dragons or Joulong (Kowloon) in Chinese English."

"But where is the Ninth Dragon?" asked the Emperor.

"You, gracious Emperor, are the Ninth Dragon" replied his companion.

The smiling Emperor continued his walk in silence.

Valiant for Truth.

Dragon boat races

Part One

Close Encounters In Nine Dragons Country

The Thompson Clan

The Hague Clan

St. Andrew's Church, Kowloon

Chapter 1

Return from Communist China to Great Britain

Oh to be in England now that April's there.
Robert Browning.

After six strenuous years in China, 1943-1949, working under my Chinese name, Valiant for Truth, and having lost two stone in weight, I had to sail for England, along with my wife, Loving Virtue, and No. 1 son, Bill, aged 4 months.

Chairman Mao Zedong and his Communist armies had finally conquered China, and we were ordered home by our missionary society. I had gone out empty and returned full, with Loving Virtue, my lovely doctor wife and Bill, aged 4 months. Bill was bonny and so small that he slept in a drawer in the cabin. Four weeks voyaging to UK, strengthened us physically and spiritually. Good rich food served thrice each day, and no rationing; the stimulating tonic of sea air, the sea and sunshine, easy exercise walking the decks and swimming in the open-air swimming-pool; the genial company from the ship's Captain downwards, and the joy of our nuclear family, soon replaced those lost two stones, ere the London docks appeared in sight. The Church Missionary Society's doctor was also suitably pleased.

As we had sailed through the Red Sea, we caught sightings of grim Mount Sinai, conjuring up thoughts of Israel's ancient great leader Moses, who 3,000 years earlier had led Israel on a desert long march, greater far than Mao's.

On arrival at Tilbury docks, Greta's elder brother Dr. John Thompson met us, and drove us like a Jehu to Appledore Kent, where we were to stay with Greta's mother and father.

Doctor H. Gordon Thompson had spent 40 years in China. With his wife Amy Constance, he welcomed us with reciprocated joy. We quickly settled in to our temporary home until, two weeks later, we travelled up to London CMS Headquarters to see Canon

Max Warren and his Missionary Committee about our past and future. It was with some relief that we heard that CMS policy was now that "first-furlough" missionaries should spend their time on seeking rather to equip ourselves better for their return overseas, than in deputation work.

In my own case, having left war-torn England in 1943, my London degree studies only half-completed, I was given leave to complete my degree in the School of Oriental and African Studies to take my finals in an Honours Degree in Modern Chinese. I hoped to do this in two rather than in three years.

Having recovered our bearings well with Greta's parents, we soon journeyed north to Liverpool, taking baby Bill with us, to meet the Hague Clan, i.e. my elder brother Charles, my twin brother Stanley, and my younger sister Dorothea and their respective families. Both my mother and my father had long since died. However, Greta and the babe had also to meet my own extended church families – my home parish, St. Cuthbert's Everton and my first curacy church, St. Cyprians, Edgehill from where I had gone forth to China during World War 2.

My wife enjoyed the ordeal and, as is said these days, 'the learning experience', with her natural charm. Young Bill came to conquer while I learned a new thing or two in the process.

Some weeks later, we had to meet Greta's many relatives. Her mother had been one of seventeen children. On first acquaintance, all the men seemed to be over 6 feet in height. It was a formidable experience even for a parson missionary used to large crowds. However, they were most welcoming and considerate, especially Greta's elder doctor brother and her younger brother working for the BBC, both of whom had been born, like Greta, in China.

Before London University's term started CMS arranged for me to become a weekend curate at Christ Church, Hampstead, under Canon Nisbett Wallace. He in return provided us with an attractive town house in Well Walk, a rather "desirable residence" near the church.

Most of my time was spent in studying Chinese at SOAS and

in burning the midnight-oil. My fees, rent and living allowance were all met by CMS.

Meanwhile, Loving Virtue, my wife, was at Well Walk looking after Bill, making friends and gossiping the Gospel to good effect. Greta and I built up a Young People's Group in our large lounge on Sunday evenings. This began to interfere with my studies and I had to ask CMS to find me a church with a home attached and less intensive weekend tasks.

CMS then discovered a strong supporter living in the Blackheath area who belonged to St. James' Church, Kidbrooke. She offered us her house for the rest of our time.

I had no official duties at St. James; we simply worshipped there. The Rector, the Rev. W. Hunniford, his wife and others became close friends. I preached there occasionally for "Woe is me if I preach not the Gospel." St. Paul's *cri-de-coeur*, was also mine.

At St. James' we met a husband and wife called Pollard. He was a former Navy man. During the War he had gone down with his ship on three occasions and survived, and became a Christian of simple and strong faith. He often came to help us in the house where his wife was of infinite help to Greta. With Greta now expecting our second child in Woolwich Mothers and Babies Hospital, Mrs. Pollard looked after house and Bill, until he was taken to Granny and Grandpa Thompson in Appledore, Kent.

I attended the University most days. My younger fellow students, a lively and somewhat ungodly crew, were part of the post-war generation intake. I was fair game for shocking tactics but as I refused to be shocked, they would occasionally discuss Jesus and Christianity. In the Final Degree examinations we had nine papers including an essay in written Chinese. Of these, I chose three subjects and prepared essays on them. For the final paper I was literally exhausted. However, I eventually scored an Upper 2nd, which pleased me, Greta and the CMS.

In my time at SOAS, a curious matter arose. Many of our students were young military or diplomatic personnel, with a future as interpreters or diplomats. They were inquisitively suspicious about Chinese nationals on the staff. The students gently probed me from time to time as to conditions in China and the possibility of crypto-communists on the staff. One such was a charming, courteous lecturer about whom these students quizzed me. Evidently I was quoted to the English faculty staff and one of them quizzed me in return. I was not amused and decided in future to keep my musings to myself. Some people in England were still suspicious about spies, even years after the end of World War II, and sometimes with reason.

In the meantime, No 2. Son, John Gordon, was born, "Gordon" after his esteemed grandfather. Later, we realised that he may have inherited a gene from his Scottish ancestry on his mother's side, and eventually became proud possessor of a Gordon Tartan kilt! His birth was a difficult one for Greta. She had become anaemic and entered Woolwich Hospital. It was not quite in sound of Bow Bells!

Once my degree result was announced, Greta and I made haste to return East. China was now defended by the Bamboo Curtain and impossible to enter. It remained so for almost 30 years. Return to China being out of the question, CMS suggested we go to Hong Kong to work amongst students at Hong Kong's English University and at Chung Ji College, later to become Hong Kong's Chinese University. However, the Lord had other plans for us. They concerned St. Andrew's English Speaking Church set in a lovely compound in Kowloon, or Nine Dragon's Country, on the peninsular side of the Colony.

Chapter 2

Return to Hong Kong, Nine Dragon's Country

If you approach Hong Kong from the sea, you will sail through a narrow channel between the Island on the South and the Mainland on the North, thus coming into the great harbour from which the island-colony gets its name. For Hong Kong (pronounced in Cantonese 'Heung Gong') means Fragrant Harbour. If you approach from the Mainland, from Communist China, you would find yourself crossing a great line of hills from which the narrow peninsula, reaching South to meet the Island, gets its name Kowloon. For Kowloon (pronounced in Cantonese Gow Long) means "Nine Dragons".

It was in the shadow of these Nine Dragons that these stories took place. Beyond those Dragons lies Communist China, perhaps even more of a mystery than the old Imperialist China with its 3,000/4,000 years of recorded history. From Communist China since its liberation in 1949, had fled nearly one and a half million Chinese people, men, women and children. They came from all classes of the community – there are professors, teachers, doctors, students, merchants, engineers, farmers, peasants, artisans, Government officials, artists, musicians – in fact, people of every profession and occupation.

They came into this free British Colony comprising an island two miles long and averaging three miles wide (about the size of the Isle of Wight); and 'New Territories' stretching for twenty miles to the Chinese border. Numerous other islands, some centres of the fishing industry, others merely barren, are included in the Colony's area. However, these million and a half refugees came mostly to live within the precincts of the twin cities of Victoria (more commonly called Hong Kong) on the island side and Kowloon, facing it on the peninsular side. They helped to swell the population of these twin cities to over two and a half million people of whom ninety-nine per cent were Chinese.

Such is the Colony of Hong Kong today, so vastly different

from that Pearl of the Orient which was the Hong Kong of yesterday. With the political changes in China and the flood of refugees, its social structure has been radically altered and its economic life has been changed beyond recognition. Trade with Communist China had dwindled to a mere trickle, so that to support its greatly swollen population, the development of local industries in Hong Kong became an urgent necessity. Old residents would scarcely recognise their former home.

It is easy to imagine the problems that such a tremendous influx of people into a city, normally the size of Liverpool, brought in its train. Where are they all to live? Where are there to be found houses and schools? Where will they find work and so, money to live? What about food supplies, hospitals and medicines for the sick?

In 1956 alone, in the Colony 77,500 babies were born and lived. Another 56,000 refugees from the Mainland also found their way over the border. The following year still more, and the birth rate figure was even higher.

Of the first-comers, many brought money and experience, and soon managed to integrate themselves and their families into the life of the Colony. At least 650,000 of them remained true "refugees", living on or below starvation level. Some 350,000 earned, as families, from 2s.6d to 1s.6d a day only. The other 300,000 existed by begging or by help from numerous Refugee Relief Associations, sponsored by Government and Christian and private groups.

The tragedy of the situation lay in this: no other country, be it Burma, Siam, Indonesia, Vietnam, Australia or the US would receive these refugees into their countries. Even Taiwan (Formosa) took only about 150,000. For the vast majority, Hong Kong was the end of the line, the point of no return. Most of them remained for seven or eight years – years of frustration if also years of freedom. They lived on street pavements, and rooftops, on staircases and tenements, in bedspaces or rooms of 12 feet by 10 feet for a family of five people (a child counted as half a person). Forty to eighty people shared one tap and one lavatory, and the water was often turned on for only three to four and a half-hours daily. Thousands lived in shacks made of bamboo or slats of wood and oiled paper, cheek by jowl on rocky, precipitous hillsides within the City, endangered by fire and flood. On various occasions, shantytown fires destroyed areas of 65,000, 25,000 and 15,000 people. Heavy rain (15 inches in one day; 28 in three days; 60 inches in one week) literally washed 10,000 people out of their homes. Fires devastate but floods last longer.

Government began, and continued to build six and seven storey tenement blocks to accommodate the victims. The blocks were built in H-formations. The bar of the H was where the lavatories and wash places were placed. The rest of the buildings were rooms. Five adults shared one room. Thirteen of these blocks were built on one squatter village fire-site; 25,000 people lived in them.

It is not difficult to believe that Hong Kong had the worst slums in the world, The incidence of TB alone (apart from other epidemic diseases) was 95 per cent of the whole population over twelve years of age, according to a reliable source.

No wonder George Bernard Shaw, looking down upon the wonders of Hong Kong at night, ringed about with a thousand diamond necklaces of brilliant light, is said to have remarked "It is the first time I have seen an illuminated cemetery!"

The sketches in this book are true stories of real people I have known and loved for Christ's sake, who "Going through the vale of misery, used it for a well" and others who belong to the other section of the population whose lot, like ours was cast in pleasant places. All of them are loved of God. All of them He seeks. For all of them, rich and poor, high or low, Christ died.

The minority Church in Hong Kong had to work and witness in these terribly difficult circumstances; in season and out of season, in the exhausting heat of summer, and the dusty months of autumn, and early winter, in rain and cold. That Church was some 40,000 strong, including all denominations, and was constantly helped by the Government and secular organisations.

At that time, in Communist China, there were over six hundred million other Chinese, and today, many, many more, indeed one fourth of the total world population, and amongst them now are sixty million Chinese Christians. What a task force!

Chapter 3

Inside News from the Chinese Peoples Republic: Behind the Bamboo Curtain, June 1957

Dear Percy, Brother in Jesus,

Thanks for your letter. I am glad you met Bishop Ding and that you were able to get a photo of all the 17 Bishops.

As to my family, we are very well. Although, I had another attack of lung trouble yet I am quite strong again. Our children are grown up. All three daughters are married. S has two girls, but John is at home at present for he is not very strong, and Sammy is doing well in college in Beijing.

Our Diocesan Headquarters moved to beautiful Guilin last December, for LL is small, away from the railway and not so good for the development of our work, as our new site is where we are now living.

I am sorry not to be able to reply earlier, because I have been busy attending conferences and visiting all the parishes. I have just come back after visiting HY, LL, DZ, NY and YM. There are motor roads to all these places now. I travel with pleasure on buses, three hours on the bus from LL to DZ instead of three days. New roads and new houses are being built everywhere. What a great change and a wonderful improvement!

Before going to H province, I also visited all the GX parishes. I travelled by bus from GZ to KY. During my last two visits, 29 people were confirmed in G province and 15 in H province. Our Christians are very happy at work and as earnest as before. Our Sunday services and Prayer Meetings are getting on nicely. In GL we also have a Sunday School for children. Every Saturday evening we have Gospel Hall preaching in St. John's Church. Christians are taking an active part in all Church activities. Thank God for the good opportunity!

All the clergy are doing good work with me in the Diocese, but the Rev. Lu passed away with illness. We have just had our

Diocesan Standing Committee to discuss and plan our work for this year. One of our catechists, Mr. Ong, is at Nanking Theological School, Bishop Ding's school, taking theological training. He will finish his course next summer, and will come back to work in DJ. Last spring, we sent two of our workers to Nanjing Theological School for a short refresher course. When they come back we hope to send another two next Autumn. Nanjing Theological School is a great training centre for church workers.

Our Christians are working in various departments, scattered all over the place. John T. and Jao HP are teaching in school. Miss T. our Bible Woman is married; Hong JY, my late cook, is working in a hospital. Chen GX is doing medical work with her husband. Wei XY is still working in the diocese, but no news of Dzeng SY or Wang YW!

I am sorry to hear that you had an attack of Polio and that your wife is not very strong. May God give you a speedy recovery and keep you in good health. What sad news about Juliet! Please give my deep sympathy to Nellie.

I am pleased to hear that Mrs. Holden keeps well and that Douglas and family are well. Please give our greetings to them.

My wife and self are well.

With best wishes,

Yours sincerely,

Addison X.

Red Light
A Chinese Bishop writes from China

> Master Tseng said, *"The true Knight of the Way must perforce be both broad shouldered and stout of heart. His burden is heavy and he has far to go. For Goodness is the burden he has taken upon himself; and must we not grant that it is a heavy one to bear! Only with death does his journey end; then must we not grant that he has far to go?"*
>
> (The Analects of Confucius – WALEY)

Dear Percy, Brother in Jesus,

Will you please pass on our message to friends in England?

When they ask what China needs, please tell them that what China needs is Christ. Whatever is going on at present in China is only transitory. We want a strong peaceful country but we can only have peace through Christ. Christ is above all nations and political parties, so the Church in China in this time of trial will only stand for the Truth. If the Church should suffer misunderstanding or persecution, we shall only say "Yea, yea: Nay, nay" to bear witness for Christ.

Pray that God will give us the Spirit of power, love and self-control. We know that all things are working together for good to them that love God. Let us go forward with St. Paul's words:

"Preach the Word, be instant in season and out of season". Preach! Preach! Is the watchword for our work.

We want your sympathy, your help and your love, but above all, your prayers, so that we can stand firm in time of trial, and be worthy to suffer shame for His name. However, we are a very small minority among the big masses of people in China. China wants Christ. The only way to present Christ is through His Church, and through His keen followers.

With love from every one of the Family,

Yours ever,

Addison X.

Chapter 4

Padre Ogilvie Meets the Hague Family

When the Japanese armed forces were defeated by China and the Allies, they left Hong Kong in 1946/47. Hong Kong was liberated by the British fleet. Bishop R. O. Hall of Hong Kong, on a happy inspiration and lacking other candidates, offered the Living of St. Andrew's Church, Kowloon (or Nine Dragons) to a Scottish Naval Chaplain, the Rev. John Ogilvie, who had come in with the British Fleet. After agreeing to receive Episcopal ordination in addition to his Presbyterian orders, John duly became Vicar of St. Andrew's.

John Ogilvie was a near elderly, cheerful bachelor and soon won the love and affection of the church members. With his naval background and Scottish ancestry, he attracted people also by the name of the patron saint of the Scottish Church. These people came to see and stopped to pray. Others who were English speaking Christians, including Westerners, Chinese and Eurasians came to thank God for victory, liberation and peace.

So, a multi-racial, multi-cultured congregation was formed and grew. After his war service and then four years as Vicar of St. Andrew's Church, Padre John, as he was always affectionately called, began to have thoughts of home and a time of furlough. Good Bishop Hall acquiesced and, with his usual perspicacity, and having learned about the coming of the Rev. Eric Hague and family to the Colony, asked CMS for the loan of this young man for nine months to make John Ogilvie's furlough possible, and it was so!

Thus, my wife and I and our two children, found a ready-made home and an immediate task awaiting us. It seemed to be the Lord's doing and marvellous in our eyes. St. Andrew's Church and Vicarage were already familiar to my wife. As a child, she had spent a holiday there with her parents and siblings. Her maternal uncle, the Rev. G.R. Lindsay had been vicar there about 1925. The children of both families had played together in the lovely garden, and enjoyed the spacious rooms with wide verandas with which the house was blessed.

Thus, my wife Loving Virtue and I, Valiant for Truth, with our two sons, Bill and John, aged 3 years and one year, set out from Southampton on Friday, September 19th 1952. We were passengers on the P&O liner "Carthage", bound for Hong Kong, sailing via the Suez Canal. We arrived at our destination after 30 days on the 19/20th October 1952.

Our voyage out had not been quite the holiday we expected, Bill and John being hyperactive and constantly on the go with excitement. The ship provided a good nursery for short day periods but John took a long time to get used to it. The liner's nurse was splendid but our two boys met older children and learned some rough ways, which they had to unlearn. The weather also grew rough. After Bombay, the ship was tossed by the tail winds of two typhoons.

According to English custom, Sunday worship was taken by the Captain. Amongst the passengers, however, was a friendly Malaysian Chinese Pastor and he and I were asked to celebrate Holy Communion at 7.15am on Sundays. We also arranged an afternoon Sunday School for the many children aboard.

Since a large crowd of returning missionaries and other Christians were travelling, various joint meetings for prayer and Bible Study were arranged. The Word of God was precious in those days. Some 80 people regularly attended. We also listened to an Indian and Malaysian, both delegates at a recent International German Missionary Conference, at Willagen.

One afternoon, the Captain invited the Hague's to tea but he professed to be afraid of Bill whom we had to leave in the Nursery!

The ship docked at a Kowloon berth and we found our way to St. Andrew's Vicarage and were welcomed by Padre Ogilvie. The church grounds had a playing area, a sandpit, and a tennis court and some fine climbing trees, which delighted the boys. The Church Hall had a flourishing kindergarten school which Bill and John invaded. They enjoyed the lessons as well as the school's slippery-bob and seesaw. John was now beginning to talk and he and Bill loved to sing songs and have shouting matches each morning before rising.

It was the end of January before Vicar John left on his nine months' furlough. He left behind him in the Vicarage a young married couple named Savage. He was Navy and played the organ at Evensong. At the end of January they also went on leave. They had become interested in the continual stream of Chinese refugees who began to come to the vicarage to see us. We were interested that he had built an electric organ, even better than the Church's. He had it 'cased' and sent home to England. Unfortunately, after arriving there safely, a British docker dropped it off a truck and it was irreparably damaged.

Sunday was a busy day. At 8am, 30-40 people attended Holy Communion. At 9.30am, a Forces Service for families was taken by the Army Padre, and attracted 200 or so. At 10am the Sunday School met in the hall, Greta helping 9 teachers with the 90 children, including Bill. At Easter, we held our first Prize Giving, to which many parents came and Bill received a prize, to his great joy. I gave the talk and asked what the children had to thank God for. Bill jumped up and shouted "Eggs"; a photographer took a photo and this appeared in the local newspaper the next day, much to Bill's satisfaction.

At 11am Morning Prayer, some 400 attended, filling the church. This included Boarders from the nearby Diocesan Girl's School in their attractive school uniform, blue edged white dresses. Evening Prayer at 6.30pm brought 50 or more people most of whom came to the Vicarage afterwards for tea and biscuits and a 'sit down'. This was greatly appreciated, especially by the service men.

There was no active Youth Fellowship as yet, but 26 young people, confirmed recently, agreed to re-start the Group. Our Navy organist and wife helped us to run the Social Club three times a week. This did a good spiritual work for a great number of Choir attended very faithfully. The 'acting Vicar' greatly enjoyed the Scottish Dancing.

On 30th November, St. Andrew's Day, we held a Confirmation Service and Day of Prayer. It was also a Gift Day and HK£2,000 (£160) was given. At an earlier Garden Party, Mongolian Dancing and a Chinese Ming Period play aroused great interest, and a further sum of $2,000 received.

Greta, apart from caring for our two boys, was now Enrolling Member of the Mothers' Union, and supported the Women's Guild.

Once a week she helped at a Nightly Medical Clinic in St. Thomas' Nissen-hut Cantonese Church in the centre of Kowloon's Refugee area, spending 2/3 hours doctoring the poor, 300-400 a time. Ten other doctors formed the Clinic Team, all giving their services free.

At the Bishop's request, I now taught 2 hours a week in Chung-Ji College. My subject was 'The Life and Teaching of Jesus'. Another task was being a manager at a Workers School, helping the Labour Unions to start such schools because Government schools were too expensive for workers' children. These were solely for Chinese children and were reputed to be Communist! This was one of the good Bishop's dream children, and I became Comrade Hague.

Of the one and a half million refugees from the Mainland many came to see us seeking help. One camp outside Kowloon held 11,000. We visited the camp and met refugees from our former stamping grounds in China but none could give us any hard news. None were Christians. All feared to return or even write home. A Guilin woman had been there 2 years and reported a rumour that our Guilin Church had been burned down, but was being repaired. Another from Tan Shia Xu near Guilin also had no news. A former Christian teacher and university graduate became a friend. We found him sleeping on the 5th floor staircase of a block of flats, and very ill with asthma. He was wrapped in a bedding roll and had not eaten for two days. He had no job and no money. We helped him medically and to find a job.

Outside the Church's fellowship generally, we soon became aware of the problems facing fellow Europeans and the serious cleavage between East and West. Westerners sometimes showed to ill advantage. At holiday and festival times, certain Armed Forces personnel, unrestrained by forgotten conventions of homeland, just indulged in drinking liquor and spirits to the embarrassment, nervousness and scorn of the local people. Christian servicemen loathed these holiday times and found places of refuge in the churches from the destructive behaviour of their fellows and from temptation.

Wives of servicemen had their own special temptations. Many had to live in 2 rooms in a crowded apartment house with noisy neighbours on either side, above and beneath them. Without a 'home' to look after, little or no work to do, since amahs minded, cared for, fed and took any children to school, these wives faced a life of complete boredom. Many could not bear it and, after a few months, chose to be parted from their husbands and return home even at some personal expense. Others filled their time with Beetle Drives, cocktail parties, whist drives, bridge and so on. Many wives found themselves in a completely different social position from that at home. There, housewives worked hard, but here, they were ladies of leisure. Cynicism, snobbishment, unnatural manners, drunkenness, marriage quarrels and unfaithfulness were not unknown. Add to this the enervating climate, an unbearably hot damp summer, and these human powder kegs were ready to explode. We felt deep pity for wives and husbands alike. To crown all, they faced the false, competitive social values of the circles in which they chose, or were forced, to move.

We could only thank God for the hard-worked Service Chaplains and local English speaking churches for padre's Hours, church working parties, clubs and study circles, all attracting the hearts and lives of these service personnel and families. The regular clergy invited many of these folk to their homes, and showed them kindness, friendship and moral and spiritual example. The needs of many others remained unmet, however, and this almost broke one's heart, and the Divine agony was beyond our imagination.

At St. Andrew's church, another aspect was both interesting and rewarding – the work amongst the youth, at first spasmodic, quickly developed under some young men with decided powers of leadership. They were former YPF members, especially Bruce Chan and Nelson Young. They were earnest and sincere Christians who, backed up by others, recreated the life of the earlier Group. An increasing number of Europeans, Eurasians and Chinese became members.

St. Andrew's Church Junior Youth Fellowship

St. Andrew's Church Senior Youth Fellowship

Chapter 5

The Communist Dragon and Solitary Confinement

One day we invited Mr. Olin Stockwell to the Vicarage. Both Greta and I had met him, separately, during our times in Chengdu, Sichuan, China, when we lived at the home of Douglas and Imogen Sargent. Douglas was an older CMS missionary and his wife Imogen was the daughter of the American Methodist Bishop, Ralph Wood. Olin Stockwell belonged to the same mission as the Bishop.

After the Great Helmsman, Mao Zedong and the Communists took over China in 1949/50, Greta and I were ordered home on furlough. Olin Stockwell was one of those missionaries who were arrested and sentenced by the Communists to solitary confinement and its accompanying brainwashing techniques, euphemistically called 're-education'. After 18 months incarceration, Stockwell was released and allowed to go to Hong Kong. Here he was interviewed by the Morning Post Reporter, and their guarded account shocked the local Christians and Hong Kong citizens, and later the American Press and Church authorities.

We invited, along with Olin, a Mr. Dart, to meet in the Vicarage for discussions, and duly informed Bishop Ward, who was in Hong Kong at the time, and the Sargents. Bishop Ward was deeply disturbed by the newspaper report and felt that Mr. Stockwell had betrayed the Christian missionary cause. At the same time, Olin seemed extremely proud and even boastful of what he described as "Out-doing the Communists".

His story was disturbing, somewhat inexplicable, and perhaps a psychological twist or of Satanic influence. Perhaps only those who have had to endure such suffering themselves have a right to judge. It also made us think more charitably of others, not least our Chinese friends who had been driven to make confessions and accusations against Christian colleagues and others, whether Chinese or foreigners – accusations which were built around grains of truth, isolated incidents and quirks of character in their missionary or national friends. But who had ever heard before, as in Olin's case, of the Holy Spirit leading a believer to tell a whole string of fabrications?

Olin told us, at one time during interrogation, his nerve gave way. He felt sick of the whole matter and confessed to one of the Chinese judges that his confessions were all untrue. The Communist judge-interrogator refused to believe him and came back to say that they would not allow him to retract anything already confessed. Olin then said that he recovered his nerve and carried on.

Greta and I wondered if he had unconsciously absorbed some Communist beliefs, e.g. 'To do evil that good may come'? Perhaps he had become aware that the Communists really sought converts to their faith, more than to punish spies and traitors, although their affirmation that "There are no good landlords, and no good Nationalists", illustrated the latter.

Olin's solitary confinement lasted 14 months. He had been arrested after a house searching, he said. Certain letters were found in his name that he said were forgeries, written by a church worker with a grudge against Olin. Later, however, Olin confessed that he had indeed written the letters, and added, "All missionary societies had information services." After having ensured that his wife and another Mission friend had left China, Olin also volunteered that this friend and he had worked out a code and had sent coded letters to US Senators and to another fictitious person in Hong Kong.

At a private trial before a Judge and 3 others, Olin described how he was constantly questioned but that the aim of the Communists seemed mostly in getting him to change his thinking.

In the book *Wild Swans* by Jung Chang, the author writes: "True communists will say 'The Revolution is not won, the War is still going on. If we break the rules, we should admit mistakes. A revolution needs steel-like discipline. You have to obey the Party even if you do not understand it or agree with it."

Olin then described how, as he stood before his judges, he suddenly heard an inner voice say, "Say this". He then began a fictitious confession because they would not hear the truth, and the words of Jesus came to him, "Cast not your pearls before swine", and again the words of Jesus, "It will be given you in that hour what you will say."

Concerning his fabrications and his conscience, Olin said he did not think about it. His was not a public trial but a private one before a judge and two or three others. He felt he was guided by the Spirit to tell these fictions. He did not understand it himself and he showed no signs of a disturbed conscience regarding his "confessions" He was not concerned, he added, with politics at all, but only with the evangelistic and religious aspects, and of how it might help others. This he would discuss with his authorities in USA.

One incident helped to convince the Communists of his sincerity. When the Communists first arrived, his wife told Olin that the servants told her there was a rifle hidden in the attic. Olin found it and suspected that it was possibly left by some American friend. Wrapping it up in red paper, he himself now hid it in a disused air-raid shelter, where damp would rust it away and where no one would ever go. Later, in prison, he told his captors where to find it and that he had hidden it because of fear of what the Government would do.

During the first 9 months of this solitary confinement, he felt, as never before previously, the sustaining presence of the grace of God. He had often preached about this but now knew it as a real experience. To encourage himself he resorted to singing hymns. Suddenly a command came to his mind, "Compose some yourself!" Never having written poetry before, he felt he could not. However, another command came, "Try!" Eventually a real poetic form took shape in his mind and resulted in religious poetry about reliance upon God and awareness of Christ. He composed in all 129 poems, memorising them all by means of a rhymed table of their titles. On arrival in Hong Kong, he had committed them all to paper.

In prison, he continued, the authorities allowed him a New Testament. He began a systematic study of its contents and found that the Gospels of Matthew, Mark and Luke, together with Paul's epistles, spoke to him forcefully. St. John's Gospel, however, was different, arousing no echo in him. Suddenly he realised that "John" was not a history but a dramatic version of Christ's life for teaching purposes. He then produced a version in parallel columns, of the teaching of John's Gospel and the historical facts of the Synoptists. He was now considering publishing them.

His wife also sent him a book of poems, with wide margins, in which he wrote the events of his life and what led up to them. He would sit with his back to the door, so that the guards would think he was writing more poetry, or studying his New Testament. When he was transferred to Prison 2, the guards put all his books in a bag without looking at them. He thought he must be the first imprisoned Christian since John Bunyan to do so.

His second prison was a re-indoctrination centre. For nine months he shared it with seven Chinese. They were given regular talks, and books to read, on Marxist Leninism. Apart from these and newspapers, they had no other reading. Regarding newspapers, they were not allowed merely to read them but, in talking about them, they had to keep the newspaper's editorial line. There was no freedom of thought. The only freedom was what capitalistic countries gave the workers – freedom to starve. His opinions about China were coloured by this practice. Even when escorted out of China by train later, Olin's two guards ensured he did not talk to anyone. He believed the Chinese hated Communism but preferred it to the Guomindang. They with Olin, recognised that the Communists had benefitted the nation, especially the peasants, by abolishing inflation, reducing prices, giving a stable currency, getting rid of rich landlords and putting down bandits.

His food was adequate but poor, the same as that which peasants received – rice, one vegetable and occasionally bits of meat. His imprisonment involved no physical manhandling, but the usual lectures and constant questioning were very wearying. The Communists were absolutely intolerant and would never let him say he came to China to preach the Gospel to help the people, for "he was intelligent and knew religion was only superstition". "He had come as an agent of imperialism and had taught the Chinese to accept and be subservient to it. He must acknowledge this and must not mention Christianity in the same breath as Communism. Only Communist logic and way of thinking were right." He was reproved for any Christian thinking or philosophy.

Realising eventually, that Communists could or would not accept any other viewpoint, he was willing to talk in their terms, otherwise he would not be allowed to go free. His greatest craving was for Freedom. Other bodily hungers and instincts completely faded away.

In the second prison, the inmates had no furniture except their bedrolls laid on the floor. At communist meals they had to listen to lectures twice a week and hold mutual criticism sessions, criticising each other as severely as possible regarding anti-Communist ideas. Listening guards would suddenly rush in and shout, "You cannot say that about the Government" and force them to retract their words and apologise. Once he was asked, "Do you pray?" "Yes, night and morning" he replied. He was then officially told, "No praying is allowed in this prison!" Another prisoner was asked, "Do you study (Buddhist) Scriptures?" He was ordered, "No Scripture reading in prison". This was to a high-ranking Buddhist general, a deeply religious man. He and Olin were left alone for a few moments. Olin asked "Do you still pray? Do you still study the Scriptures?" The General replied, "If we did not have religion, life would not be worth living." This man had lost his only son in an air-crash.

Only when Olin was ready to make confession of sins in Communist terms, did he see any hope of release. Realising this, he made such a confession. He was then ordered to write a condemnation of American life; and wrote a statement condemning all that he saw as wrong and felt ashamed of, but including things of which he personally approved.

Whilst awaiting his release, Olin and others had to give their impression of China. To make it more interesting or different, he began by saying he came out to China as a church worker to help the Chinese people. He was immediately reproved. They said, "You have not really benefited from your prison course, your thinking has not changed." The senior prison warder then lectured him for half an hour. Olin had nearly prevented his own release.

All this time, Olin had no contact with Christians. Only one other prisoner seemed to be a Christian, one who sang Christian hymns. He did, however, discover his former young Chinese secretary had been imprisoned in the prison below him. This man sent him a note mentioning the departure of Olin's wife and his friend "S" from China to safety. Although it was dangerous, the young man later sent Olin a Christmas card.

Olin believed he was not the only foreigner to undergo this prison indoctrination. He also believed that only he had brought out a written record (in his poetry book), which would be listened to with hostility in the USA, where Communism was as bitterly hated as Capitalism was hated by Chinese communists.

The missionary zeal of the communists was apparent. Even his two guards on the train to freedom, took him aside independently, to urge him to be a good Communist back home, since this was the world's only hope. The Party also told him they were surprised how quickly he had learned their teaching, saying, "No other foreigner has done this so well!"

Finally, Olin showed us specimens of his written poetry, viz:

To Him

To Him who gave his all for me,
I would not ungrateful be,
But turn and thank on bended knee
The One who cleansed my leprosy.

To Him who spoke His piercing word
And cleansed my soul as with a sword,
For Him I spill the precious nard
Anointing the feet of my dear Lord.

To Him whom I have oft betrayed
Adding to the debt He paid,
In sorrow and in thanks arrayed,
Before my King all life be layed.

To Him who cleanses hate and pride
And ever keeps me by His side,
To Him I open life's gate wide
That He may enter and abide.

The Magi

The Magi who followed the distant gleam
Of Bethlehem's guiding Star,
Did not have the dream;
It led to lands afar.

The Kings who brought their presents to give
To a Babe in a manger stall,
Express the love whereby men live
Who offer to Him their all.

Wise men who returned a secret way
Thwarting an evil King,
Were but the first of many today
Who risk their lives for Him.

Olin Stockwell was a strange character. As we listened to his testimony, I could not help comparing the tone of his voice to the plucking of a highly pitched violin string. Was he a man of God or a man deceived by Satan? There were many in Hong Kong and in the USA ready to defend either answer. Who knows who was right? I suppose only God alone, in his infinite love and mercy.

After some time in USA, answering his church's juries and still believing that the Holy Spirit had told him to lie to the Communists, Olin eventually returned to the Far East and we heard of him once again – as a missionary-ambassador for Christ his Lord in Malaysia.

About the same time, another Western missionary was released after 18 months solitary incarceration. Her name I have forgotten but she was, I think, a 'dour Scotswoman' with typical firmness of character, love of truth and loyal faith in God. She told her story at a public meeting. Do what they might, the Chinese Communists were unable to break her indomitable spirit. She bore without flinching all attempts to indoctrinate her. In due time, the Communists gave up the struggle and she was allowed to leave China and to proceed to Hong Kong and freedom.

We met yet another person who had been given 'solitary'. He came to our Sunday Evening Fellowship in St. Andrew's, and demonstrated the size of his cell by walking silently across our Drawing Room carpet: six slow strides, forward and back, forward and back, forward and back, forward and back, again and again. We all watched silently, deeply moved.

"The Saviour of the world is born"

Chapter 6

Multi-racial Church in Over-crowded British Colony

My wife, Greta or Loving Virtue, to give her Chinese name, soon discovered a new problem – our boys' education. Was it unfair for European children to take up precious places in Chinese schools or those for Eurasian children? Therefore, from 5 years up, the Hong Kong Government European schools seemed the only possibility. For No. 1 son, Bill's age group, there were two such schools when we lived on Kowloon side, and later, when we moved over to Victoria Island, we chose to send him to a school on the Peak. Our petrol consumption nearly doubled, even with a rota of families who took it in turn to "take up and fetch down" seven young rascals.

No.2 son, John, had to attend a kindergarten school on Robinson Road which was a long way from the nearest bus stop, so a second group of "takers and fetchers" was formed. We both seemed to spend our time acting as chauffeurs. We even envisaged later, when air-travel became cheaper and safer, allowing our two sons to attend an English Public School as weekly boarders and to return to the Colony for weekends!!

This became a particularly sad time also. Dean Temple's son, aged 5, died during an operation. A Methodist Parson friend and his wife had the tragedy of a second baby son in succession dying within two days of birth. Another lost her babe at birth, and an American friend and wife had a stillborn child. Two other friends had miscarriages and two more had malformed babies who died within a few months.

The touch of death is certainly a 'close encounter' of tragic proportions, a puzzle and mystery of life difficult to bear. The only consolation was the joyous reality of Jesus' resurrection and his eternal power and glory. However, where do average Chinese parents in their folk religion or Buddhism, or foreign agnostic non-believing Westerners, find consolation and hope?

We were also involved in work outside St. Andrew's Church.

Under the pen name of 'John Mark', I was asked to get as much information as possible about the Church in China under totalitarian rule, and about our own Christians in particular.

Bishop RO Hall also asked me to help at Chung Chi College the future Hong Kong Chinese University. This involved me in lecturing twice a week in Christian Philosophy, using both an English textbook and both the English and Mandarin languages.

I also took prayers twice a week at the Diocesan Girls' School whilst a continuous stream of Chinese refugees from the China Mainland called at the Vicarage seeking help. Finally, I made a regular weekly visit to see church people in hospital.

On her part, Dr. Greta helped twice weekly at a Refugee Clinic and volunteered three months doctoring at another clinic where they had lost their only qualified doctor. This involved three hours each morning from Tuesday to Friday doctoring Chinese refugees and other poor folk, free of charge. To help in this work, she began learning Cantonese to acquire more facility in talking to patients.

Regarding St. Andrew's Church, we began to develop the Sunday Schools. Fifty children now attended our Kindergarten and 50 our junior department. A new Youth Bible Class, taken by Greta, increased rapidly also – all this was on Sundays at 9.45am. 'Give us the tools and we will finish the job' was now the plea. Teachers' lesson books were in short supply, as well as teachers. No sooner were new teachers enrolled than others had to leave on furlough. When we insisted on Teachers' Preparation Classes, on Fridays in the Vicarage, a new idea to some, it was accepted with reluctance but only one teacher resigned.

Youth work was our weakest point. Members of uniformed organisations, like scouts or guides, were not necessarily Christians, nor their leaders. The Girl Guides were an open group led by an odd Guide Captain and did not really belong. Both Scouts and Guides had a monthly Sunday Parade and we hoped the truth about Jesus might perhaps sink in. The Diocesan Girls' School sent 30-40 boarders each Sunday, but this was backed up by the school Head and staff.

Of all groups the Choir, now under an excellent choir master organist, grew in numbers and ability and reality in worship. Some indeed, with understandable pride, believed they were better than the Cathedral choir since ours attended both morning and evening Sunday services (!) Works v. Faith is a Biblical struggle.

Our first Christmas Festival, however, was a crowded and joyous occasion, with the Incarnation of Jesus, Son of God, being powerfully proclaimed. Then at its heels came the Chinese 'Winter Festival' on the 23rd of the 12th Moon, seven days before Chinese New Year. According to Chinese legend, this was the day when the Kitchen God, conceived as living above the kitchen stove, with his wife – as witnessed by their printed portraits in many Chinese homes – were said to go up to heaven to report on each family to the celestial Emperor. This superstitious folk religion was observed only amongst pagan or Buddhist Chinese. A good report from the Kitchen God would bring abundant food to the kitchen in the coming year. The participants would kow-tow to the pictures of Lord and Lady Kitchen God, and even burn life-like miniature horses and models of servants made out of grasses. During the following days all sorts of food were prepared for the Chinese New Year holiday of 15 days, like pork, chicken, beef and other dishes, with powdered rice and soya beans for making buns, rolls and dumplings.

The food was stored in the cellar or the lofts of homes, which acted as natural refrigerators in the winter temperature of January and February – whilst in the cities of Victoria and Kowloon, electric fridges were possessed by many Chinese.

At midnight on Chinese New Year's Eve came the first day of the 1st Lunar month, at the beginning of February, and the expected exploding of huge bursts of fireworks, lasting into the early hours of the morning. Greta and I decided to go to the highest point of Kowloon. We stood and listened amazed to the continuous roar, from all points of the compass, for hours on end. Excitement filled the air. It is said, led by their superstitions, people would go outside to Kowloon, to meet the approaching God of 'Good Luck' and bow to one another with the greeting 'A happy New Year: May good fortune be yours'. Family members and friends would give each other presents of money wrapped in red paper (intended to last for the coming year). Illuminated signs wishing all 'Good Luck' filled the streets much as, at Christmas, there had been 'Happy Christmas' signs lighting up buildings everywhere in unprecedented profusion to Western eyes.

On the 15th day of the 1st Moon, the New Year Festival ended with the Lantern Festival when, after dark, carnival processions were held with lighted lanterns. Pictures of the God of Fire would be carried round the neighbourhood to 'inspect' safety precautions and warn the populace of the danger of fire. Some times the 'God' would be a giant figure with red hair, beard, eyebrows and cloak, carried in a sedan chair by a team of men, whilst figures appeared of dragons, lions, with floats, people on stilts and dancers.

The Lantern Festival is usually a special and separate honouring of the mystic Chinese Dragon. The Chinese words for Lantern are 'Den Lung', meaning Lantern Basket, and each character including the symbol for Dragon. The festival dates back 2,000 years to the Han Dynasty (206 BC – 219 AD), and celebrates the return of light, the lengthening of days, and the coming of Spring.

All this with a splendid Dragon figure of bamboo framework, covered with silk or paper, was supported by local men. The Dragon may be over 100 feet long and it processed through the streets as it performs fantastic dances thrilling to behold, whilst money is collected to cover expenses. The evening twilight is lit up with lanterns. The dances end as the Dragon is taken to a local temple for a final ritual and a somewhat superstitious final dance.

If the Dragon is made of a fragile construction, it is ceremoniously burned. If made of stronger materials it is stored in the temple for another year. Often other 'Lanterns' appear representing those other mythical creatures beloved of the Chinese, the Phoenix, Unicorn and Tortoise. Many give up work for the 15 days of the Festival, visiting their parents and other members of the family clan. Chinese are only too ready to do so, still holding to the traditional Confucian precept, "Honour thy father and thy mother."

There would be lavish meals prepared for such incursions.

Great would be the courtesy of the formal greetings, and joyous the sharing of the feasts and merriment. Even foreign friends might be included, as with Greta and me.

It was just about this time that Padre Ogilvie began his nine months furlough – rather later than at first arranged. However, I now became Acting Vicar of St. Andrew's whilst Greta, and the children, took over the Vicarage as home.

Padre Ogilvie takes a baptism

The choir and organist

Chapter 7

More Cross Cultural Encounters

It was February 19th. As one vicar left, another arrived on a nostalgic visit to the Colony. It was no other than Loving Virtue's maternal uncle, Canon Reginald Lindsay. He had married Miss Thompson, sister of Greta's father, and now came for a 3 week holiday to revive old memories, not only of the Vicarage and Church, but of his niece and her husband, his former curate in Liverpool!

The Canon was quite excited to remember his ministry at St. Andrew's and preached a number of powerful sermons, which moved the congregation deeply. It was with some regret that he eventually said 'Goodbye'.

Lent now came upon us and we held a week of midweek services to complement Sunday's worship with teaching sermons on the theme of Salvation. This was well attended by members of the Armed Forces, who evinced great interest.

Muslims amongst the Chinese population in the Colony were not so visible then and we saw little of their observance of the Fast of Ramadan about that time also.

Easter 1953 soon followed on from Lent, and the Easter Thanksgiving Festival was attended by over 315 communicants, whilst the other services were crowded too. The Resurrection of Jesus was joyously proclaimed. A new event was also included – an Easter Breakfast shared by many, especially the now very enthusiastic Youth Fellowship of the 14-21 age group, and older Christians too.

This Youth Fellowship, influenced by active believers, had now written a Constitution. This ruled that only local youth within the age limits could become members. This ensured that members were of similar if varied cultural and educational background, with real roots in both the local church and the local community. It promised well for the future. These young folk desired to be a point where God's grace could touch the immense non-Christian society of which they were part. Being a mixed group, ethnically and sexually, sanctified by their church connections and guided by the Group's faithful Christian leaders, both sexes were also able to meet openly with the happy consent of parents. The shy adolescent interests of both boys and girls were also met and satisfied in good clean fun and recreation.

Their leader was overheard one day to say it was his deepest joy to go to the weekly meetings because he felt he had left behind the outer-world of Hong Kong in which rivalry, insincerity, self-interest and evil prevailed, to enter a world in which he could find goodness, purity, good fun and comradeship. The powerhouse of this was the regular half-hour of Quiet Time, held halfway through the 2 plus hours long sessions.

Another great social and cultural event had meantime burst upon the Colony and its millions of people, on February 25th of 1953. It was the Coronation of the young Queen Elizabeth 2, an event surrounded by deep Christian spiritual realities. On the preceding Sunday, the churches of the Colony, and St. Andrew's in particular, were very crowded, and on the Day even more so. The streets were splendidly decorated, not least the immense and ancient banyan trees lining both sides of Nathan Road and festooned with electric lights of every colour. At the major junctions, huge triumphal illuminated arches had been erected – a very Chinese touch. Immense crowds came sightseeing. On the afternoon of Tuesday and Wednesday, huge processions crowded the roads and streets, the final showpiece being a gigantic dragon, performing spectacular dragon dances en route. Over 1.5 million people watched the scenes on either side of the harbour.

Instead of spending money on illuminations, the Anglican churches gave the equivalent cost to help build a Coronation 'Church and Clinic' at a medical centre where my doctor wife assisted. All over the Colony splendour, gaiety and sincere rejoicing reigned.

Coronation or no Coronation, however, refugees continued to visit us and we shared in their harrowing tales, sometimes touched by 'divine encounters'. One from our former China diocese, hoped to go to Malasia to help in new missionary work in new villages. His father and mother had died through Communist ill treatment, but he escaped to Hong Kong and strove to earn enough to live on. His latest method was to hawk around a travelling library of Chinese classics and other books, having already tried coolie work or being a boat watchman. He had already completed one year at a Chinese University but the hard conditions of life and unemployment soon began to cause evident deterioration of character.

Another university graduate had become simply a beggar in which poverty and hunger spurred him to try anything. A recent ruse was to call on clergy, say he had had no food for two days and ask simply for bread and fruit. He would then go on to call at the other missionary homes or churches; who could blame him?

It was on 13 February 1953, that news reached us of the death in England of Greta's father, Dr. H. Gordon Thompson, at 75 years of age. He had served in China for 40 years for which he had received a jade medallion from Generalissimo Jiang Kai-shek. Greta's great sorrow was that she was so far away, knowing her mother would have been much comforted with Greta at her side. We rejoiced, however, that the Great Doctor Tan (as his Chinese friends called him) had served Jesus the Lord and his beloved Chinese people to the uttermost. We inwardly hoped to prove as worthy, and were upheld by many letters of sympathy.

The weather in Hong Kong now heated up and on Whit-Monday we had scorching sunshine and received many minor burns whilst relaxing at the sea side. Bill and John also developed bad chills and bronchitis. As the months went by, Hong Kong's climate became more difficult, with high temperatures and the damp atmosphere. To escape this we occasionally visited Stanley on Hong Kong Island, where we had spent our honeymoon. There the sea breezes meant a six degrees lower temperature. Later, for our summer holiday, we enjoyed the 2-hour ferry journey to Lan Tau Island.

There on Lan Tau Island we climbed the 3,000 feet peak and lived in a concrete bungalow (able to resist the typhoon conditions). A canteen was run by the residents of these bungalows. Summer in Hong Kong sapped one's vitality, which could lead to depression. In spite of care over food, it seemed easy to get fever or dysentery of varying severity.

To counter-act the climate and to avoid over-work, Greta and I made it an unbroken rule to have a day off every week. Nevertheless, I had two bouts of dysentery and fever, which lowered my vitality and even prevented me from taking two Sunday's church services. So hot was it that I had to change my clothes and church robes after each of the day's three services. Our two sons had very bad chills, some bronchitis and other mysterious illnesses for no apparent reason, whilst Greta had been off-colour trying to do too much, not realising that caring for two tough little sons and a busy husband is a work in itself.

Economically, we found the cost of living very high, but we were never short of money at St. Andrew's, for the church gave us free lodging, light and fuel.

Psychologically, Greta and I were conscious of not being 'at home' here. Our ministry was largely amongst English and English-speaking people. We knew Mandarin Chinese, but not Cantonese, thus limiting our contacts with local people. Our present work was also temporary and not that for which our Society had sent us out, although I loved the opportunities of pastoral and preaching work. We also had a deep conviction that 'Abba Father' was using us here not a little.

Politically, we existed in a complex situation. At the back of our minds was a conviction, not yet thrashed out, that British possession and control of Hong Kong since the Opium Wars of 1860 had no sound moral justification. Yet, 1.5 million Chinese (5% of the population) would not wish the Colony to be handed over to the present China Mainland Communist Government.

Some years back there seemed to be more folk in favour of the Mainland Government, but the recent 'China Day' was not so well celebrated as before, whilst Nationalist China Day was better celebrated. Over 2 million people also joyfully celebrated the Coronation. Many of the Camp Refugees were bitter opponents of Beijing and there was a strong wish for a Nationalist invasion of the Mainland by the Formosa/Taiwan Government and Armed Forces.

In local Government there was a very strong desire for more representative and democratic Government but great difficulty in achieving it. One bone of contention was that material assistance was given to the refugees but not education, and no religious teaching. The many and diverse churches working in the camps also did not touch, nor wish to touch, this problem.

However, now all the excitement in the Colony centred on the Dragon Boat Festival, celebrated with great excitement by the Chinese and enjoyed as a spectacle by the non-Chinese too. It was held on the Double Fifth, i.e. the 5th Day of the 5th Moon, about June in the solar calendar, and no doubt in Communist China also, for even Communists love their political heroes and martyrs, especially a People's martyr.

It is an annual festival commemorating a famous statesman called Chu Yuan, a Prime Minister of great moral courage, under King Huai of Chu State. Chu Yuan loved the people but disagreed with the evil policies of his King. Like many such men in China in those days, such as Confucius, China's greatest Sage, and Mencius, the Sage's later disciple, Chu Yuan sought in vain to guide his King and the Court in the ideals of good government. He was at the same time, a great poet and wrote a poem entitled 'Li Sao' meaning 'falling into trouble' in which he said:

> But I am just an outcast.
> I think of my Prince
> But all in vain.
>
> (After H.A. Giles)

As a last final protest, Chu Yuan deliberately drowned himself, clasping a heavy stone and plunging into the Milo River, to be seen no more. Annually, therefore, on the 5th Day of the 5th Moon, the common people of Chu State, who revered their minister greatly, re-enacted the search for his body and this extended year after year to the whole of China. The search developed into a series of boat races. Many boat crews from different areas of China, vied to reach the mythical spot where Chu Yuan had disappeared, and a special kind of rice was cast upon the water as an act of remembrance. These teams of men wore their own special uniform, they built their own boats, the prow being always a Dragon's head, and the boats were paddled at great speed. It became a very exciting spectator sport.

In Hong Kong in 1953, it was commemorated in the lovely fishing village of Aberdeen on the East of the Island, and I was privileged to witness the festival with my sons Bill and John. Crossing over to the Island on the car ferry, we drove along the seven miles of hilly country on a fine evening. There were several long, dragon-headed boats, some with as many as 50 rowers, or rather paddlers, since these were used and not oars. Each boat had a drummer in the prow or stern or even amidships in a boat, who gradually increased the stroke speed beating time. Last year's champion crew, sporting their winner's red waistcoats duly appeared , to great applause. Their excited drummer stood on his head and kept time in that position.

Some eight crews competed in the Festival. At first they cruised up and down the estuary, warming up and showing off. Two crews would suddenly find themselves at the starting line. They would then set off, the drummers would begin their drumming, paddles would flash and the dragon boats race down stream and tide. Faster and faster beat the drummers, louder and louder shouted the spectators from the banks or anchored house-boats, higher and higher grew the excitement until both crews crossed the finishing line, with drummers and crews going at a fantastic pace.

The successful crews would compete again until finally a winner was found and the Dragon Boat Festival came to an end. The ultimate winners were then given their Red Waistcoats, and the crowds, some thousands in number, returned to their homes excitedly discussing the contest.

The Festival is now observed, not only all over China but also overseas. In Aberdeen, Hong Kong, a crew of British soldiers even appeared and almost beat the champions, at which many spectators amongst the thousands lining the banks of the narrow estuary, almost fell into the river! So ended a very happy Festival experience; and a special thought struck me. Chu Yuan died and only his memory and example survives, unlike Jesus who died by crucifixion but returned to life on this planet Earth for 50 more days and then returned to the Heaven from which he had come. From there He now sends out his followers to celebrate in almost every corner of the Planet, His life, death and Resurrection, year by year.

Chapter 8

Problems of the Refugees

How happy a thing it is, when friends come from afar
(Analects/Confucius)

The Double Fifth also celebrates the Ching Ming Festival. Ching Ming means 'Bright and Clear' and refers to the coming of Spring and brighter weather. Since it also concerns the caring for the ancestral tombs, it is very important to the Chinese who venerate their ancestors. So it is also called the Festival of the Tombs and becomes another occasion for family outings. If the tombs are in the hills or distant countryside, boats are hired for the journey and the whole operation may take a week. The graves are swept and made tidy and respectable after the ravages of the winter and early spring rains. It is an act of filial piety and, with Chinese practicality, the family takes plenty of baked and boiled meats and other foods.

In China, we had been very aware of the Festival, but in Hong Kong with its intermingled cultures, we were not so aware of it. What we realised however, was the large numbers of Chinese refugees who dared not return to the family tombs. They also had their own problem of just managing to exist in an over-crowded Colony with massive unemployment.

One of these refugees was Shu Nai-an. Like Chu Yuan that early Chinese martyr, Mr. Shu had also disagreed with his country's rulers and fled to Hong Kong. He had studied at the Sun Yat Sen University in Canton. The Japanese invasion of China compelled its 1,000 students and university staff to remove, hook, line and sinker to West China – including Shu Nai-an. His degree studies in Sociology convinced him of the need of reform in China. When the atom bombs fell on Japan in 1945, and she surrendered, the Nationalists resumed government and Mr. Shu hoped that a great future for China lay ahead. However, the fierce civil war between Nationalists and Communists broke out again. Mao Zedong and his communists eventually took over China in 1949, whilst Jiang Kai-shek retreated to Taiwan.

With trepidation, Mr. Shu had tried to work with the new regime. He had to undergo indoctrination. He saw that their ideology was not his and their god not his God, for he was a Christian., brought up in a Christian school in Kaifeng, Honan. Witnessing the sufferings of his fellow countrymen, he fled to Hong Kong along with 1.5 million other Chinese who had chosen the self-same banishment.

Having witnessed the Aberdeen Dragon Boat Festival, he chose to walk back the 7 miles to the City, for the evening was fine and he could use the bus fare to get a decent meal. He kept 10 cents for the ferry-fare to Kowloon where he lived on a staircase window ledge. However, the steep hills tired him and left him gasping for breath. As he paused to recover, he noticed a Chinese food vendor with his tiny shop on wheels, selling noodles and pork scraps, piping hot in a pan over a charcoal fire.

The vendor looked appealingly from his emaciated face. Mr. Shu guessed that he had no license to sell – just another refugee from a nice home and good family in China. He lived by doing odd jobs and gradually spending all his savings, his gold ring, watch, fountain pen, and even his clothes, to keep alive. If caught selling food, the police would confiscate his cart and food and he would be fined.

Buying a bowl of noodles, Mr. Shu squatted on the roadside and saw another young Chinese eating noodles and recognised a fellow refugee from Gwangxi province. They had both been teacher-headmasters, on the Mainland, and met at the Refugee Centre for Chinese Intellectuals in Hong Kong. The two men returned their empty bowls to the vendor, who moved away with his little mobile shop. The exertion shook the vendor's frail body and he coughed, spitting blood. The two friends looked at each other. They knew the signs – TB. They should not have bought that food. TB, that white dragon, devoured many lives in the slum conditions of the Colony. They shrugged their shoulders.

"Is your honourable surname not Wong Li-chuan?"

"Not wrong! Wong is my humble surname" replied the other. "And you are Shu Nai-an, are you not?"

They both spoke Mandarin, the "King's English" of China, the dialect, north of the Yangtze River, now being used as China's first language in all schools, colleges and universities by order of Chairman Mao. Unconsciously, the two dropped into the ancient dialect of Gwang-dong Province, dominant in South China and amongst Hong Kong Chinese too. It has no written form nor literature, but is extremely expressive.

"Are you still hoping to go to Taiwan?" asked Wong.

"Yes. My name is on the list since the project began" said Shu. "I hope to go as an interpreter in the Generalissimo's Army or the Government there. And you?"

"My missionary friend in Kowloon, Pastor Ho, hopes to get me a job as a teacher in Malaysia. He knew my father –in-law in China and when I escaped, I found his address and asked his help. He became my sponsor to the police who gave me a Residence Permit" replied Wong. "I now earn a few dollars as a ship's watchman, and also work as a labourer on a building site. An old well-to-do Gwangxi family also know me and the dowager grandmother occasionally employs me. Living on a rooftop in Kowloon does not cost much. Hundreds of others live that way. Some 15 of us live that way on my roof. What about you?" Mr. Shu signed. He was tired and not very strong.

"I was private tutor to a family but they have left the Colony. I also wrote and translated for the newspapers but that work gets less. One can only trust God and pray for help. I am living in an old block of flats on Austin Road. The caretaker lets me sleep on the 5th floor staircase landing. My bedding roll just fits into the window ledge."

The two men were silent. Wong stirred:

"I must not be late for my watchman's job. See you again. My friend Pastor Ho lives at the church near where you sleep. Go and see him."

"Perhaps I will. Thank you. See you again." said Mr. Shu.

Mr. Shu was glad to reach the ferry and pay his 10 cents to travel 2nd Class on the lower deck, with a dense crowd of others. The upper 1st Class deck was crowded too, with well dressed Chinese,

Eurasians and Europeans. The fresh sea breeze and a seven-minute passage to Kowloon was sweet joy. It made Mr. Shu's half-mile walk from the ferry to his home just possible.

Summer with its hot sticky climate made Mr. Shu's asthma worse. A long drought had recently reduced the Colony's water supply to 4 hours daily. Then the rains burst with a vengeance as a typhoon passed near the Colony. Gale warning signs were hoisted and given over Radio Hong Kong and Rediffusion. Ferries stopped running. Winds of 80 mph shook the Colony, followed by torrential rain, 12 inches in one day. In the night, Mr. Shu heard a frightening rumble like an earthquake but he felt too ill to care. Next morning he heard that a hillside, undermined by rain, had slipped into the harbour waters and a whole building had collapsed. Some folk were injured and everyone was evacuated for safety.

"How many more refugees are homeless again?" wondered Mr. Shu. "Only God would know what had happened to the thousands living in the wooden shack villages and those hundreds sleeping on pavements with but a tarpaulin for cover. What about friend Wong on his roof top?"

However, Mr. Shu was past caring. His fever grew worse, and his asthma. His rice bowl lay by his pillow. The little rice water that it contained was all he had had for two days. Another friend Mr. Gao tried the hospital. There was no available bed and at the moment two patients slept in each bed. Then Mr. Shu suddenly remembered Wong's missionary friend and asked Gao to find him.

Mr. Shu was half asleep and delirious when a shadow fell across his bed. A foreigner's voice spoke, "We must get him into hospital!" Hours later, Mr. Shu was disturbed again. Kindly hands lifted him. When he became conscious, he found himself in a hospital bed. Slowly, with tender nursing care from kindly Chinese nurses, medical treatment by efficient Chinese doctors, and adequate meals, he grew better and stronger. In a week he was out of hospital to find there was a teaching job waiting for him at St. James' Settlement.

One of the joys of the job was that he could sleep on the premises. The Chinese girl in charge at the Settlement told him that he could begin to teach a class of local harum-scarum youngsters from the neighbourhood, the most densely populated square mile in Hong Kong. They responded to his teaching. He taught them the '3 R's'. Others taught them gardening, carpentry, printing on a small printing press; repairing cars and other practical skills, all of which would help them to get jobs when they were old enough. However, Mr. Shu also taught them about Jesus and the Christian Faith. It was only a temporary job but it was the salvation of Mr. Shu. He recovered his health and self-respect.

Nor had God forgotten him. One never to be forgotten day, a letter arrived from "Aid Refugees Chinese Intellectuals" giving him permission to enter Taiwan to help in Army and Government administration. A year later, as Chinese New Year was celebrated once again, Mr. Shu boarded the liner taking him to his new home and a new life. As the liner sailed, some 20 miles away was Canton where he had been born and perhaps where his mother still lived. Further still were the vast provinces of China where his father, former Inspector in the Government department of Communications, had sometimes taken him. Would he ever see them again? As a Christian, he left them to God who knows all things. He determined to be more faithful himself in his new life in Taiwan.

Wong Li-chuan, Mr. Shu's fellow teacher-headmaster, had also had his own close encounter. He came to the home of his friend Pastor Ho one day, after having escaped from China, via Macao, further up the coast than Hong Kong. He had spent weeks hiding in the mountains and, using his savings, made his secret way to the Portuguese port, found a solitary fisherman there on the shore, and paid him his 100-Yuan to smuggle him to Hong Kong. This left him with 5-Yuan to buy food for the long sea journey and other eventualities on arrival. After four weeks in Macao he again contacted the fisherman. "Come tomorrow morning at dawn" whispered the man.

The sea voyage as he lay hidden and cramped under the deck of the fishing boat was very unpleasant compared with his journeys by sampan up and down China's rivers. The violent rocking of the fishing boat and the smell of fish and bilge water, nauseated him. He fell asleep in his cramped quarters – a Chinese can sleep anywhere if he can curl up, and wooden boards commonly formed his bed at home.

Awakened by the fisherman's voice, Wong crawled out of his prison and looked about him in the gathering dusk. It was a small-secluded bay. No Hong Kong Maritime Police were evident.

"The main road and a small village are just behind the hill" said the fisherman. Wong thanked him and jumped ashore. At the village inn, he paid his last 3-Yuan for his bed and a bowl of fried rice with scraps of chopped meat and egg, steaming hot. He found his bed and fell asleep.

The next day he set off for the City. In Kowloon and Hong Kong there was plenty of building work. He found a job carrying rubble or breaking stones. Not much for an ex-headmaster and son of a magistrate, but better than starving. Another coolie introduced him to a rooftop and there, he staked out a bed-space. Smoke from a chimney vent and the smell of the communal lavatory bucket were unpleasant and noxious. Water, carried up four storeys from the nearby street tap, was also a problem. It was Christmas Eve and he fell asleep, suddenly remembering that Mary had only a manger in which to lay the child Jesus. Wong, just remembered to say a prayer.

Next day he found a Cantonese church and looked in, astonished. There were 600/700 Chinese crowding in for the Christmas Day services, a joy to behold. Three weeks later he found the name and address of the missionary friend he was to seek out. They had met in China. Plucking up courage he called at the house and was given a letter of introduction to the police. They were very helpful and gave him an Identity Card. A Relief Agency Official provided him with a mattress, a blanket and an overcoat. His new friend also suggested he write immediately to Malaysia where a Chinese teacher was needed in a Church school. It would be a race against time, for new regulations restricting Chinese entry into the Federation were due in 6 months time.

Wong Li-chuan went to sleep dreaming about jungles, bandits, his wife and their first baby who had been a still-born son; and his father, shot as a tyrant by the Communists, and the mystery of God and His providence. A few days later, his casual coolie job ended, but he found work as a watchman on a junk. News from Malaysia was slow in coming. The Hong Kong authorities were willing enough and a Relief Agency had promised to pay his ship's passage money. Hope struggled with Despair but when time had nearly run out, Emigration officials sent for him. Everything had come through at last.

As Wong Li-chuan boarded the ocean-going cargo steamer, I stayed with him until the ship was due to sail. As I returned down the gangway, Wong called out "The Lord be with you". "And with you too" I replied. The ship's engines throbbed and the ship itself moved away to the open sea, to Malaysia. Wong would soon be teaching in Ma Wah School in one of the new villages. A year later he became Assistant Resettlement Officer in another new village.

Postscript: 1993; 41 years later.

Wong Li-chuan's eldest daughter came alone to England to visit Greta and me. She stayed the night and shared in our Bible Study Group, which met in our home. She was petite, 31 years of age and married to a Chinese Christian husband back home. She took our Group members by storm with her joyous love for and simple faith in, Jesus the Christ. She also prayed for us each in turn, deeply perseptive of our spiritual needs and longings.

"When friends come from afar, is it not a joyous thing?"

Chapter 9

The Wanderer's Return and the Fire Dragon

We were learning many things at St. Andrew's which we had not experienced during our years on the China Mainland. One of them was the colour problem, hardly noticeable in China, either in the nationalist regime under Jiang Kai-shek or during the short time we spent under the threat of Mao's Communist regime's victory. The vast population of ethnic Chinese swamped from view the question of yellow and white and even brown peoples. Memories of the danger of European attempts to carve up China had faded. China now really belonged to the Han race and they began to take up the Whiteman's burden of Education and Medical Health. Europeans like ourselves were welcome to help the Chinese to grapple with these immense problems. Foreign investment was also encouraged to help deal with economic/industrial matters. In agriculture, the Chinese are possibly the best farmers in the world. Greta and I even thought of ourselves as half Chinese.

In Nine Dragons Country and Hong Kong generally, colour and race did not appear to matter, either. Canon Fison, an English theologian, published about this time in the West, a book entitled "Christian Hope" in which he wrote about the middle wall of partition, or the colour problems in the Western half of the world. It almost seemed out of place in Fragrant Harbour and St. Andrew's Church, Kowloon. Our congregations of Westerners, Chinese and Eurasians, mixed together very happily in worship, and also on a less regular basis in social and recreational events. One churchwarden was a northern Chinese, the second, an Englishman, whilst the treasurer was an Eurasian. The Church Council included all three groups very happily in the close fellowship of their common faith in Jesus Christ, and even on such occasions as the Vicar's Annual Garden Party. It was in eating habits that separateness found place, for at Harvest Festival time, the church held three separate Suppers, one with a Western menu, another with a Northern Chinese menu (Shanghai or

Beijing food), and a Cantonese food Supper at the third. English was spoken at the first, Mandarin at the second and Cantonese at the third! Quite a number went to either two, or all three occasions, doing their humorous best with the language problem. The price was the same, an 'entertainment' followed each, and all ended up with a short service in the church.

Much of this Christian camaraderie was due to Padre Ogilvie who, being a Scotsman, had his own brand of "English", as well as eating Haggis and Porridge! In addition to these peculiarities, he had a great sense of humour, a big laugh, and charming manners. People loved him and he loved people.

Greta and I had both grown to love St. Andrew's multi-ethnic life and people; we had been given 'pastoral hearts'. Now in the saga of our life in Nine Dragons Country, we came to another turning point – John Ogilvie's return from furlough. Imagine our surprise and consternation, however, when our dear and saintly Bishop R. O. Hall came to see me and said:

"Eric, when John Ogilvie returns, I would like him to accept another appointment, and I want to ask you to continue as Vicar!"

I was absolutely astonished. However, I have never been scared of Bishops, and I expressed my own reaction forth-rightly.

"Bishop! You just cannot do that to John. He loves St. Andrew's, and the church folk love him because of his simple and joyous goodness, and in spite of his Scottish Presbyterian ways and worship. I could not accept your offer myself."

The Bishop, whom I respected as a real Man of God, and of transparent holiness, paused and accepted my refusal with a smile. John Ogilvie returned in November 1953 and we began to plan our move to and our work on Hong Kong Island. No easy task, but we did so with eager expectation at working amongst Chinese students in the University and Colleges and other commitments.

Greta and I were the only 'pukka' or freelance Anglican missionaries in the Colony, being under the authority of the Church Missionary Society, London. They also paid our living allowances. We were, therefore, not directly under the jurisdiction of our dear Bishop. He was once heard to say:

"I have no control of Eric and Greta Hague!" with faint irritation. However, he graciously accepted the inevitable. All other missionaries, i.e. foreign personnel in the Colony, were called by the Diocesan Educational Board to specific tasks in their institutions and so under the Bishop's guiding hands.

When the day came for us to leave St. Andrew's and move to pastures new, the Church members very kindly presented us with an electric fire and a cheque for HK$1,000 (£62) with which we bought a Mongolian carpet rug. It looked well in our new flat in St. John's Hall.

Greta and I had now to move house to a very different scene. At the Vicarage, we had been looked after by the cook and his wife. In our new home, we wished to experiment and have no servant. However, after our move we soon decided that this was impossible. Instead we found a very nice Chinese girl to act as Amah and come in daily to help us. Greta and she decided to share the cooking and washing up between them. Her name was Ah Lin, and she was to do most of the house cleaning and all the laundry. This was a big task because, in the hot weather, a change of clothing was necessary almost every day, and washing men's linen suits was not easy. We agreed that Ah Lin should not take charge of the children. Other influences were so strong that we were sure that parents should be in charge. An Amah also finds it difficult to be firm enough when children do not understand her language. We ourselves, having been given the responsibility, privilege and joy of children, accepted that Greta, while she might like to do more medical work, go to church with her husband, and attend social events, felt she could not leave the boys to others.

Ah Lin came of a good family, formerly prosperous. Her brothers studied at St. Paul's Boys School, and her sister at St. Stephen's Girls. Ah Lin had married a nice young man, until he suddenly disappeared without trace. The family felt he had gone into China. The husband's family had been quite kind to Ah Lin and were loath to see her become an 'amah'. However, she quickly became one of our family and grew very fond of the boys. Our only difficulty was to prevent her from working too hard.

With Padre Ogilvie already back at St. Andrew's, we moved over to St. John's Hall on the Island. The Governors, no doubt guided by Bishop Hall, offered us the use of a flat in the building. As the Christmas Festival was approaching, our move coincided with the outside broadcasting of Christmas Carols in Chinese from St. John's Hall on an outside loudspeaker system. We took this as a sign of real welcome. It went on for several days, reaching out to the surrounding population, including the English University. So penetrating was this broadcast that it could be heard above the noise of traffic, as well as over the sounds of excited children, enjoying the freedom of holiday. This was no mere respectable radio broadcast such as that of King's College Cambridge's Service of 9 Lessons and Carols (which was heard over the Hong Kong Radio Station), but a bold public proclamation to the Colony's population of the Good News of the birth of Jesus the Christ, Son of the Eternal God, whom world Christians worship.

Christmas day, 1953, was duly celebrated with all the joy that Hong Kong Christians usually showed. However, it ended with a disaster of gigantic proportions. We were still feeling our way and finding our feet and exploring the life of a freelance Evangelist amongst the student population and seeking a new spiritual home in the life of the Cathedral and the Chinese churches.

Bill and John were also discovering that Father Christmas was still at large, still making his mysterious visits and filling stockings – all because of the history shattering event of Jesus' incarnation almost 2,000 years earlier.

It must have been early evening when I saw the great red glow spreading along Nine Dragon's skyline across the harbour like a stealthy Dragon. I set out to investigate. Crossing the harbour by Star Ferry, I made my way up Nathan Road's 3 miles of light and colour. It stretched resplendent down the centre of Kowloon Peninsula. Smaller links of light reached out on either side at main crossings, ablaze with lights from shops and hotels. On either side of the four-lane highway, massive ancient Banyan trees, their gnarled branches almost touching, glowed with multicoloured lights. I passed St. Andrew's Church campus, a welcome oasis of green grass and trees.

Brilliant shop windows displayed everything man, woman or child could desire, succulent foods, exquisite curios, Chinese fiddles, beautifully glazed china, toy tanks and jet planes, Chinese scrolls, and a plump Santa Claus with dashing reindeer. Window gazers, young and old, enjoyed just looking at the feast of good things – not least a magnificent Tiger skin in the Siberian Fur Shop and the warm colourful bedding ready for the winter's cold. A modern cinema's gigantic poster advertised the current films and the price of a seat, enough to feed me for two days.

A clock showed 9.30 pm. Grills began to protect the shop windows. The night sky was now glowing a fiery red; an earnest tocsin cried a warning. Human voices began to shout alarm, "Fire! Fire!" as I reached Shek Kip Mei and Pak Im, two villages separated by a hillside. Families of poor refugees began to stream from their huts in panic, dragging hastily packed bundles. The village's fire-squad were helpless. A fire engine clanged its desperate way, police sirens wailed, and an urgent ambulance raced along. Crowds grew, pushing and shouting, and children crying. Flames roared and crackled, smoke billowed high. A small soap factory and a paraffin store exploded. Other dwellings burst into flame.

Fearful cries now rent the air "The wind has changed … the fire's getting nearer, hurry! Hurry!" Firemen dragging long hoses, carrying axes and bars, tried to clear free lanes. Police and Civil Aid Service men directed fleeing refugees. St. John's Ambulance Brigade, and soldiers on leave hastened to the disaster area, answering a radio broadcast.

The Red Fire Dragon was now leaping to the sky, pouncing on flimsy huts, pursuing fleeing crowds whilst thin ropes of water tried to restrain it. It was now 1am and the fiery dragon began to tire. By 1.30am it was struggling for its life, 2am and it was finally overcome. A strange quiet settled on the scene. One solitary fire engine and a traffic policeman stood guard whilst 60,000 misery-worn victims dozed down anywhere, as Christmas Day 1953 ended and belonged to history.

I forget what time I returned home.

St. Andrew's Sunday school

Baptism of Baby Tiger

Chapter 10

Encounters and Happenings in Fragrant Harbour

1954, the year of the Horse seemed to speed by. Too soon, it was again Christmas and we were celebrating Christmas Eve Midnight Eucharist in the St. John's Cathedral with 1,000 people present. Six hundred of whom were communicants. Dean Freddie Temple and his staff's hard work were being blessed. The Hong Kong Chinese were taking the Birthday of Jesus to their hearts – and to their eyes. The Colony's public illuminations glowed brilliantly everywhere, rivalling London's Oxford Street and Piccadilly Circus. The Chinese churches were also very much alive, not least St. Matthew's, where Canon Edward Lee had invited me to preach at the Christmas Day 11 am. Family Service, in the Cantonese tongue, to my joy and deep apprehension, and no doubt his too! It was not quite an unqualified success but the loving acceptance of my efforts overwhelmed my inner shame.

On the family's side, with that curious schizophrenia which affects even committed Christians, our boys wrote to Father Christmas c/o the Pacific Airways Corporation. An accepted and harmless part of our Western Culture, enjoyed without necessarily swallowing completely that semi-historic fable! To their delight, our sons received back replies post-marked "Alaska" from that Jovial Personage and equally and gleefully enjoyed finding their hung-up stockings loaded with gifts. It was 6.30am when these were opened, breakfast being a definite after-thought.

Ah Lin, our Amah, to our great joy, also went boldly to St. Stephen's Church nearby, without comment from her family, and arousing no doubt intense family interest.

Our lunch guests added to the Day's joy. They included Doctor Sturton of CMS, Dr. Hadow ex Hangchow; Dr. and Mrs. Vaughan Rees ex North China; and the menu was roast chicken, plum pudding, ice cream, fruit and coffee. We had a happy time.

The afternoon's visitors were the Runcorn's (CMS), the

Spekes and Father Christmas in his red and white robes. Sunday, next day, seemed to be Christmas all over again and why not? Greta took No. 1 son to a Sunday School Entertainment at St. Matthew's Church. At the Cathedral later, Bill sang in the chorus of an excellent play, whilst Greta gave out prizes to 250 children! On Monday (Boxing Day in our culture), Ah Lin, her elder sister, two younger brothers and two of our refugee friends, shared our midday meal.

In the final week of January, the Universal Week of Prayer was celebrated. For my sins and to my joy, I was now Secretary to the United Missionaries and Clergy Group for the Colony. This met once a week at the Dean's house and this year many more Protestant churches joined in. It ended with a wide exchange of Sunday preachers followed by a United Service of Christian Witness, one at the Cathedral on the Island side and another at the Union Church on the Kowloon side. Chinese pastors, exhausted by their own multi-meetings in Christmas week, asked to be excused.

In the first week of January, just before Chinese New Year exploded round our ears, I held a short Retreat for six CMS missionaries and 7 Diocesan workers. This was at the Hoh Fuk Tong Centre, which was greatly appreciated and was an island of calm before the First Day of the First Moon Festival. As usual, this latter erupted with its uproar of firecrackers, family parties and school holidays – and a week's holiday for Ah Lin. This was a 15-day celebration and if it had little "religious" content, it did proclaim the Chinese cultural Filial Piety theme, "Honour your Father and your Mother". This is the cement of the Chinese nation and written up in strong and beautiful 'characters' on the four walls of every Confucian temple. Chinese Christians also used the Festival for Gospel Preaching with great fervour and conviction.

As Chinese love to quote, "Time flies like an arrow through the air", so the 1955 year crept, no, sped on to Christian's Lent, Good Friday and the great Easter Festivals. Soon Summer burnt its way into our bodies and minds, soaking our clothes with sweat. Lan Tau Island beckoned imperatively to us to come for our Summer retreat with the family.

However, suddenly, history was stopped in its tracks. Padre

Ogilvie took a swim too many in the warm, welcoming waters around the Colony. A sudden heart attack shook even that great frame and heart, and he died after making it to a nearby raft. Multitudes were devastated by the news and deeply mourned his passing. In due course, our Holy Bishop R. O. Hall, having sought my consent and that of CMS, instituted the Rev. Eric Hague as the succeeding Vicar of St. Andrew's Church in Nine Dragons Country on September 2nd, 1955. We then duly moved back to our former home in St. Andrew's Vicarage, Nathan Road, Kowloon. We were both glad and sad, but it seemed to be the Lord's doing and marvellous in our eyes, and I felt that it truly was more my scene.

Chapter 11

From Confucius to Christ

"The Master said, "It is only the very wisest and the very stupidest who cannot change."

The Analects: XVII,3. (Waley)

James Lam is a printer. He is also Chinese, trained by his father in the old Confucian tradition. For both reasons he cherishes words and ideas, and loves to hear in the workrooms outside his office, the rhythmic thudding of the great printing presses at work. They are his life. It is not only that his salary as works manager depends upon them; the printed or written word is precious to him, as it is to any educated Chinese. Words clothe ideas and give beauty of form on the receptive paper (especially if they are written in the beautiful Chinese script): They are creative, living things, living on and on into the future, moulding it and refashioning its peoples. Had not the words of Confucius, handed down from generation to generation, moulded his own people, giving them a poise and inner courtesy equal to withstanding all the buffetings of others?

Nor is it unexpected that finally James should discover and reverence Him who is the Word of God and the Reason behind all existence. However, it is terrifying that words also nearly kept him from the discovery, almost separated him from Christ.

From his boyhood, James learned from his father and teachers the treasurers of their ancient Confucian culture, the old classics edited by the Sage, and the sayings of the Master (as Confucius is called). James' mind and character nourished themselves on words like these, said five hundred years before Christ: The Master said: "The good man does not grieve that other people do not recognise his merits. His only anxiety is lest he should fail to recognise theirs."

The Master said: "Never do to others what you would not like them to do to you."

From a boy, James had also grown up within a non-Chinese

culture. A culture in which money and efficiency, technology and science, even race and colour, seemed to him to be the features, the culture of a race and people inconsistent within itself. For had not the Christian British, more than a hundred years before, allowed their great ships and merchant adventurers to bring opium to the Chinese people, which had gravely threatened not only China's economic structure but the bodies and minds of his people too? The first war between Chinese and British resulted largely from this very evil, and forced China to cede Britain the Island of Hong Kong – for China's moral principles, plus a few junks, were no match for British determination, guns and men-of-war.

Yet in such ships as these came also the Christian missionaries, the friends of the Chinese people, bringing their dynamic faith in Jesus, God's Word, the answer to life's riddle, for which James himself had long and restlessly searched. With this new hope they brought also healing and knowledge, hospitals and schools, health and cleanliness, all the spiritual riches of the Christian West.

However, James remembered there were other things. There was that English lady whom James had encountered as a youth. Strolling quietly and contentedly along the road one day, he noticed her coming behind him. He did not stare at her, even at her curious clothes, her fair skin, eyes and hair. That would have been discourteous, and good Chinese are never discourteous. Her strides, so unlike the short steps of his own Chinese womenfolk, brought her quickly up behind him so that he was in her way. Then she had used her walking stick to whip him sharply across the legs, speaking abruptly in her monotonous language, telling him to get out of her way. When he did so and she walked on without further ado, James was left both angry and confused. Was this also part of the teaching of Christ? He did not find the answer until much later in his life.

Armed with his receptive and quick mind and unfailing courtesy, James went on to conquer his world. Schooling and his own mental alertness gave him a ready command of both Chinese and English, and bi-lingualism is a key to many doors in commerce and trade in the world of Hong Kong. He found his way into one of the big newspaper offices in the Colony. Words, language and news, and the great machines churning out the daily reading matter of a great Colony, became his life. Through the outstretching tentacles of its printed columns, East and West were brought together beneath his eyes and even by his own hands. It was exciting and creative work.

Then James married a Christian girl. His wife longed for him to become a Christian but he consistently held back. However, the children when they came, were duly baptised.

James had his doubts about Christians. These were not removed by the closer contacts he had with them through his wife or by the fact that he now met Chinese Christians. Perhaps if the Christians had been able to present a united front, he might have been won, for he had learned to reverence the teaching of Jesus. However, the Christians were so divided amongst themselves. There was this church and that church and the other church. Why were there so many? They competed with one another, maligned one another, criticised and disliked one another. How could their words be true? Why did their deeds not match their words? Their Christ, if he was God and alive, did not seem to change them, unite them, or make them much better people, any more than He had been able, apparently, to change that English woman who had whipped his legs with her stick. Nevertheless, this Jesus, this Christ, this Son of God – if He were such indeed – attracted James almost against his will. Sometimes he would get a New Testament and read His words and His teaching. What if he had really risen from the dead after being crucified and killed? However, James would shrug aside the tantalising idea, thinking of those uncharitable, complacently divided churches. He went on with his own job of sowing good news in the daily newspaper.

Another opportunity confronted him, a change fraught with some possibilities. He was offered the position of Works Manager in one of the Colony's largest printing firms. He accepted, and it was there that we met, for his firm printed the parish magazine of my church. From the beginning, we were attracted to each other. We met, talked and became friends. We talked business and religion, Confucius and Christ. We talked often and long, for many were the problems, which James wished to talk out. Then, one day, he suddenly decided: "I want to be baptised." About three months later, having attended preparation classes held in the Cathedral, James was duly baptised into Christ and the great Christian family, making his spiritual home in the Chinese church, St. Mary's near his home. Here he began a new pilgrimage, learning to walk in the Way, which is Christ.

James was sitting back in his office chair one morning, his fingers idly turning over the engagement calendar on his desk. A momentary lull in the busy day's work was very welcome. Even the telephone seemed to be taking a rest. From beyond, in the workrooms, came the dull rhythmic music of the printing presses at work, like the bass undertone to some modern symphony.

The calm was broken as a workman brought in a sheaf of proofs. James' momentary relaxation gave way to efficient attention. His long, finely cut features bent down over the rough proofs. His delicate nostrils twitched to the familiar loved smell of the printer's ink: his practised eyes ranged quickly over the page, noting the mistakes of spelling and line.

When the door opened to admit a customer, James put his proofs aside and, as courteous as ever, stood up to smile a welcome. Soon he was in the midst of discussions on type, blocks, paper and costs. Then the demands of Western efficiency satisfied, he leaned back in his chair to exchange the gentle more leisurely tributes of friendship.

Hardly had he bidden his customer good-bye and sat down again, than a commotion outside caught his attention. The door swung open suddenly and in strode an irate Englishman, a big business man from a near-by office. His face was flushed with anger and coming up to James, he shook a bundle of proofs in his face. "These are no use to me. They're all wrong." He shouted, and ripped them across several times with angry jerks. He then flung the pieces into James's impassive face and walked out.

James sat still for a moment and then, picking up the torn fragments, put them into a waste paper basket. Had James been an Englishman, this man would never have behaved in such a way. James had had experience of him before. Important, clever and superior in his own eyes, the man was yet uncouth and rude, just another un-Christian Englishman. However, this now had no power to disturb James' faith, for James himself belonged to Christ, and Christ he knew was not a Western Christ, but the Lord of both Englishmen and Chinese, and the Saviour of all who come to Him of whatever race, colour or clime. In this lay the difference between Christ and the great Chinese sage. Confucius belonged to China, but Christ belonged to all men and women everywhere, and they belonged to Him.

Indeed, it is a pilgrimage to travel from Confucius to Christ. Occasionally, James would attend the Cathedral services where his command of English enabled him to worship in that language, and to understand the sermons. Eventually he began to attend a Chinese Church along with his wife and children. This rejoiced their hearts too. I suppose that in Hong Kong, there are more clergy, ministers and church workers per square mile/per head of the population than in most other places in the world!

This will probably still make little difference when the Pearl of the Orient ceases to be a British Colony on July 1st, 1997, for "In the four seas, all men are brothers", says a China Proverb.

Chapter 12

Back to the Future at St. Andrew's

Our return to St. Andrew's brought a new realisation of an immense task facing us. Before, I had been Deputy Vicar with no power to change things. Now I was Vicar and with wisdom, able to bring change. I became more aware of the size of the parish – probably 200,000 people lived in blocks of flats or high-rise dwellings, a small percentage of whose inmates was English speaking and interested in the Jesus faith. My task had changed radically because Sunday by Sunday, week by week, I was now involved in disciplined and continuous worship, building up the Christian "Body", compared with spasmodic Evangelism or teaching amongst groups of students, Christian or otherwise, challenging them about God and Jesus.

Now I had to build up the Church congregation in the faith, in Sunday Schools, Youth Groups, Bible Study Groups, Baptism and Confirmation Classes. There would be days of Prayer and Giving; Festival celebrations, Choir practices and the editing of the Monthly Church Magazine. There would be the Mother's Union to foster, Church Council's business and Annual Church Meetings to review the work and elect new officers; shepherding strangers and new members would be necessary, the tasks were legion and I had no regular assistant. Occasionally visiting preachers came to my help.

I now saw St. Andrew's in a new light. Originally, it had been a Colonial Chaplaincy, dominated by the East India Trading Company and UK Colonials. I remembered Henry Martyn, a Colonial Chaplain on the Indian continent. Against opposition by the Company, he reached out to local people. Now at St. Andrew's we had inherited a multi-racial, multi-coloured and multi-cultural congregation. Along with UK members, we had Americans, Australians, South Africans, Chinese and Eurasians – all sharing in the life and tasks involved, such as sidemen, lesson readers, PCC members, Choir and congregation. I had become an English Parish Priest again, but with different problems yet similar advantages like receiving the traditional Easter Offering, a Vicarage home and a salary (I was no tent maker like Paul of Tarsus). However, I had little time for improving my Chinese language, except my contacts with the ubiquitous mainland refugees, drawn to a foreigner who spoke their language. Many of these became our friends.

One such was Mr. Liu Tien-dz. Having discovered that we were away on holiday, he came 16 miles across the Island to find us. After only nine months in St. Andrew's, we were already weighed down by a flood of refugees, ever needing help, work, food, lodgings and friendship. We thought we had escaped but he flushed us out. I felt angry and must have shown it. With a polite gesture, he turned away. With shame I called him back and wrote him a letter of introduction to a friend in the Army Barracks. With a gentle smile and a 'shie-shie' (thank you), he went off and duly found work. Although a son of a magistrate in the Chinese National Government, he accepted a job clearing out Army latrines. The Communists had shot his father but he himself had escaped. Since then, he had never had news of his wife and two children. That was four years ago.

When our No.3 son, Baby Tiger, was born, Mr. Liu would come, hold him, take him out in a wheeled chair, play with him and make him laugh. Occasionally, out of his little, he would bring us a gift chicken. Joining a distant Chinese church, he asked for baptism. Later he was confirmed quietly in a city church. Never once did he ask for money, but only for friendship.

After our return to England, we helped him to get a job as Hospital Porter. Qualifying for a residence permit after 4 years, he moved to London where he opened a small Chinese restaurant. Every Christmas, he would visit us 'bearing gifts' – noodles, rice, Chinese delicacies and yes, a turkey!

On 12th March 1959, we had received a letter from him:

"Dear Rev,

I devoutly pray God that I place my future and my life into His Hands. Mankind has no power. Everything is under our Lord's guidance. Nothing can accomplish without His permission. I pray God help me to fulfil my hope, obtaining His grace and unmerited mercy towards this miserable and poor creature. More than 9 years I have passed in Hong Kong. I alone (of my family) escaped from Red China. My whole family members are lost and my personal property ruined when the Communists over-ran China.

Now through your assistance I may have the chance of going to England for work. Is it not God's power had delivered me from these cruel Communists? How can I not believe my safe coming to Hong Kong is not God's grace?

Best wishes to you, your lady and three little brothers.

Respectfully yours,

Liu Tien-dz"

Post-Script, 1994 (Cambridge)

Mr. Liu has just been to see us, bearing gifts as usual. He told us he had just sold his "Take Away" shop in London. After being attacked by three men, one with a knife, he had decided to retire and live at peace with his new wife and son, whom he had found in London, who was also of Chinese origin.

After lively conversation and a meal with us, he said he must return to London and his family. As he headed for the railway station, he said a cheerful 'good bye', left us a brown foolscap envelope and departed. Later, we opened the envelope and found inside 20 fifty-pound currency notes, i.e. £1,000, from the sale results of his shop. We were humbled and astonished at his loving generosity. God is no man's debtor.

It says in Ecclesiastes, in the Old Testament, Chapter 11, Verse 1:

"Cast your bread upon the waters and it will return to you after many days."

Greta my wife and I went to see him and his new wife and family recently. He was all cheerfulness and rejoicing in his British Government's old age Pension!

Chapter 13

Baby Tiger at Heaven's Gate

With its humid weather and semi-tropical conditions, Hong Kong was not very good health wise. With my entire student work and preaching engagements, my throat began to be affected. We also began to experience family ills. Bill had a bad throat, John began vomiting and Philip – "Baby Tiger" – had diarrhoea, vomiting and fever. Greta had to doctor us all and to deal with illnesses in St. Stephen's Girls School where one dormitory resembled a hospital ward. Added to this, she had to give a talk in English to Heep Yunn Girls School on Nine Dragon's side. We began to feel exhausted. Therefore, we decided to take a week's holiday in Cheung Jau, a small island 30/40 minutes away from the Colony, where there was a CMS bungalow.

At first, all went well. Relaxation away from Hong Kong's vast activity was just what we needed. Baby Tiger's fever, however, refused to abate but rather grew worse. Bill and John improved considerably but Philip became very ill. Greta kept calm, but I could see that she was alarmed. Cradling him in her arms, she kept him as still as possible, lest severe coughing damage his lungs and heart. Greatly alarmed myself, I decided to phone a doctor friend at the Nethersole Hospital in the Colony but there was no telephone connection. Going to the Police, I sought their help and they allowed me to send an urgent telegram to Dr. Ted Paterson. He telegraphed back, "Coming early morning ferry with oxygen equipment and medicine."

As soon as I heard the sound of the early ferry's hooter, I raced down to meet him in the grey shadows of dawn. Soon we were both hurrying back to the bungalow carrying the oxygen cylinder and other packages. As we arrived breathlessly, Greta carrying Baby Tiger in her arms kept shouting excitedly, "It's happened! It's happened! The measles has just broken out and the fever declined." Soon Doctor Paterson had confirmed her tearful-joyful diagnosis. "I thought we had lost him," she cried with a quiver in her voice. "Thank God you have come." Dr. Ted smiled reassuringly, we were encouraged, Baby Tiger began to recover, and the necessary medicines were handed to Greta. I prepared breakfast for all and the crisis was averted. Soon, the doctor was returning to Hong Kong.

No.1 son, Bill, was now attending Primary School at the Kowloon Junior, proving himself to be a voracious reader, perfectly at home with his Bible, Prayer Book, many children's books and classics, and speaking extremely correctly. He took to it like a duck to water.

No. 2 son, Johnny, was also doing well at kindergarten, showing himself good at numbers and ABC and quite a rascal. However, one day at Sunday School, his mother found him crying very tearfully, "I can't find Bill anywhere." Mum went seeking Bill at the other end of the building. Seeing her, he suddenly burst into tears, crying "I can't find Johnny ANYWHERE!" No.3 son, Philip, however, on his part, was all joys, smiles and fun, riding his little "seat on wheels", or walking cheerfully anywhere. All three of them were normally jokers – in which they take after their father!

However, it never rains but it pours. The mid-Summer holiday was soon with us and early in July the weather becoming severely hot, Greta, the boys and I, with Ah Lin, went to Lan Tau, by ferry. From the pier, we proceeded to climb the 3,000 feet to the summit and the camp, with Philip being carried 'a la huagan'.

Having settled in, we put the bungalow in order and arranged for our meals at the Canteen, and then enjoyed a good cool sleep. Next morning, I left to return to Hong Kong for a Student Christian Conference, and then returned to Lan Tau peak and the family. I was very glad to escape Hong Kong's sizzling heat.

Bill and John loved the mountain and even more the swimming pool, fed by a mountain stream, which also provided our drinking water. Bill could now swim and dive, Johnnie had also learned to swim a few yards, whilst Philip ventured bravely with Mum or Dad at hand. Whilst some of the older folk were talking at the edge of the pool, Baby Tiger on his own initiative, decided to walk on the water and stepped out. He was no Peter, however, and sank immediately.

Although clothed, I immediately jumped into the water and handed him out. A few minutes later, he tried again and I got wet again. Unbelievably, the Tiger determined to achieve his aim. Stepping between adults, busily talking, he was going down the 3rd time. Seeing him, I quickly leaped into the pool again and did another rescue act, my heart racing. However, Baby Tiger seemed undisturbed!

A whole crowd of holidaymakers now joined the camp, glad like us to enjoy the peace and quiet. With no warning, the wind blew with tremendous force. To reach the Mess Hut, I crawled gingerly to our bungalow. A violent gust of wind swept me some 20 yards. Making the bungalow, I went around securing all windows. Finding a window open, I pushed it hard into place but my right hand went through the glass and I gashed my thumb. Dr. Greta came to the rescue with a darning needle but no anaesthetic or painkiller. Sterilising the needle, she tried stitching the gash. Two stitches were all that either of us could bear. "The hand is the most sensitive part of the body" she said. I agreed! She made an arm sling, which I wore for two weeks, but no blood poisoning developed, but only some restriction of hand movement.

Back at home, a doctor friend gave me some short-wave therapy, easing blood circulation and movement of the thumb. I was reminded of Bishop R. O. Hall once saying:

"God Himself put an element of chance into human life – and all this makes the wonder and miracle of Christ's birth, life and death and resurrection, even more wonderful."

Back in Nine Dragons' Country and Fragrant Harbour, we learned that the typhoon had left the Pearl of the Orient somewhat scarred too.

As for my thumb, I was unable to play the piano for many months to come.

The Shek Kip Mei fire, Christmas 1953

Putting out the fire

Chapter 14

Riot and Vengeance

The next six months from October 1955, proved to be quite dramatic. It began on the Double Tenth, the 10th Day of the 10th Moon. To Chinese, this needs no explanation. It is the day in 1911 AD upon which the Chinese Revolution broke out under Dr. Sun Yat Sen, father of China's Nationalist Republic and the Ching Dynasty lost the Mandate of Heaven. Chinese look back to that day as Englishmen look back to Magna Carta, and Americans to July 4th.

Chinese are just as history-minded as the Westerners, but they add a little mystery and poetry to their celebrations. Chinese Communists also look back to it but celebrate a day of their own, October 1st. A person's loyalty thus becomes clear-cut. There can be no doubt, where Chinese stand politically in Hong Kong, Taiwan or on the Mainland. Passions and hatreds, bitter memories and ideologies lie behind dates and mystic numbers.

My friend Yueh Ming, Chinese by race but a British subject, could look objectively on both Chinese factions and might have said "A plague on both their houses," knowing some Shakespeare. He had married a Chinese girl and they now had a dark and brown eyes happy baby. Yueh Ming had a local Government job and his wife did a half-day's work, so they could keep an Amah. One large room served as sitting room and bedroom, and off this was a bathroom. There was also a veranda. Not very spacious, but thousands in Hong Kong had less. They had waited long for it. A privileged few had more. It was always so in Hong Kong.

It was the Double Tenth when the alert sounded. Yueh Ming went over to the Police Station immediately. The alert meant trouble. He looked strong in his smart blue uniform and he was no mean athlete. Nationalist refugees had stuck paper flags on a Resettlement Block in Kowloon. An officious resettlement officer, unable to persuade anyone to remove them, rashly tore one down (what hidden passions lie behind the mystique of the flag). In a moment, all was

"Bubble, bubble, toil and trouble."

The frightened officer fled into his office. The crowd grew quickly, threatening violence. Two thousand people lived on the six floors of the block. The police restored order, but the trouble spread to the other 12 settlement blocks. Nationalist and Communist provocateurs joined the fray, tempers broke, fighting began, and Triad members and hooligans infiltrated, passions ran high. Yueh Ming sent word to his wife – "Stay indoors".

Public disorder now broke out. Roads were barricaded, cars were stopped and the occupants forced to buy Nationalist flags. Pickets stopped buses running. A bus driver drove straight through the area without stopping. Strong forces of police arrived. Pitched battles took place. Tear gas was used. Shop shutters were broken, looting began. Occupants of cars were roughly dragged out and the cars overturned. Using minimum force, the police cordoned off trouble spots and by early morning, control was achieved.

Yueh Ming slept little that night. Having ensured all was well at home, he added, "Keep indoors. Do not go out on the street!" Patrols reported to the Police HQ. Instructions were given out over the loudspeakers of the station.

Yueh Ming pondered the foolishness of humans. What pleasure was there in destruction? Maybe 7 long years of frustration had damned up anger and hatred in the hearts of refugees; the frustration of hand-to-mouth existence and living on charity, and existence without work.

Some policemen were arguing: "I've just been waiting for a chance like this! I want to smash up these rioters" His disgust was aroused. "Why do they allow such men in the Force?" he thought. "They are not worthy to be Policemen, let alone Chinese. Police training only makes men fit and tough." He had seen men broken and weeping, through the brutal training. There were some decent policemen, like him, who cared for law and order, loved children and laughed gently, "real Chinese", like Yueh Ming himself.

Next morning, trouble again broke out. At 10am the station loudspeaker called all men to duty. Reports indicated a new recklessness and savagery abroad, in outlying districts and factory areas. Police were attacked; Triad gangs were refuelling the flames using paraffin and petrol. Madness seized the rioters. A taxi trying to escape was pushed over, pinning the driver underneath. Paraffin and petrol were poured over it and set alight. The driver was burned to death, the woman passenger died in hospital, a man escaped with severe burns.

Yueh Ming tightened his belt and put on his steel helmet. The military were called out. Tanks rumbled into the area. Troop lorries appeared. Barricades were set up and districts were cordoned off. Yueh Ming was on duty in the station and breathed a sigh of relief. He watched patrols bringing in arrested rioters, who were taken upstairs to the CID room. The police were not gentle – their own lives had been in danger out there, as concrete blocks were dropped from seven storey buildings. Deaths and arson were reported.

Seeing the quiet savagery meted out to suspects, Yueh Ming was dismayed. Rioters were flung into the room, ringed by policemen, then beaten with steel helmets and truncheons, boots and fists. "Don't beat their heads" someone exclaimed (blood on the walls was whitewashed over).

Yueh Ming was not squeamish, but as a Christian, if only for four years, he was already Christian in outlook and principle, hating revengeful strategies and relieved when orders were given over the loudspeakers, warning that policemen who beat prisoners would be punished.

Day wore on. Military control tightened, a curfew was lifted at times to allow people to buy food. Some 6,000 arrests were made and order gradually restored to both the City and the outer districts. On the skyline, the Nine Dragon Mountains gazed impassively as rapacity and murder were bound and banished.

Yueh Ming returned home in the early hours of the morning. The streets were quiet. He pondered on the evil he had seen, the five men charged with murder, and the beatings in the police station. What could he do, if anything, to amend things?

His report, written and sent to the authorities, was sent anonymously, naming no names, for vengeance might even cloak itself in the Law's uniform. Later he heard that another eyewitness had corroborated his story and that the police authorities were investigating thoroughly.

Master Kung said:

> *"If you raise up the straight and set them on top of the crooked, the commoners will support you"*
>
> The Analects of Confucius 11, 19. (Waley).

Jesus in Gethsemane

Chapter 15

'Heaven Knows'

"No doubt it was Heaven's Doing"
The Book of Songs, 272. (Waley)

As it was just before nine on a school day morning, the red single-decker bus was crowded to suffocation, but the cheerful conductor let on an extra passenger and rang the bell. As the bus jerked forward, I took a second look at the newcomer, who was hanging on to the nearest rail. It was indeed James Pong. His eye caught mine. "Hello. 'Morning. Just caught it. It will save me a few minutes." There was, however, no evident sense of anxiety in his voice. He is an extremely imperturbable character even for a Chinese.

Among the massed crowd of schoolboys and girls packing the bus was one who, noticing James, half rose to offer him a seat. James smiled and shook his head, muttering a polite refusal. "Don't trouble. I get off the bus in a moment." He turned to me. "Must be one of our college students – or was it perhaps my 'dog collar'?" he murmured.

At the next stop we pushed our way off the bus through the ebb and flow of students and turned down the tree shaded path leading through Glenealy (a steep road in the City Centre not unlike a glen just at this point) and made our way to the college. We did not hurry – it was too hot and damp. Even the strong breeze stirring the great trees overhanging the road, failed to fan away the perspiration that began to trickle down our brows.

"We could do with some more rain rather badly" I said.

"Yes – all this dust lying about is not healthy" answered James. "Rain would bring the temperature down too. Have you seen the reservoirs? The water level is a record low. The newspapers say this morning that the Government will cut down the water supply to three hours a day only. Five hours at the moment's bad enough!"

We came to the College Chapel. The local Chinese Vicar had

kindly let the College use his Church for the weekly Friday Chapel Service.

"I must go in" said James, "To see everything is ready." The Chapel was peaceful and almost empty as we entered. In the chancel, the Vicar's small familiar figure was to be seen. He came with a word of greeting.

"Good morning. Still no rain. Rather serious, I'm afraid." We were all beginning to be rain conscious. What with the rain figures very far below the average for the time of year, and on top of that the million and more extra thirsty mouths and sweating bodies of the great influx of refugees from the Mainland, the water situation was critical indeed. "It must rain soon", I thought hopefully. "A couple of typhoons would do the trick, but they might do some damage too, especially in those flimsy refugee shanty towns. Icing the clouds has not done any good, either. Perhaps we ought to pray for rain."

The Vicar had departed, James had put everything ready for the service. The students began to come in and soon the church was full of the buzz of quiet conversation, the tread of feet and the rustle of clothing. As the college staff took their places there was silence. Only a minority of students were Christians but all shared and mostly valued this weekly worship together. They were the inheritors of the tradition of the former Christian universities on the Mainland.

The Chaplain began the service with an introductory sentence followed by a hymn, and nearly four hundred voices filled the church with the echoes of "Praise to the Lord, the Almighty, the King of Creation." It is a noble hymn in Chinese as well as English. Some students sang in Mandarin, and the majority in the local Cantonese dialect. As the organ sounded the "Amen" James Pong stepped forward to take prayers.

"Let us pray." The students were quietly attentive as James led them in thanksgiving, followed by a prayer for the needs of the community and colony.

"... O heavenly Father and Creator Spirit, send, we pray, the rain which we need ..."

Before he could proceed, the whole student body burst into loud and continuous laughter. Taken aback, James could only stop his prayer, waiting in dignified patience until the laughter died away. I was astonished too. "What can have come over them all?" I thought to myself. James in the meantime continued, "... and grant, O Lord, that the reservoirs may soon be filled ..." Again, startlingly loud and unbelievably shattering, that wild, wild laughter ...

* * *

It was later in the day that I met James again. We had both tackled the students in our classes on the reason for the extraordinary scene in chapel. Except for an odd one or two, none of them believed that God and the weather had any immediate connection at all. The Chinese propensity for mirth, sometimes ill timed, had been too much for them.

As we walked out of the school, a gentle rain was falling!

Chapter 16

The Scottish Ship's Engineer's Romance

Naturally, Chinese girls in Hong Kong, sometimes have secret hopes of marriage to young Western men, in spite of some misgivings about race and colour. However, backed up by Christian faith and church allegiance, such liaisons resulted in good, if not always, infallible friendships.

Such romances occurred also outside regular church life. Such was the extraordinary story of the Scottish ship's engineer. His ship called regularly at the Colony but only for one or two days, every 6 months. Here he had met a Korean girl whilst on shore. Neither could speak the other's language, but he had courted her and they had fallen in love. She had come to Hong Kong on a six-month visa and had stayed with a Chinese friend who spoke Korean. The latter's flat was near St. Andrew's Church and she occasionally attended our services.

Since the Engineer's ship did not return within the six month's, the Immigration Department generously extended the girl's visa, but only for an extra six months. In due time, a week before the expiry of the extended visa, both ship and engineer arrived for only one day in port. The Marriage Ceremony was fixed at the Registry with all concerned unaware that beyond 4pm it was illegal. Bride and Groom duly arrived, but too late. Returning to her friend's flat, the Bride wept bitterly, whilst the Engineer, went out to drown his sorrows. His ship was due to sail that night at 9 pm.

The Bride's friend came to the Vicarage seeking my help. I phoned the Colony's Registrar who said, "If the Registrar General is willing to extend the time, I will issue a certificate".

Alas, the law was the law. On an inspiration, I telephoned Bishop Hall. He said that marriages could take place in his chapel up to 6pm, and that I could take the wedding. The Registrar mentally kow-towed and issued the license.

All was excitement and haste. The parties rushed to the flat, however, the Bridegroom had not returned. It was now 5pm. I waited at the Bishop's House-chapel. At 6.30pm, they telephoned. The Bridegroom had been found, but too late. With some trepidation I decided to phone the Governor of the Colony. He listened courteously and promised that if his Registrar General concurred, he would issue a Special License immediately. It would, however, cost HK$150 (£10).

The Registrar General telephoned me, "A Special License must state the place of the Marriage Ceremony. May I suggest you are all welcome to my own home on Hong Kong Peak." It was 7.20pm.

Rounding up the Bridal Party, we sped across the harbour by "walla-walla" boat and reached the Registrar General's house. His wife welcomed us into the Drawing Room, waiting for the Registrar to return, with license and Bridegroom. It appeared that the Governor had been attending a State Dinner and was delayed in signing the license.

Meanwhile, at the house on the Peak, I went through the English Prayer Book Marriage Service with the Bride. She had no English but listened to her friend who interpreted into Korean. Where necessary, I explained in Mandarin to her friend. The Registrar General, who had returned, and his wife acted as witnesses. The Bridegroom, who had raced up in a taxi, was an Anglican and was acquainted with the Prayer Book service. The Promises were made. The ring was placed on the Bride's third finger of her left hand, I finished with the Blessing; the Marriage Register and the Certificate were signed. I gave the certificate to the Bride and she, her husband and her friend, raced away in the taxi back to the flat. There, collecting his own things, the Engineer, his wife and I, drove at speed down to the harbour, in the taxi. The ship already had steam up and the gangway was still down. The Engineer raced up the gangway, which was immediately drawn up. The ship's anchor was loosed and the ship began to move on its six-month's voyage to Australia. The couple waved good bye vigorously. The impossible had been achieved, with all the parties exhausted but utterly thankful, and not least to the divine Lord.

Being now a British citizen by marriage, the young wife was

free to remain in the Colony as long as was necessary. What the angels in heaven said, I cannot imagine. However, history had been made. Never in the long history of the Colony had this happened before. Anticipating the mad curiosity of the Press, I kept the whole matter a secret, but I quietly thanked the Lord God our heavenly Father for His infinite mercies to two of His children, and inwardly cried "Laus Deo".

I never discovered the facts of the eventual re-meeting of that Romeo and Juliet, for I must have left the Colony and returned to merry England before their reunion.

> *"A wedding took place at Cana in Galilee ... Jesus and his disciples had also been invited to the wedding ... His mother said to the servants, "Do whatever He tells you ..."*
>
> St. John's Gospel, Chapter 2, vv1-5.

Jesus with the woman at the well

Chapter 17

Air Hostess in Distress

St. Andrew's Church Choir, Kowloon, was well known and much appreciated. A visiting young man once described it, not incorrectly, as a glamorous choir, composed of school girl sopranos, and young men of the forces as well as local inhabitants. Eugene Shih the young organist, an excellent musician, following others, had moulded them into a good choral group. Above all, the choir members were faithful Christians. Amongst them was Ma Mei-ling, or Mei-ling Ma (using the Western fashion).

In those days of 1956 AD, the Colony was very overcrowded, following on the vast exodus of one and a half million refugees from the Mainland and other places. Mei-ling's mother, however, was a regular Hong Kong resident, half British and a widow. Her English husband had died when Mei-ling was young.

There were two other children. Mei-ling being an orphan and Eurasian, was eligible to attend one of the Colony's large Anglican church schools as a boarder. At home she spoke Cantonese, but in school the basic language was English. Thus, she grew up bi-lingual, a great advantage in that British Colony, equal to the advantage of having British nationality.

Only a small percentage of the 700 girls of the School came of Christian families, but in addition to the good teaching, they also received regular tuition in the Christian faith through religious knowledge classes, assemblies and a Students Christian Union. Many of the girls attended our St. Andrew's church. Our good Bishop Hall also arranged yearly Conferences for all the Colony's Christian Union members. Mei-ling Ma loved these occasions where she was able to meet hundreds of the other students and share in Bible Studies, Prayer sessions, special speakers and not least the recreation times, including "Rags". It all helped her to think out her faith, and she became a convinced and intelligent Christian, like many others and was duly 'confirmed' by the Bishop.

Eventually, Mei-ling was old enough to leave school, and seek work. Her competence in two languages, her good manners and looks, and quiet assurance learned at school, and the school's reputation in the Colony, enabled her to get an office job. Although she enjoyed the work, her wages were low. Her widowed mother had been compelled by circumstances to live in a large tenement building, and to rent part of a covered veranda, where she cooked, worked and brought up her family. The toilet was communal, but at least the living space was better than living on a staircase landing, or on a roof-top, or on a pavement covered by a tarpaulin, or in a road-side shack built of pieces of wood, with oiled paper covering the window spaces. Thousands lived that way in Hong Kong. Moreover, Mrs. Ma's TB played havoc in such conditions and as Mei-ling now became the family breadwinner she knew that she needed work to bring in better wages. She quickly made up her mind. She must try the Colony's Airlines as an air-hostess. They were well paid and it would be an exciting adventure, with a chance of seeing the world. When she was accepted, she was excited and overjoyed. Her increased wages also enabled her to move her mother and two brothers into a small three-roomed flat in one of the seven storied buildings which the Government was erecting with commendable speed to meet the desperate needs of the rapidly increasing population.

Mei-Ling, by nature a friendly and charming girl, also looked most attractive in her air-hostess uniform. With the glamour, alas, there came also the danger. There seemed nothing wrong in taking a small gift for an acquaintance in Honolulu for someone in Hong Kong, Bangkok or Singapore. Her Chinese genes made her respond to such an appeal. Then, before she knew what was happening, she became involved in a large smuggling racket. Unknown to herself, a small suitcase she took with her into the plane, contained hidden dutiable goods and even strips of gold, sewn into the linings. Already implicated and unknowingly involved, she tried without success to escape the net.

She realised frantically that exposure would certainly mean dismissal and even prison. The gang involved cared nothing for innocent stooges, and her life was threatened if she refused to cooperate, and especially if she told the authorities.

Exposure did come. Mei-Ling was terrified. Contraband goods were found in her suitcase. The Borneo Police acted and took her into custody. Afraid for her life, she dared not confess. Other air-hostesses and pilots and big names were involved. Although the police knew she was merely a stooge, a term of imprisonment and a huge fine faced her. With the knowledge of the airline officials, the head stewardess saw her secretly and urged her to confess everything, promising her protection and even the continuance of her job. She confessed secretly but they went back on their word; she lost her job. In any case, she would become an obvious target to her enemies if she continued as a stewardess.

Hearing of her desperate plight, her Christian friends in Hong Kong gave some of the money to pay the fine. Our good Bishop and other church leaders wrote on her behalf to the authorities, and we all held her up in prayer to Jesus. A frightened and deeply repentant girl secretly returned to the Colony. Ashamed to meet her old friends; too scared to go out even amongst the thronging millions of Hong Kong, lest some unknown assassin strike to kill, she no longer lived with her mother, nor even visited her. Therefore, she crept about the City, going to worship at other churches where she was not known.

Only one way seemed to be left. Mei-Ling must leave the Colony and secretly begin a new life in London. Helped by her friends, she collected enough money to pay the sea passage to England. Here, sustained by caring and praying friends, she found another job and a new life. A businessman took her into his office at a good salary.

Today, somewhere in England, lives an attractive, charmingly dressed Eurasian girl, with her own English home. Every Sunday sees her worshipping in her parish church. Every week she sends a part of her salary to her mother and brother, who, through ill health, is regularly in and out of work. She might well have married. It was not for want of a proposal. However, for her, the Christian and her Chinese (Confucian) teaching of "Honour your Father and Mother", is an obligatory necessity.

Mei-Ling loved the quiet beauty and peace of England, yet from time to time her thoughts strayed into cosmopolitan "Fragrant

Harbour", its scenic beauties, its warm climate, its thronging millions of colourfully dressed people, even its ubiquitous refugees, existing on roofs and staircases, or in a squatter village or the forest of Government multi-storey blocks, amidst wealth and poverty., its Triads, its suicides, its 'call-girl' hotels and lively churches. To some it is Paradise, but for Mei-Ling, it aroused sighs too deep for tears and longings for home.

Then Grace and Faith came to the rescue. She met again a courteous and caring young Englishman, whom she had once met in St. Andrew's Church, Kowloon. He had fallen in love with her, and now asked her to marry him. He was a Christian and in one of the Professions. Loving-virtue and Valiant-for-Truth became her proxy parents; the Wedding was a beautiful and joyous occasion and Jesus the Lord was also invited to the Wedding, and we remembered the ancient words of the Psalmist:

> *"Though I take the Wings of the Morning, and fly to the uttermost parts of the earth, even there shall Thy hand lead me, and Thy right hand shall hold me."*
>
> (Psalm 139 vv 8/9)

Chapter 18

Old Mrs. Lee – First Wife

Before Padre John died in the swimming accident, he had introduced me to dear old Mrs. Lee, a Chinese Christian, whom he had encouraged to attend church. She looked Chinese but she had been born in Jamaica. Her husband was Chinese too, and had brought her to Hong Kong, finding a house in Nine Dragons' Country. Here she remained all her life. She was really an Old Testament Christian, baptised as a child in her Jamaican home. I never could discover how old she was! When she married, she never had a child and determined to act as Sara to her 'Abraham', separating from him totally, although still living in their home at 19a Tak-Wing Street. In her place, she persuaded her husband to marry a younger Chinese wife. It was never a peaceful solution. Second wife bore her husband a son, named George, and a daughter Dorothy (Gift of God), before her husband died.

Now old Mrs. Lee was strong-willed and had some education. The second wife, on her part, had a sharp tongue and was illiterate, and was much younger. When the husband died, old Mrs. Lee, first wife, took over the family affairs. Sub-letting the apartment brought in just enough money to keep them all going. Like the Padre, I also visited her and gave her Holy Communion from time to time, for she was now too infirm to get to St. Andrew's.

On my latest visit just before Christmas 1956, I found old Mrs. Lee lying half-asleep on the low bed against the wall. The room was ill lit.

"Who is that?" she asked in her high pitched toothless voice.

"It is the Pastor come to see you", second wife said loudly in Cantonese.

"Oh Vicar, have you come at last? Please sit down. I have not seen you for a long time." The words came slowly in a loud singsong tone, as if she were not used to speaking in English, and as a deaf person speaks.

"I thought the Lord was going to take me – and I would never see you again." Her wrinkled old face puckered and tears filled her eyes.

"Well here I am, and how are you today?" I asked.

"I'm not very well. I'm going to die. My old head is dizzy and if I try to stand, I fall over and none of them will help me." Her voice took on a sob. "Last night, going to the toilet, I fell and lay on the floor, unable to get up. My body is too heavy and my heart has a pain." Her ungainly form shook as she wept. "That 'other one' wont help me. She only shouts and gets angry, and she lets the children do as they like!"

On the veranda a youth and a girl sat at a table, he reading a book, she doing embroidery. They took little notice of us.

"George is a good lad," I said. "He attended the confirmation classes quite regularly and was very attentive. Dorothy too. They were both at church on Sunday."

"Yes." She intoned. "Yes, he's a good boy but sometimes he is disobedient and speaks sharply to me. I've brought them both up and loved them as my own children ..."

She had told me the story often, so that I knew it off by heart. "Perhaps you can come to church on Sunday," I interjected, changing the subject.

"If only I could come and the Good Lord would let me, or take me Home!"

"Now Mrs. Lee, the Lord Jesus knows about you and the children. Trust Him. I want you to promise me something!"

"What do you want me to promise, Vicar?"

"I want you to try to laugh every day and to be cheerful with George and Dorothy. Don't scold them. Rejoice in the Lord! That is what St. Paul said."

"I could not promise to laugh", she began, a faint smile beginning at her eyes.

"Yes you could! Count your blessings every day. You do have some blessings, don't you? Laugh and rejoice!"

Her old face lit up and she almost laughed. "Laugh! Fancy asking me to laugh!"

"Yes! ... and every day too! Do you promise?"

"Yes, I promise" she said, and laughed aloud, murmuring to herself. "Laugh – and every day!" almost chuckling. "Rejoice in the Lord! Yes I will."

"I've come to bring you your Christmas Communion," I added.

"Good. I knew you would come, although you are very busy."

"George," she called, "Bring me a candle please. Here is the white cloth for the table, and here is a kneeler for you," she said, turning to me.

Therefore, the table was spread, my tiny silver chalice and paten arranged, her one candle lighted, her old eyes closed, and her stiff fingers joined. I knelt down and began the ancient liturgy:

"Our Father who art in heaven ..." Line by line, on and on, she repeated after me, up to the well remembered words:

"The Body of our Lord Jesus Christ, given for Thee ... the Blood of our Lord Jesus Christ shed for Thee ..."

As I put away the vessels after the service, her old hands caught mine, "God bless you and your wife and the little ones."

"We return to England soon now." I said.

"Yes. I know. Pray for me, wont you?" she said. "Wait, I have a little gift for your wife. Please give it to her from me."

She rummaged in a drawer and brought out a little box. In it were two small pieces of Jade. She pressed the box into my hand and said, "Good bye."

"Thank you dearly," I responded. "The Lord bless you and keep you, and don't forget! Rejoice and laugh every day!"

She laughed delightedly again. She was probably still laughing as I went carefully down the gloomy rickety staircase and the doors were closed by Second Wife. On my way home I thought of Abraham, Sarah and Hagar.

The other day, I noticed Greta was wearing a pendant. It looked very nice indeed. Jade suits her. Her engagement ring was made of Jade too. Dear old Mrs. Lee, first wife.

The Master said,

"It is Goodness that gives to a neighbourhood its beauty."

Analects IV, 1. (Waley).

Mary and Martha at Bethany

Chapter 19

Our Holy Bishop Visits the Red Dragon

In August 1956, Bishop R. O. Hall and his wife were invited to tour Red China by the Mainland Communist Government. His visit and his reflections upon it caused some controversy. "What mattered" he said, "was that for Anglicans world wide, it was necessary to understand what Chinese Anglicans in China – bishops, clergy and lay folk – felt about that country under its new Government. Roman Catholic brethren in Hong Kong have their different interpretation of the Church and Government situation but many China Roman Catholics differ. It was necessary to agree to differ and resolve to love."

The Bishop and his wife spent three weeks in China. He told us what they saw. They saw what they were shown – new worker's housing; new kindergarten and nursery schools, and a vigour and health among children everywhere. Hospitals and medical colleges had expanded too. In Shanghai they saw no beggars and in Beijing only one. A Yorkshire wool-spinner spoke of the miracle of moral transformation in Shanghai and, best of all, pensions for their old workers. Old China friends spoke with pride and confidence about the new Government "Atheist in theory, theist in practice." They could never be Communists but were grateful to the Party for bringing at last a good, strong Government. They were amazed at the successful moral reform of the people compared with the little that the Christian Church had done.

The Bishop insisted that in China, the Church, Theological Colleges and Sunday Schools, continued to exist, also Men's Societies and Young People's Associations. Some Shanghai parishes had several Family Prayer Meetings each week in Christian homes, as well as Sunday worship. The Bishop of Shanghai had confirmed 600 adults that year. Now, after the Japanese war and surrender, China had become a peaceful, orderly country. Nevertheless, it was important to remember, urged Bishop Hall, that Chinese Christians are all products under God of faithful Missions: the faith of Chinese Christian leaders came via missionaries along with their parents, grandparents, pastors and friends. They believe that they themselves can do more and greater things, without the old international controls. A new inter-church fellowship was already taking shape.

On his first day in Beijing, Bishop R. O. Hall and his wife met the beloved Bishop of Beijing, Timothy Lin, a strange mixture of English Public School manners and Chinese traditions – a scholarly 'un-arrogance'. They went to the Altar and Temple of Heaven. Not since 1933, had Bishop R. O. Hall worshipped God in that most Holy Place. He felt it was to the Altar of Heaven, rather than the Cathedral that they needed to go first. Mrs. Hall had visited it 30 years earlier. They were now both amazed, having forgotten its incredible beauty, dignity, simplicity and grandeur. For them, it recorded all pure art and true religion, and God's demand for obedience and self-naughting in natural life and answered by the Chinese people. Bishop Lin often went there to meditate on the mystery of China's ancient history and God's demands today on the Chinese people and Chinese church. There, Bishop Lin prayed for Bishop Hall and for the Chinese people, asking for God's mercy on Church and People. As he prayed a soft rain fell, a reminder of God's mercy which falls as gentle dew, and a parable of Christ's love for His church in China today. Years before, the great giant Christian General Feng Yu-xiang had told them how China loved the symbol of water and of its greatest use to man because it is always restless to find the lowest place. So God emptied Himself in Jesus, even in the shameful death of the Cross.

Bishop and Mrs. Hall were later invited to the Visitor's Gallery of the National Assembly of the Chinese People, to see the delegates assemble, including the Chinese Presiding Bishop C. T. Chen and others. The assembly rose to its feet, clapping the entrance of Chairman Lui Xiao-chi and officers, followed unobtrusively by Chairman Mao Dz-dong, General Chu-deh and the Prime Minister Chou En-lai.

"Here", stated Bishop Hall, "was another Government in Power in Beijing, on a scale and lavish dignity making Versailles look like bric-a-brac!" At last Beijing had a Government which knew how to rule and control, and make other nations take China into their reckoning. "Here," Bishop Hall continued, "he saw Communism as Christ's minister, passionate in its pursuit of honesty and the welfare of the people rather than its own power." A Chinese friend told him, "Our Government is a good Government, concerned with the people's welfare, and expecting the Christian Church to have an equal concern, and deserve protection."

The Bishop and his wife were also invited to visit Hangzhou, the pride of all Chinese people, a superb example of China's skill in making nature's beauty still more beautiful. There in the old temple of Yu-fei, was expressed the perfect balance, – loyalty to nation and to family, and to honest integrity in public life, preferring eventually death to compromise, the loyal and faithful son, perfect husband and ideal father.

"In China" the Bishop believed, "was a Government strong and remarkably enlightened, the nearest approach in history to Plato's 'Philosopher Kings', depending on the education of it's people and perfecting the work God had done in remaking China, through the family, the Nation and the Church."

Not unnaturally, this panegyric excited some comment. At a later meeting of Bishop Hall with the clergy of the diocese, one American chaplain asked, "And what does the Bishop think of the Satanic Government of the West?"

A Chinese priest indicated that prior to the Bishop's visit to Canton, a meeting was called to plan for it. The Bureau of Religious Affairs made a list of all those in China with whom the Bishop had worked in past years, whom he might wish to see. The Bishop was taken to all his various friends. The smallest details of their livelihood were anticipated, even the food in the kitchen was prepared in advance. Those visited would be very careful in their statements to the Bishop. Any possible desire or wish was anticipated and prepared for.

"In China," The Bishop urged, "the struggle was not against Paganism, Buddhism and Religionism – not a 'secular' v 'spiritual' issue – nor one between Capitalism v Communism – but a Church involved in the nation with power to influence Government. However, the Church was beginning to find its feet."

In Beijing, the Bishop said he found a set of ivory chessmen –

but no 'bishop', instead a 'Grand Vizier'. When chess came to Western Europe, the Grand Vizier was replaced by the Bishop – the Bishop's assumption of office was as a King's Chief Minister – not as a Friar Shepherd of the flock of Christ. However, today in China, there is no Bishop, no Council of Churches, no Lambeth, no World Council on International Affairs. However, God's influence, through Jesus Christ, 2nd Person of the Trinity, is present.

The Church should now make sure of the existence of the Family, the Nation and the Church, in God's ordering of the World. The Family and the Nation today are basic factors in China. Contemporary, political and economic thought are 'passing away'! Indeed, the Presiding Bishop of the Anglican Church in China is now an elected member in the National Assembly – nominated by The Party. The strength of the new Chinese Government lies in a remarkably high level of efficiency and sweet reasonableness in local Government, with some heart-breaking exceptions.

Bishop Hall indicated his deep personal assessment of the state of China at that time. He also intimated that he had had an interview with Premier Jou En-lai, and the Presiding Bishop Robin Chen and discussed Bishop Xu's imprisonment, following an 'arson incident' in Lingling. This had aroused indignation against the unknown but real culprits.

Bishop Robin Chen had then written to Bishop Xu, telling him that Bishop Hall, after a short delay in Hengyang, was returning to Canton on a certain train. To Bishop Hall's great delight, Bishop Xu suddenly appeared in the dining-car and they went on together to Canton.

Apparently Bishop Xu was bent and thin but as spiritually alive and able as ever. Nine months earlier he had had an operation in Lingling hospital to deal with his lung. Apparently it proved unnecessary for him to use a tube for the rest of his life, so it was removed.

He was now well and living in Lingling with a retired priest to help him. His wife was also with him; one son was studying in an Engineering College in the North East; two of the girls were married and the adopted daughter was in school.

However, some time later, Bishop Stevens in England heard that Bishop Xu and his wife had died.

Chapter 20

Harold Smythe – Another Barnabas

Bishop R.O. and Mrs. Hall had now returned to the Bishop's house and we had returned to lovely St. Andrew's Vicarage, Kowloon. Here we found our other bachelor friend, Mr. Harold Smythe, kindly Christian eccentric and retired business man, son of an Anglican vicar. Having continued to look after Padre Ogilvie until the latter's untimely death, he became a sort of lay-vicar during the interregnum and continued as our guide and friend. Formerly, when Greta and I had married, way back in 1948 in Hong Kong Cathedral, he had been my best man. It was a joy to renew our old acquaintance, whilst Harold rejoiced to be able to look after his erstwhile bridegroom and bride, and great were his kindnesses.

He was also an eccentric in some ways and a modern Barnabas, full of the Holy Spirit and faith. I suppose for this reason he would often parade about in the vicarage wearing a sarong, and with great sang-froid. Most of his religious interests had been centred upon the Cathedral, where he had regularly worshipped, and gave it his devotion and common sense, as a Council member.

During the days of Internment Camps under the Japanese, he quietly exercised his practical and spiritual influence. However, after the liberation, he took up residence in the Dean's house and ran it as a Guest House in his own efficient, competent and kindly manner, making it a great opportunity for doing good works to help many people. It was here that I first had the pleasure of meeting him.

When the Dean and Mrs. Rose returned to the Colony, they took him into their house in their own loving way and he became as much part of their home as he seemed to be part of the Cathedral.

When Dean Rose resigned as dean and the new dean was appointed, Harold very naturally felt that he ought to find another place to live, and my wife and I were extremely pleased that just at that time we were at St. Andrew's Vicarage (whilst Padre Ogilvie was on furlough) and that Harold accepted our invitation to him to come and live with us.

From that time began his closer association with St. Andrew's, for Padre Ogilvie was extremely pleased on his return to have Harold with him in the Vicarage. I suppose that Harold rarely if ever missed the regular weekly Wednesday Communion Service and Evensong in the church, and in his quiet way he was able to help many people who came, both practically and spiritually. Yet he never forced himself upon St. Andrew's (being too much a Vicar's son, to make that mistake). However, when dear John Ogilvie suddenly collapsed and died, Harold (although feeling the loss very deeply) went on to do the work of a vicar at the Vicarage. He arranged baptisms, weddings, launch picnics and preachers for each Sunday, and entertained visitors and the different organisations using the church, I suspect largely at his own expense.

He told me privately that in one month he had given 600 bottles of orange squash to the various people calling at the Vicarage during one of those hot months. He was also a genial host at the Fellowship held in the Vicarage every Sunday after Evensong.

He was a good man full of the Holy Ghost and of faith, when on the Eve of St. Andrew's Day, 28th November 1955, towards midnight, Harold came to the banks of life's Jordan River and quietly passed through the waters to the other side.

We all missed Harold when he died and we thanked God for him, and we may all be sure that in that other Kingdom, on that other shore, he is still serving and following his Master, as he did here, with cheerfulness and faithfulness.

Chapter 21

A Spate of Visitors

It was January 1st, New Year's Day, in 1957 and our first visitor, courtesy of Radio Hong Kong, was His Majesty, King George VI of Great Britain and Northern Ireland and the British Commonwealth. With a memorable and moving call, he welcomed in the New Year.

"Put your hands into the hand of God" said King George. His slight stammer emphasised his message, which well illustrated the saying of Genghis Khan "It is better to light one small candle than to curse the darkness."

A spate of unusual visitors led us through Chinese New Year up to Easter. First of all Mrs. H. Gordon Thompson, my wife's widowed mother, came to stay with us for over a month to our mutual joy. She had not yet met Baby Tiger, No. 3 son, but had cared for Bill and John in England. She was not very well during the flight nor at the time of arrival, so we were allowed to meet her on the tarmac as she alighted from the BOAC plane, and to lead her to the Airport lounge. Mother was so excited at seeing us that she forgot about 'not being well' and Greta had to ask her to be more sedate! She met some old friends whilst staying with us and made some new friends too. We were loath to say good bye when she flew home to England by BOAC on Friday March 16th.

Another unusual visitor was Dr. George Ademola, son of a Nigerian King. One Sunday morning near Easter, he arrived at church in his very colourful robes. We invited him to stay with us before he went on to Manila, which he appreciated since we were able to share experiences of Jesus in Africa and China, and he also had opportunity to experience Chinese New Year.

To that same service came also an American Negro, some Phillipinos, Malaysians and our own cultural mix of Chinese, Eurasians, Europeans and Commonwealth citizens, a warming example of the Church Universal and a foretaste of Heaven.

From Manila, the Doctor Prince wrote a charming and humble letter:

"My dear Friends,

Firstly let me apologise for not being able to see you the Saturday you went on holiday. I was so involved in buying and packing. Please pardon me.

I was among you as a member of the Family and enjoyed my stay. I am grateful to you for your friendship and love of the Family, where the People of God are, and the children of God find a home.

I arrived here on Saturday to be met by a Christian man, a Professor of Law at the University, a friend of a friend. Later at church, I met a past President of the Medical Association, who was also in Amsterdam for the World Council of Churches 1948.
Manila is expensive and, I am afraid, not so picturesque as Hong Kong, but the people are friendly.

Greetings and love to you all.

George Aderemi Ademola"

Two other distinguished Christian visitors were Dr. Howard W. K. Moule, Archbishop of Australia and Bishop Marcus Loane of Sydney. They came to assess the situation in the Chinese Peoples Republic vis-à-vis the former Mission Churches, such as the China Inland Mission and the Three Self-Patriotic Church, under Communism. We had to hide the Archbishop from a predatory Australian reporter of an Australian Church Newspaper. The reporter became very angry when we refused to tell him where the dignitaries were staying, but we kept him away with kindness, for a rather bad reputation had preceded him.

Another event was a Recital of Sacred Music by the Russian Orthodox Church Choir, supported by 120 of their members and led by their gracious Priest, Father Elia Wen. Our St. Andrew's Senior Fellowship had arranged the visit, which proved very inspiring. They regularly used our church hall for monthly services.

As Bill and John, our older sons, grew up, they found some fresh delights. Any day of the week, introduced by Harold Smythe and taken by Greta, they were able to visit Hong Kong Cricket Club on the Island side, of which Harold was then a member. Here they were taught how to play cricket by Billy Tyldesly, well known in the Colony. Of even more importance, he used to read to our two and other children, the classic boys' adventure books of R. M. Ballantyne and not least my own favourite, 'The Dog Crusoe'. When in my earlier China days I was given an Alsatian pup as a congenial friend for a lonely bachelor, I named my constant companion 'The Dog Crusoe'.

At the Kowloon Cricket Club, they also had entrance through a great Eurasian friend, an officer in St. Andrew's Church, Freddie Wong. Here they could not only play cricket, but enjoy the open swimming pool. Freddie, indeed, was 'a brand plucked from the burning'. His parents were not church goers and left Freddie to play in the streets, and to his own devices, on Sundays. An RC Christian nearby, noticed this and took the boy to St. Andrew's Church, where he joined the Sunday School and youth activities and the regular congregation. In due time, Freddie became a member of the Church Council, then Church Treasurer, and a most regular worshipper.

Jesus calls Zaccheas to come down from the tree

Chapter 22

St. Stephen's College, Stanley – Eton of the Far East

St. Stephen's College was well known to me and my wife. We had spent our Honeymoon there in the summer vacation of 1948 and the Prison Governor allowed us to use his private beach nearby, which, in the hot weather, was a real joy. After our month's honeymoon, we returned to China.

A year later, we were back in Guilin where Greta was the Hospital Superintendent in our small Christian "Way of Life Hospital". Mao Zedong was now threatening the City, and our nursing staff, when our No.1 child was due to be born, did not wish to take the responsibility of looking after the birth. Happily, Greta's parents were due to arrive by plane and fly on to Hong Kong, and from there to England. They were only too ready to look after their daughter in the circumstances and I duly went there by plane, nearer to the birth time.

No.1 son was born on June 29th, St. Peter's Day, but we named him William because of the death at the time of that great Archbishop of Canterbury, William Temple. We were also invited by one of St. Stephen's College senior staff members, to use her bungalow, until we were ready to return to China and to Guilin. The staff member was Miss. Griffin and we had to take care to keep Bill from crying too much. We achieved this by keeping him in his small pram at night, and if he whimpered , we pushed the pram to and fro across a piece of rope on the bedroom floor. It worked splendidly.

Kindly Miss Griffin looked after us very well, and we had plenty of time to share with Grandpa and Granny Thompson. Miss Griffin also shared a strange experience with us. One early morning, she saw a tiger paddling across the sands near her home! Where the stray creature came from, we never discovered.

When, therefore, we were sent back in 1952 as missionaries to Hong Kong and not to China, where all foreigners were expelled by the Mao Government, we were glad to return to Hong Kong, of which we had many happy memories, not least of Stanley on the East coast of Victoria Island, and of St. Stephen's College, the Eton of the Far East.

Stanley possessed a good school beach and pier, a welcome refuge in the hot weather. A few fishing junks were usually anchored near the shore, and the fisher-folk, with their brown bodied, barefooted children, looked content and peaceful enough. The CMS Day School there, catered for only a few of them and was being enlarged to accept more children.

The College was an attempt to transplant the British Public School idea to Hong Kong and the Far East, and the College at Stanley depended on fees and subscriptions. It had no financial help from local Government.

Alfred Sung, who had now finished his time at St. Stephens, was sitting on the pier, looking at the bay. It was too early, he told us, for sharks. However, during World War II, a British soldier was sitting on that very pier, his legs dangling in the sea, and he had his leg bitten off. The sharks had become more common at that time since the Japanese, it was said, dumped dead corpses at sea and this attracted the sharks.

Alfred was now joined by his friend Francis. They were both sixth formers, and had now passed the Hong Kong English University entrance examinations and were enjoying their summer vacation before going up.

The first week at University was exciting. Amongst the 800 or more undergraduates there were some of their former College friends, now in their second and third year. They had been cheerfully welcomed. The University campus was palatial. The big hall had solemn panelling and oil paintings of former patrons and vice chancellors. The fine lecture rooms, the modern science laboratories, the goldfish lily ponds; and the great library, muffled and quiet, were all very attractive. Even the wearing of the student's gowns, oddly green and half-length, gave them a literary air and sense of importance.

In the letter rack, they found letters addressed to them from the University Christian Fellowship, inviting them to the Fresher's Tea. Perhaps, they hoped, some of those good looking girl students would be there! After the very male atmosphere of their old college, it would be pleasant to mix with their female counterparts. Two of these now came up and introduced themselves.

"May we say 'hello'? We are glad to meet you. I am Barbara Fong and this is Kung Xu Wa. Are you from Ying-Wa or where?"

"No, we're from St. Stephen's College, Stanley", said Alfred.

"Oh, I saw your names in the Freshers List. You're Christians aren't you? We hope to see you at our meetings."

The days went by. Alfred studied hard and yet found time for recreation in the Students Union. He also shared a study-bedroom with Francis, in St. John's Hall, the Anglican hostel. They began to take an interest in the University's religious activities. At first a little restless, they began to enjoy the Student Christian Fellowship meetings. The rather aggressive belief of some students was annoying, but less so than the chorus singing of American revivalism.

Alfred's religious faith was formal as yet. Now on Sundays, he attended the Cathedral's Communion Service. The dignified liturgy worship appealed to him and to some of his friends. Alfred himself was quiet and reserved, but he had a ready wit too. As the familiar pattern of worship unfolded, one of the prayers suddenly struck him with compelling power:

"We do not presume to come to this Thy Table, O Merciful Lord, trusting in our own righteousness but in thy manifold and great mercies ..."

It came like a revelation, a flash of deep insight; the secret that had revealed itself to Paul, Augustine, Luther and Wesley – the secret faith and trust in Jesus alone and utter distrust of one's own resources and spirituality, came upon Alfred with overwhelming power.

In the weeks, months and years that followed, Alfred grew in wisdom and in favour with God and man. With conviction and joy, he began to speak openly about Jesus to other students at the University, and went on to leadership of the Students Christian Union. After his graduation, he began to teach in one of the bigger church schools in the Colony. It was there at the Summer Students'

Conferences that we met him and realised that Satan's ramparts had better beware.

A well-known Chinese classic puts it very graphically:

> *"In order to rise like a Roc to the highest regions of the skies, one must first study more than ten years by the light of the snow and the firefly.*
>
> *When the times are out of joint, how can a man pursue his hopes?"*
>
> (From: Story of the Western Pavilion)

Chapter 23

Farewell

In 1957, the news of our departure for furlough and our decision not to return to Hong Kong, had now been notified to the Church authorities and to the congregation of St. Andrew's. They readily understood our problems of finding good schooling for our three sons in the Colony. They also realised that, after five years of energetic pastoral and evangelistic work, we ourselves were beginning to feel under stress, partly the effect of Hong Kong's climate. And our hearts had also begun to turn towards home.

As the news spread around the Colony, so also it spread around the Church at home. However, my heart lay in the work of ministry as Vicar or Rector. St. Paul's words re-echoed in my heart – "Woe to me if I preach not the Gospel."

However, no prodding from the Lord came and I determined to wait until we reached home before making any promises, and immediately experienced peace in my mind and heart.

From the many faithful lay warriors in St. Andrew's Church came moving letters of loving appreciation and farewell.

The Church gave us some precious farewell gifts. One was a Chinese round carved table with a nest of four stools, which we watched being carved in a shop near St. Andrew's.

Ah Lin, our Amah, was deeply moved by our departure for England. She loved the children, especially Baby Tiger, No. 3 son, who became her own special care from his birth. She loved him as if he were her very own, and taught him to say his child's prayers in both Chinese and English.

When the day of our departure arrived, Ah Lin's heartache was no less for having been so long expected. Tenderly, she packed away Baby Tiger's clothes and toys. She held her excited charge closely in her arms and stood on the deck of the great liner. Finally, the ship's siren blared out its warning and cries went up, "All ashore, All ashore". Lotus kissed the fair head, took a last look at the unsuspecting blue eyes, then plunged down the gangway with aching heart. Soon the great ship moved majestically away. A little cry rang out, "Ah Lin, Ah Lin" and little arms reached out in vain. If God sees a sparrow's fall, He also knows the tears of an Amah and heals broken hearts.

Chapter 24

All At Sea

Breathes there the man, with soul so dead,
Who never to himself has said.
This is my own, my native land!
Whose heart hath ne'er within him burned
As home his footsteps he hath turned
From wandering on a foreign stand.

Surging up the English Channel, we saw the incredibly red soil and green grass, the white cliffs beneath the blue sky, and then the inquisitive pilot-ship coming to meet and take the ship home to London docks. My eyes could not stop the tears rolling down my cheeks, nor could I stop the racing of my heart.

It was Greta's younger brother who met us this time and drove us helter-skelter back to Greta's mother's lovely ancient cottage in Appledore, Kent, where the garden of England was at its peak of beauty. For sons Nos. 1 and 2, it was a renewal of acquaintance, but for Baby Tiger it was a joy unspeakable and full of glory; for Greta a reunion with her dear Mother, but alas! Not her Father.

For me, I was relishing the promise of a two month's holiday, with Nine Dragons Country far, far away. However, my mind, still 'all at sea', wondered what the Good Lord and the Missionary Society had in store for us. However, there was no whisper yet from the Holy Spirit, and I had determined to wait until our arrival home before making any promises, and had experienced immediate peace of mind. Suddenly, however, the General Secretary of CMS, the Rev. Dr. Max Warren, came to the rescue. He wrote saying, "Go and look at Christ Church and Parish in Woking, Surrey. They need a new Vicar and I believe it is the right appointment for you and Greta."

He was our personal friend, and had a fine Christian mind. Greta and I set off immediately for Woking, a town unknown to us at the time. Secretly we toured the parish and saw the vicarage and then finally looked at the church. There we spent some time in prayerfully seeking guidance, but experienced no close encounter with the Lord.

We wrote frankly, but courteously, to our friend, saying we had no deep convictions. His reply was speedy and direct. "Go and look again. I believe this is for you!"

We returned to Woking and on arrival first entered the church. It was of French architectural design and attractive. We were drawn to the side chapel and immediately noticed a bronze plaque there, dedicated to a former curate, the Rev. John Bacon. His wife was Doctor Charlotte Bacon, and she had preceded Greta as the Superintendent of the Way of Life Hospital for Mothers and Babies in Guilin, China.

All doubt vanished and a certainty that this was indeed the Lord's doing, filled our minds. Eventually, I was duly instituted as Vicar there in 1957. So began a new era in our lives.

Part Two

Venture Into the Red Dragon's Den
or
The People's Republic of China
October/November 1982

Part Two

contents

Part Two illustrations

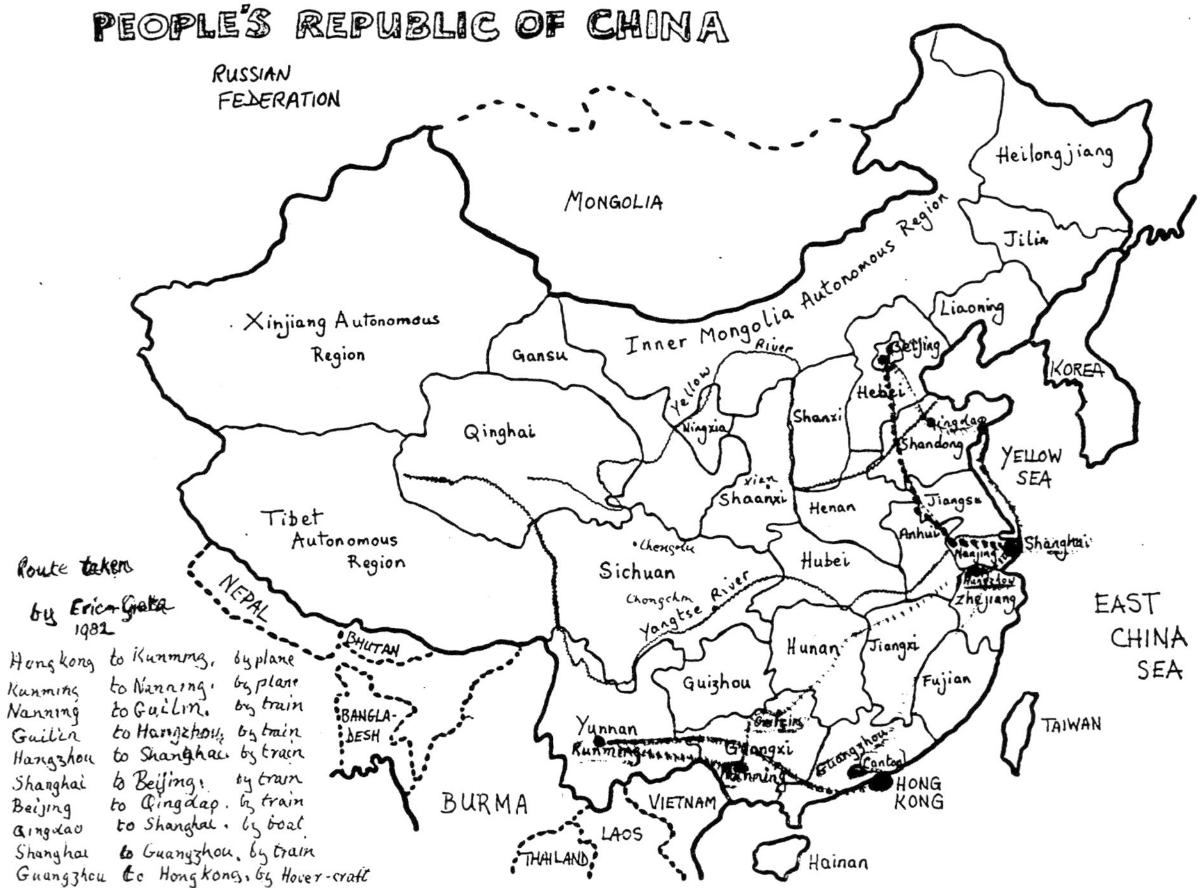
PEOPLE'S REPUBLIC OF CHINA
RUSSIAN FEDERATION
MONGOLIA
Heilongjiang
Jilin
Liaoning
KOREA
Inner Mongolia Autonomous Region
Xinjiang Autonomous Region
Gansu
Yellow River
Ningxia
Qinghai
Beijing
Hebei
Shanxi
Qingdao
Shandong
YELLOW SEA
Xian
Shaanxi
Henan
Jiangsu
Anhui
Nanjing
Shanghai
Hangzhou
Zhejiang
Tibet Autonomous Region
Chengdu
Sichuan
Hubei
Chongchin
Yangtse River
Hunan
Jiangxi
Fujian
EAST CHINA SEA
TAIWAN
Guizhou
Guilin
Yunnan
Kunming
Guangxi
Nanning
Guangzhou
Canton
HONG KONG
Hainan
VIETNAM
LAOS
THAILAND
BURMA
BANGLA-DESH
BHUTAN
NEPAL
Route taken
by Eric 1982
Hongkong to Kunming, by plane
Kunming to Nanning, by plane
Nanning to Guilin, by train
Guilin to Hangzhou, by train
Hangzhou to Shanghai, by train
Shanghai to Beijing, by train
Beijing to Qingdao, by train
Qingdao to Shanghai, by boat
Shanghai to Guangzhou, by train
Guangzhou to Hongkong, by Hover-craft

Introduction

'The Dream'

The dream came to Greta and me in the summer of 1981. Greta is my wife and we met and married during our work as missionaries in China before the Chinese communists took over in 1949. She had been born there in 1917 in the Kunming Hospital which her father had built, and which he used as a centre for healing and evangelism.

Greta's father, Dr. H. Gordon Thompson, had met her mother, Amy, and married her in the leprosy colony in Pakhoi, on the coast of Guangdong. They joined Dr. Neville Bradley and his wife Daisy. Neville Bradley was Amy's brother. All four later went to Kunming to begin work there. Later still, Dr. Thompson went to work in Hangchow (Hangzhou), and then in Shanghai, accompanied by his wife and Greta and her brother Peter.

It was very much later that I arrived in China. That was during the Great World War II. Along with some other civilians, many of them missionaries, I went out by troop convoy in the summer of 1943. We left port on the day after my 30th birthday, on American Independence Day. Had I thought about it that might have been significant to me. My arrival at my future home (or station as they called it) in Guilin, Guangxi Province, some four months later, is a slightly astonishing story in itself, but will not be told here. I arrived on All Saints Day and noted the fact in my diary.

After about four years of much wandering and some adventures, and being back once more in my 'missionary station', I met Greta, and we were married in 1948. Bill, our first-born, was born on St. Peter's Day 1949, at a hospital in Hong Kong, and we called him William (after William Temple). All three of us flew back into China about a month later. However, the Chinese communist army came hard at our heels and, much to our regret, we were ordered home to England. I had been six years in China.

It seemed better to our CMS missionary HQ in London, that we should return home and, after a rest and preparation, do a five year stint in Hong Kong – from 1952 to 1957, and finally return home to England for good, with three young and growing sons.

In England, during the War, Greta had qualified as a medical doctor. In Guilin, China, she had worked at the Christian hospital full-time, but in Hong Kong, she had been vicar's wife, busy mother and part-time doctor. When we were back in England for good, she continued as an even busier vicar's wife and mother and only later, when the family had grown up, did she begin her medical work again. She continued the latter even when I retired and we went to live in Wirral, by the Irish Sea, in 1979.

So it was that in the summer of 1981, we had a dream. The situation in China, after the fall of the Gang of Four, had changed. The more liberal Chinese Communist Government began to allow Christian churches there to open their doors. Slowly but surely, churches were opened in city after city. The Government allowed two churches to function: The Chinese United Protestant Church and The Chinese Catholic Church. Each of these two bore the title "Three Self-Patriotic (or Love China) Church". They had government recognition and certain government guidelines to guide them. News was received of very large congregations worshipping together. In addition, there was also news of large numbers of House Churches, gathering regularly for worship but a little more secretly. There was talk of an explosion of Christian faith.

So then we began to dream of revisiting China and seeing this for ourselves, if we could get visas. In the summer of 1981, on the day before we returned from a holiday in Scotland, thieves broke into our house in Hoylake. Three months later, in the severe winter conditions, we suffered three burst pipes in the loft. For these inconveniences, the Insurance Company made us a payment of just over one thousand pounds. About the same time, we received our first letter from China for 33 years, and we were invited to go out to see them if possible.

Our dream, and may I say our prayers, had become a possibility. We were ready to go; we thanked the Lord for His strange answer to our prayers; and we were inclined to think that He had a delicious sense of humour too.

Chapter 1

Sir Francis Bacon: BA 003: Jumbo Jet Boeing 747

Early on Thursday morning, September 30th 1982, Howard and Dillys, my wife's cousins, took us by car to the Coach Station at Skelorn Street, Liverpool, to catch the London coach to Victoria Coach Station in the metropolis. Bob and Edna Roberts of Holy Trinity Church, Parr Mount, St. Helens, had already taken up residence to look after our home in Hoylake and deal with correspondence from distant Cathay, if any arrived, and to send out copies to family and friends.

We felt excited and eager, even at my ripe age of 69 years and my wife's, some four years younger. In any case, travelling to Liverpool, the city of my birth, always sets my pulses going. Its people are gay and witty and smiling under all difficulties, even at 9.30 am. With a cheerful and thankful goodbye to our cousins, we entered the coach station and found ourselves a place in the queue, along with two lightweight nylon travelling bags – one of them a brilliant red, a courteous tribute to Red China and to the Liverpool football team. Other baggage included a British Airways shoulder bag by means of which we hoped to fly the flag and identify ourselves in my wife's first, and my own second, native land (we both have 'China' written across our hearts).

The Liverpool-London coach left almost on time at 10.30 am., delayed slightly by a rather seedy man who tried to steal a lift. He was harmless really – probably a man of the road hoping to gain a lift out of town but he was spotted and put off at the first possibility. Indeed, he seemed more harmless than some American tourists of middle age, dressed up like teenagers with Stetson hats and very colourful shirts and of loud conversation. A pity really, for they were probably very nice people, and God certainly loves them as much as He loves the quieter and more reserved English people, not to mention the man of the road.

Soon all tickets had been taken and the driver took his seat, started the engine, and off we went. The driver was a colourful man, a real 'Scouser' (like me – only he spoke the dialect perfectly). He was the 'captain' and in charge, and made easy for himself the difficult job of seeing to all the seating, and the passengers, as well as driving at a regular 70mph, once we were on the Motorway. He rolled and smoked fragrant tobacco cigarettes all along the journey but slowed up just a little when rolling his cigarettes. He could manage the coach quite easily with one hand as he did a quick 'roll'.

It was sunshine all the way as we sped comfortably down the M62, the M6 and the M1, and arrived at Watford Gap Services at 2.00pm for lunch. To drink with our own packed lunch of a pie each, we bought 2 cups of tomato soup, which was delicious and cost 82p. Like the price, it was piping hot. We arrived late at Victoria Coach Station at 4.15pm, but the London traffic was very difficult and our expert driver had shown great skill nevertheless.

Bill, our number one son, was waiting for us at Victoria, and took us for what seemed, a long walk of a third of a mile as we lugged our baggage to get to the Underground. Something had gone wrong with the ticket machines and there were long queues. It took us at least 10 minutes to get our £1 single tickets to Northfields Station, where Bill's wife, Ros, plus Jonathan and Joy, had the car waiting. Bill went off to do his doctoring at the hospital, and Ros, looking very fraught after looking after two exceedingly active children for 20 minutes, drove us to their home. It was good to be there.

A cup of tea and a crumpet soon restored us at Bill and Ros's home. We had decided to lighten our luggage after the experience of carrying the bags at the station, and ended up leaving some warmer clothes for wearing on our return in November. The result was good – only two nylon cases, a canvas grip and our shoulder bags, weighing about 19 kilos in all, to go with us for the journey.

Coming downstairs for supper, we were pleasantly surprised to find Philip, son number three, there with his wife Marilyn and their baby Esme; and number two son's wife Anna, whilst number two John phoned, and number one, Bill, had returned meanwhile, from hospital. All to wish us 'bon voyage'!

After a good supper, there was much looking at each others recent photos and a lot of talk together. Then up to bed early to finish the packing and to get a good night's sleep.

Next morning we awoke early to face 'der Tag', October 1st. All the family were soon about and breakfast was served. Ros took Jonathan to school, Bill went off to hospital and I stayed to have everything ready. John 'phoned up again from Stoke to say goodbye and Ros took us to the airport by car and we said goodbye.

Heathrow terminal was already busy, and after some difficulty in finding the ticket booth, we duly registered our arrival and received our flight cards. Our luggage was well under weight and there was no excess charge. We walked around, bought two Mars Bars and a packet of Brittle Treacle, and made for the departure gate. At the ticket and passport control our luggage was x-rayed and I (but not Greta) was frisked and we were allowed through to the aircraft. First handicapped people, and then families with children, were allowed to board the plane and finally those like us. Our own seats were just forward of the rear section, near a porthole and just over the port side wing.

Greta had been busy with her two cameras, one for colour prints, the other for colour slides for future use in England. She managed to get one of 'Sir Francis Bacon' and later one of Biggin Hill and a third of the English coastline.

In the meantime, Captain Nightingale appeared to tell us that our departure was delayed by the engine failure of the jeep towing our plane. Eventually we taxied off 44 minutes late. Soon we were above the clouds and headed along the French coast, and then South East.

Drinks were served twenty minutes before lunch. The meal itself was more than adequate. The first course was very nicely done – chicken, croquettes and assorted vegetables followed by ice cream with cherry.

Turbulence occurred, but we were always above the clouds and in sunshine. By 3.40pm we were over the Bosphorus and could see the sea below. The jet engines' noise was not too obvious.

It was 7.25pm London time when we arrived at Abu Dhabi.

We were allowed to walk around this splendid air terminal in the Gulf States, which was built, I guessed, on oil. Many fine clean shops encircled the ground floor. One could buy, at a price, Arab brass-ware, modern Japanese clocks, amazing modern sophisticated toys, a variety of costly perfumes, and refreshments at a café-estaminet type. A young Arab male, dressed in white flowing robes, lounged there, very cool and imposing and smoking a cigarette (!). Greta took his photograph – without permission.

After some delay, waiting for air clearance from Bahrain, we boarded the Sir Francis Bacon at 23-plus hour's local time. We soon climbed up 29,000 feet and then to 33,000 feet, and over the Arabian Sea to Karachi, on to Calcutta, and then across the Hump/Burma and over China to Hong Kong.

On Saturday morning we had two lots of turbulence, but neither ourselves nor the other 420 passengers (including the 12 crew members) were unduly disturbed. "We must be over China," I said to myself, "and probably over Kunming where Greta was born". However, Greta's birthplace brought into my mind a couple of lines of George MacDonald's poem:

'Where did you come from Baby dear?
Out of everywhere into here.'

Mystery of mysteries. Where do I come from, and go to? I was to use that poem quite a number of times in China later, and it proved quite significant in a supposedly atheistic culture.

About midnight local time, we were given dinner. It seemed as if we never stopped eating, and that's a good way to pass the time. Dinner consisted of rice, slightly curried with nobbles of pork and varied vegetables and a sweet of chocolate blancmange and peaches and coffee (or other more potent liquids if requested and possibly paid for).

With 2 hours 15 minutes to go, we were served with orange juice. With one hour to go we were given breakfast and at 4.30pm London time, we touched down in Hong Kong at Kai Tak aerodrome. We had no difficulty with customs, and our friend the

Rev. & Rt. Honourable Joyce Bennett, member of the Hong Kong Legislative Council, headmistress and woman priest of the Hong Kong Anglican/Episcopal Church, missionary with the Church Missionary Society, met us at the barrier of the Friends Waiting Area. With joyous gusto she escorted us to her waiting Mini and drove us through the unbelievably hectic Hong Kong traffic, as to the manner born, and to her flat at Kwun Tong on the Kowloon side.

We had arrived.

Chapter 2

Fragrant Harbour – Hong Kong

The Rev. & Rt. Honourable Joyce Bennett's flat on the peak of Kwun Tong Hill, Kowloon, overlooked the Kai Tak airport runway, the wide harbour, and beyond, Victoria Island, the hub of the Colony. From the wide, stone verandas of the flat, we had an unbelievably beautiful view by day or night. At dusk a fairyland of a million multi-coloured lights revealed itself on every side, almost rivalling the sunset. Firefly lights moved and zig-zagged every way as ferries, walla-walla boats, junks, ocean-going liners, customs and police craft, water-borne cranes, ships of every kind, weaved their secret ways across the darkening waters of the harbour. Great skyscrapers, crowding the nearby Kowloon peninsula and the distant hilly slopes of the island, were transformed into fairy palaces of lights of varied hues.

At dawn all was clear as crystal and soon, every few minutes, giant jumbo jets of every nationality began to roar down the airport runway and up steeply to clear the looming hills and then to turn to all the four quarters of the compass on their journeys to distant corners of the world. And out from the distant horizons came other giant birds of commerce or pleasure, swooping gracefully on to the mile long runway stretching out into the harbour and coming gently to a halt outside the airport terminal buildings.

After a welcome lunch Greta and I took a much need siesta, awaking about 5pm, refreshed and not too troubled by jet lag. A perfect full moon climbed slowly up the sky and firecrackers began to explode, as some eight or nine million inhabitants celebrated the Moon Festival.

Gossiping, we breached the gap of 25 years absence, but slowly gave place to weariness once more and we retired early to bed about 10pm and crawled under the almost forgotten luxury or defences of our mosquito net.

Next day being Sunday, we rose at 7am, had an early cup of

tea and then a light breakfast. Then off into Kowloon city on the MTR – meaning the 'Mass Transit Railway', to get to St. Andrew's Church for the morning service. We found the nearby Metro station and a small bank in the station, I changed a Hong Kong $10 note. Then to an automatic machine for smaller change and a second machine for 50 cent pieces. Finally, to the ticket machine where for $2.50, the requisite fare, we received a plastic ticket.

Armed with our plastic tickets, we went to the turnstile, put the tickets into a slot and awaited developments. The ticket suddenly shot out of another slot and the turnstile moved to let us pass through. At the end of the journey, we put the ticket in another slot and it disappeared (to be collected and used again – an excellent economic and hygienic device!) There was a fine of some $500/$1,000 for destroying any ticket!

On our journey, as we boarded the almost spotless Metro train, the closing doors triggered off an air-cooling system. Small loudspeakers emitted announcements before arriving and after leaving every station. There was a door microphone by which, if necessary, one could speak with the train driver.

The train had perhaps 12 or 14 coaches, all crowded with people, as many standing as sitting, and 99.9% Chinese. At Argyll Station we changed trains, merely by walking across the platform to get another 'silver-bullet' express to Jordan Road Station. From there the train would proceed under the harbour to Victoria on Hong Kong Island. Trains ran about every two minutes with most punctual precision. Both stations and trains were extremely clean, attractive and smooth-running – perhaps a tenth Wonder of the World!

We emerged from the station in to the already warm atmosphere of the streets, already crowded with pedestrians, shoppers, buses, taxis, cars and some motorised rickshaws. St. Andrew's Church was near to hand, and we walked up the drive to the church, where twenty-five years previously, I had been Vicar. There were few vacant seats left and Chinese, Eurasian and Westerners seemed to be in equal proportion. The two ministers, one of them Australian, were dressed in shirt and trousers but wore no ecclesiastical robes. The 400-plus congregation sang heartily, assisted by splendid piano accompaniment. Hymns included some modern Renewal Songs as well as older well-known hymns, and the Liturgy was modernised. The good teaching sermon lasted 25 minutes, everyone listening carefully.

The same sparrow that usually flew into the church in our day, and the same slow-moving fan in the chancel, were both still there. We recognised only one person, a young mother, the sister of a boy who used to be in the Youth Fellowship of our day. Almost everyone stayed for coffee or orange drinks available in the space under the rebuilt Church Hall, alongside the Church itself.

An interesting illustration from the sermon remained with me. The Vicar described his experience of going up, with his family, in his brother's plane in Australia. He was invited to take over the controls. So long as he let his brother guide him, the plane was okay. Perhaps we sang the hymn 'Jesus, Saviour, pilot me' – but I forget.

The return journey on the MTR was again fascinating, and even more crowded. We were glad to get back to the coolness of the flat and an appetising lunch prepared by Joyce's amah, Ah-yee Chick. After a lazy afternoon on the bed under an electric fan, which induced sleep, we were aroused by a welcome cup of tea. A young Chinese nurse joined us for supper and for Chinese checkers. That night I did not sleep too well for thinking about China, the Red Dragon's domain, and trying out my Mandarin vocabulary. Sleep finally came and then up at 6.40am for 7.30am breakfast.

Skyscrapers galore!

St. John's Cathedral, Hong Kong

Chapter 3

Uncle Tom Cobley and All or The Red Dragon's Whiskers

Monday 4th October. We went into Kowloon again on the MTR, and to the China International Travel Service offices. We had to enquire about visas to enter China, our travel tickets and our itinerary. We saw a Mr. Wong (The Chinese equivalent of Mr. Smith or Mr. Jones). He was very helpful. There seemed to be no hindrance to our entering china, so we filled up visa forms. Greta described herself as a tourist, and as a retired Medical Doctor of British nationality, and I wrote 'tourist and retired Church of England Clergyman'. I am not sure whether they knew what a clergyman was, but it did not seem to matter. They were perfectly happy for us to travel as individual tourists and not as members of a tourist group. The fact that we both spoke the Mandarin language seemed to help matters. We had to state where we had travelled before. Greta gave her birthplace as Kunming, China, and mentioned childhood days in Shanghai and Hangzhou, whilst I gave the dates of my six years, 1943-1949, helping the Chinese Church in China.

Mr. Wong encouraged us to travel by plane into China, to Kunming. Other routes seemed to be filled up, in terms of available passenger seats. Passenger traffic from Hong Kong to Canton, Nanning and Guilin was now quite heavy, and train, boat and plane services fully booked.

Our visas cost HK$60 each, the air tickets cost HK$860 each, and the booking fee HK$40 each, in total equivalent to £192.00. We asked for visas permitting us to visit Kunming, Nanning, Bei-hai (Pakhoi), Guilin, Lingling, Hangzhou, Shanghai and Qingdao (in Shandong).

Mr. Wong told us to return the next day at 10.00am to collect our passports and our tickets, for which we had to pay in cash, in Hong Kong dollars.

We duly returned next morning to the China International Travel Service and received back our passports and visas to go to

Kunming and then to Nanning. Visas for other places would be negotiable in Nanning.

We were asked to return the following Monday, October 11th, to get our air tickets to fly on Tuesday 12th from Hong Kong airport to Kunming – travelling Economy Class on the China Government's Civil Aviation Air Service, Flight CA 342, departing at 12.55pm and arriving at Kunming Airport at 14.55. The price of the ticket included a served meal. Mr. Wong also arranged a hotel reservation for us and telegraphed the office in Kunming reserving tickets on the 12.15pm flight 3402 on Thursday 14th October. The cost would be 88 Yuan (China currency) each, or ¥167 for two. This in English currency would be approximately £55.40 (the exchange rate being about £1=¥3). We were to be met at Kunming by their CITS Agent, who would arrange for a taxi to take us to our hotel, and later would arrange a taxi or airport bus to take us to the Nanning plane. For this service we would pay a regular fee. The Red Dragon's whiskers seemed very sensitive and reliable!

Having set the stage for our China visit, we returned to our hostess where I helped her at the school afternoon Holy Communion Service. Joyce, as an ordained woman priest in the Hong Kong Episcopal Church, celebrated at the sacrament, which she took in excellent Cantonese. I gave 'The Peace' and distributed the wine at the service, speaking in Mandarin Chinese. The Prayer Book we used was printed in the Chinese National Language, the printed characters being the same for both dialects. The girls were also taught spoken Mandarin in school.

Some of my clerical colleagues in England would certainly have been taken aback by a woman priest celebrating Holy Communion, but in the event, it seemed entirely natural to me there in Hong Kong.

The School Swimming Gala the next day, held in warm bright sunshine, was quite a spectacular event. It aroused great enthusiasm amongst the more than 1,000 girls of the school. Joyce gave a very forceful speech in Cantonese, which was greatly applauded.

In the afternoon, Joyce took us into Hong Kong Victoria by way of the great Harbour Tunnel. She drove fearlessly and Jehu-like through traffic which was more crowded than London's. A Mini will get you anywhere! This time we visited Swire Travel (part of the old firm of Butterfield and Swire, and now housed in one of Victoria's enormous and palatial skyscrapers with air-conditioning, plus carpets, express lifts and charmingly dressed girl clerical staff).

Swire's were able to give us a definite booking, and tickets for our home journey back to London on November 22nd, some six weeks later. This would be on a Euro-Charter flight on a British Airways jumbo jet. It would be a little cheaper than our outward flight, since our seats were more towards the rear of the plane. There seemed to be little difference, and we were told that if we were to go early and ask for good side seats, in the non-smoking zone, our seats might even be better than on the outward flight, being not so near the wings and the jet engines.

We duly bought out tickets for about £380, paying in Hong Kong dollars. The whole matter was arranged most courteously and efficiently by those most presentable Chinese girl and men clerks.

From 'Swire's Travel', Greta and I went to meet Joyce at Government House, where there was to be a meeting of the Colony's Legislature, when the recently appointed Governor was to give his first major speech on the 'State of the Colony'.

Arriving early, we found good seats but the Council Chamber was almost too cold, due to air-conditioning. I buttoned up my shirt to the neck, rolled down my sleeves to the wrists, and felt a little better.

In due time, the Council, including our friend Joyce Bennett, processed in, followed by Sir Edward Youde, the Governor. We all stood up and bowed to his Excellency, and remained standing, whilst first a Chinese lady took the oath of allegiance to the Queen and Governor, and then whilst a Chinese man swore allegiance to the Colony.

We now sat whilst the Governor began his 'survey' speech. He spoke quite quietly but earphones, provided at every seat, picked up the speech very well, and also a Cantonese translation as well. The speech took one hour and 35 minutes, and the Governor needed only three sips of water (?) from his glass tumbler. We were very wearied by the speech, although it became more interesting towards the end when he spoke about traffic problems, including the proposed new Harbour Bridge; about the Police and security, and also the talks with China's leaders about Hong Kong's future. It was most comprehensive.

We were glad to emerge from the Council Chamber and then went to consult the China Travel Service, Foreigners' Section in Queens Road. A very polite and painstaking male clerk tried to give us details of train services covering our itinerary in China. These seemed to involve very long and time-devouring journeys, night travel and middle of the night stops. He could not give us details of the fare prices.

We left the office, somewhat disappointed, and made our way to the harbour front. Here we saw the Kwun Tong ferry terminus, bought tickets (about 15p each) and boarded the ferry. It was a most pleasant harbour crossing sail, cool and taking us west up the harbour, and after perhaps half an hour, to the Kwun Tong terminus just beyond the Airport Airstrip.

The view, crossing the harbour, was spectacular. On both sides we were surrounded, not only by fine mountains and ranges, and the Nine Dragons or hills from which Kowloon gets its name, but also by many hundreds of twenty to thirty floor skyscrapers, which seemed to reach halfway up the mountain sides. There was a stream of ferries, hovercraft, motorised junks, giant crane barges, naval craft, freight liners, police harbour motor boats, all busily going to and fro in apparently random manner. To cap it all, there were the great jet planes, taking off from, or planing down to, the long 1½-2 mile runway that juts out into the waters of the harbour.

Then, after we alighted from the ferry, there were the buses, large and small, setting off from Kwun Tong chock full of passengers, roaring deafeningly down the traffic crowded streets, seeking to make their hindered way to their destinations. Ours seemed to stop and start, stop and start *ad infinitum*, taking half an hour to make its short and noisy journey. But what can one expect for a mere 50 cents – 5p English money?

How glad we were to get home, and to collapse into a chair or on to the bed, to relax and rest. Surely we have never seen so many people and so much traffic all at the same time, and such a conglomeration of young, middle-aged and old people all apparently cheerful in the heat and in the press. The temperature was 76°F.

Finally, came supper, and then a writing up of the details of air flights, journeys to our distant and different destinations in China, and a consulting of timetables and working out of travel and food costs, so as to prepare for our exodus next week.

Cheerfully weary, we eventually made our way to bed and mosquito nets and, in spite of the heat, to sleep, there to dream about China's Red Dragon which seemed to breathe out not red flames, but clear and cheerful encouragement to visit its mysterious den.

Chapter 4

In the Forecourt of the Red Dragon's Den

After an early cup of tea at 7.00am with Joyce, we all went to the Clergy Holy Communion, followed by breakfast at the Cathedral. An American woman priest celebrated, assisted by the part-time priest from St. Andrew's Church, Kowloon, who is also a missionary of the Overseas Missionary Fellowship. This OMF was formerly the China Inland Mission, but after the expulsion of all missionaries from China by the new Communist Government, the CIM changed its name, since it no longer works in China and has spread its ministry to Malaysia, Japan and other Far East countries.

It did not seem at all incongruous to have a woman priest celebrating. After all, the first woman priest to be ordained in the world-wide Anglican Church was a Chinese deaconess in the Hong Kong diocese. When the Japanese capture of Hong Kong took place, not only were Western church workers put into prisoner of war camps, but other church workers were unable to travel to distant congregations. Bishop R. O. Hall was determined to ordain as a priest Miss/Deaconess Li so that she might give Holy Communion to the scattered groups that could not be reached by ordained men from his church. Later, the Bishop told me that he had based his decision on the action of St. Peter in the Acts of the Apostles, who, faced with the problem of the Centurion Cornelius, a Roman and Gentile, being baptised into the young Christian Church, had felt that he must do so since the Lord had affirmed his own acceptance of the Centurion by pouring out his Holy Spirit upon the man as Peter preached to him and his household about Jesus. Moreover, Peter had had direct command from the Lord in a dream vision, paralleled by Cornelius' own dream vision in which he was told to send to Joppa and invite Peter to visit him. Just as Peter's vision and action resulted in the infant Christian Church taking a new step in its pilgrimage and growth, so Bishop Hall believed that the Lord was directing him to lead the Anglican Church of today to take a new step in the ordination of a woman to the priesthood. Although the South East Conference or Synod of Anglican bishops later asked Bishop Hall to rescind his action, and to order Miss Li to revert to her position as deaconess – to which the Bishop regretfully concurred – subsequently Miss Li was reinstated with the consent of those same bishops.

There were a large number of the Chinese clergy present both at the Communion Service and afterwards at the breakfast in the Cathedral hall. The Rev. Denham Crary, an old friend, was absent, along with one or two others. Denham Crary was an Eurasian who had also married a Chinese girl, identifying therefore with the Chinese people. He was a brilliant preacher in English or Chinese language, and a radical in every sense of the word. He scorned the Bishop's lackey-boys and western imperialism. For him, the working man's family were most important and each man (and woman) unique and equal before God.

The Bishop, Peter Kwok, was the first Chinese bishop of Hong Kong diocese, and in that ultra-British Colony, seemed yet very capable, efficient, and authoritative. He was dressed in a dark lounge suit, whereas his British predecessor, R. O. Hall, would have appeared dressed in his purple cassock (not unlike the Chinese long gown worn by officialdom in the China of yesterday), but he might possibly have appeared also in simple khaki shorts and shirt. Bishop Kwok not only wore a dark lounge suit – it was early winter after all – but he was also very business-like, his spirituality hidden under his efficient manner and logical mind and speech. His manner was most self-confident; there was no doubt that he was bishop.

After breakfast, the Dean of the Cathedral, a charming American named Caspar, who would have made a good 'wise man' or Magi (he was certainly a magician with the English language), gave an interesting talk on 'In the world but not of it'. He concentrated on the other worlds in the social order, of which priests tend to know little, such as the differing worlds of a priest's own people in his congregation, the business world, the diplomatic and social worlds, and so on.

However, the Chinese clergy – who all mostly spoke in Cantonese, although understanding English – were not content or happy with this unusual interpretation of the New Testament phrase and brought to bear the more obvious Biblical meaning, this world's life and spiritual life, or as Watchman Nee, the great Chinese evangelist, described it in his book 'The Normal Christian Life', opposing it to the normal life of the worldly man.

Since all the Chinese clergy, except the bishop and one or two brave men, talked in Cantonese, the discussion was sometimes difficult to follow. The Dean spoke no Cantonese but had an interpreter by his side all the time the others were speaking. It would probably be fair comment that they agreed to disagree, but the Chinese brethren certainly stood where the New Testament writers stood.

Following the discussion, all went their various ways. We had a short conversation with the eloquent Dean, who was also very charming – and the first American Dean in that British Colony. Asked about Denham Crary, he said he had not yet met that elusive and individualistic priest but was most interested in our own appraisal of the man and assured us he would try to make contact. Then, saying goodbye, we visited the cathedral office and obtained details of the addresses of churches in the various cities in China which we hoped to visit, and also the local address of Asian Outreach in Causeway Bay, where the latest news of the Church in China was carefully, and prayerfully monitored. There were also obtained some good Christian literature in Chinese, to take with us on our coming journey.

We had lunch out at a Macdonald's café – a kind of superior Wimpy Bar, at which the meals were 'chips with everything' – they were called 'French Fry'. The café was very clean and colourful, even including the menus, and behind the serving counter were quite a number of assistants, so that one's order was provided very promptly. In the Chinese way, there was courtesy combined with efficiency and the whole thing attracted large numbers of customers, especially the young and late teenagers, with their cheerful conversation and good manners. Greta and I had a sundae with our French Fry and found it adequate and filling.

Causeway Bay is on Victoria Island side of the harbour and almost opposite Kwun Tong on the mainland side, so we decided to go back home on the North Point Ferry. As we tried to make our way to the ferry through Victoria Park – an attractive green oasis amongst the towering office blocks and flats – we soon found ourselves walking along crowded streets of busy open shops and street vendors of everything from fruit and noodles to ivory carvings and incense sticks. So we changed our direction and made our way back to the famous Hong Kong Victoria electric tram system, which runs along the coastline streets for at least seven miles for something ridiculously cheap like ten cents, and which you can get on and off where you wish.

The trams almost followed each other in procession and all were crowded with passengers, who take a multitude of purchases along with them. At one stop, a prospective passenger had one or two baskets, and from one of these protruded a goose's head and neck. The bird followed all the commotion with perfect calmness and a beady eye.

It was a cool and fresh ferry journey across the busy harbour, the ferry captain avoiding all the multitudinous craft sailing in either direction, with experienced skill. Once back at Joyce's flat, however, we were glad to relax until a light supper came and bed time. I also worked out something of the possible costs of our China itinerary, including plane and train fares, hotel charges and food, from the information we had managed to glean. No one seemed certain of anything except plane fares. There was certainly no central office of information when it came to China travel.

In Kowloon there was a Chinese Study Centre, a Christian organisation, which we enjoyed visiting. It wasn't exactly a secret organisation, but neither did they advertise their work too openly. They were not anti-China's Communist Government but they tried to monitor Chinese government attitudes towards religious groups in general and the Christian Church in China in particular. They provided good Christian literature in Chinese, written by Hong Kong or overseas Chinese that would not be available in mainland China. Many Hong Kong Chinese take such literature with them when visiting their families in mainland China, and folk from mainland China visiting relatives in Hong Kong presumably, if they are Christian, take some of these books back with them.

The present China Government attitude is now more liberal in this matter, so long as no one tries to take large quantities of Bibles, New Testaments and general Christian literature in their luggage. The same applies to tourists, like ourselves. Discretion is the password. Some foreigners do occasionally try to take large numbers of these books to give them away to people they meet. If the Customs men find these, the books are simply confiscated and held until the travellers return to their exit point, where they are recoverable. However, the Chinese Government and Customs are equally vigilant about visitors taking costly consumer goods into their country. Goods like watches, pocket radio sets and the like. Whilst anyone bringing out of China any kind of antiques, large or small, or China products without a receipt from the shop or store where they were purchased, may find these 'presents' confiscated without any financial redress.

After our morning at the Study Centre, we made our always exciting journey on the MTR, to the Royal Garden Hotel, Kowloon, where we were entertained to lunch by Dr. and Mrs. H. P. Yew, together with his mandarin speaking Chinese nurse/companion – for he was of advanced age and formerly worked with Greta's doctor and missionary father in mainland China. It was a joyous and courteous reunion for all of us. We enjoyed an absolutely stupendous meal – roast beef steaks half an inch thick, roast pork, Yorkshire pudding, jacket cooked potatoes and all kinds of bits and pieces like chopped bacon, potato salad, peas and sauces; then green salad followed by various occidental sweets like melon and pineapple slices, and finally, coffee. To us, commonly used to simple and tight budget meals, it was delicious indeed. Greta exchanged family news and history with the good, gentle and amusing Doctor, whilst I practised my Mandarin on Mrs. Yew and the nurse. I was quite encouraged to see how much I remembered and could understand after 33 years absence.

After lunch Dr. Yew, wife and nurse went off in a taxi, whilst we walked around the Star Ferry area and looked in some amazement at the wonderful buildings and the modern set out of the area. Finally, we determined to take a 1A bus back to Kwun Tong, partly for the experience and also because it only cost a dollar in Hong Kong currency, which is equivalent to ten pence sterling. For the first half hour, our bus amazed us by its speed through the crowded roads, but then came a traffic jam and we just crawled along for another half hour. I suppose the distance to Kwun Tong would be some four or five miles. However, we duly arrived at Kwun Tong ferry and caught a No. 19 bus up to Joyce's school and flat, via Crocodile Hill. The reason for the name escapes me but since there is a Lion Hill, which looks like a crouching lion in the vicinity, presumably this other hill, before it was covered from head to foot by the gigantic scales of modern workers' flats and apartments, may have looked like a crocodile!

We returned to peace, quiet, coolness and a cup of tea, but we could not each much of our Chinese supper!

The great catch

Chapter 5

New Wine, New Wineskins
Other Times, Other Ways

Saturday is a rest day for Joyce, so we accepted her invitation to go with her to a Conference for Heads of Hong Kong schools. This was to be held at St. Stephen's College (the Eton of the Far East), in Stanley on Hong Kong Island and facing the China Sea. It was here that we had spent our honeymoon in 1948. The Conference began with a service of Holy Communion although I imagine that not all heads of schools, or their schools, were Christian.

The service was held in the attractive chapel of the school – all light with the many windows, and the sun shining even at 9.00am. The east window shows St. Stephen as a tonsured monk, in what looked like celebrant's robes, he being only a deacon however! The usual ceiling fans kept us cool.

Bishop Peter Kwok celebrated. The address was given by a Roman Catholic priest – ecumenical relations are excellent in the Colony. He introduced his sermon by asking us to sing a modern renewal song-hymn 'Abba Father', accompanied by his cassette recorder (a device I often use myself). He began by describing how he came to take over the head-ship of his college. The supervisor of the school came and asked him for his appointment certificate, which he had brought. Then for his personal examination certificate and other documents. Father Deignan (I hope I have his name correct) grew angrier and angrier. Not a word was asked about what he hoped for Wah Yan College. Finally, he had gone to his still unpacked trunk and dragged out his certificates. This feeling of anger remained with him for some days, until he began to ask himself 'Why?'. He realised he was doing something he knew to be wrong; he was not trusting his heavenly Father about it. He then recalled seeing and hearing an Arab boy call out to his father 'Abba! Abba!' – hence the song. His point sank home.

After Service, we met the Headmaster of the school, Mr. Yip, an overseas Chinese from Canada, who was very charming and competent, also the Chaplain and his wife, both attractive English people who were living in the school bungalow where we had spent most of our honeymoon. They took us back to their home and rekindled many secret memories.

Whilst the various heads of schools went into conference, we went to meet Freddie Wong, an old friend and former treasurer of St. Andrew's Church, Kowloon, where I was formerly Vicar. He took us in his car around the Island, looking in at well known places like Repulse Bay and Aberdeen. As he drove us round, he poured out his heart about St. Andrew's Church which, for him, had changed. Renewal of the form of worship and the style of preaching had altered the church life, and Freddie did not wish to be changed himself and wanted the church to remain as it was of old. New types of services had replaced the old 1662 Prayer Book and not for the better. Before, during and after the services, all was noise and bustle. The ministers officiated in lounge suits and even in shirt sleeves. To replace the old familiar church hall, they had built a modern five story building, with an open ground floor (for refreshments and casual conversation after service), a very attractive top floor flat for the minister and his family, and on the intervening floors, offices for various missionary and other church societies and including a very good Christian bookshop. In doing all this the church had incurred a large debt, and incidentally had spoiled the former lovely surroundings that had been like an oasis in the concrete jungle known as Kowloon.

Freddie waxed bitterly especially at the closing of the old Mothers' Union, the Scouts, the Youth Club, the Badminton Club and all former social amenities, spoiling the former homely atmosphere of the church. Freddie refused to say who was responsible for the changes, but another old acquaintance was not so reluctant to point the finger and assert that it was done against the desires of many church members. It is a familiar story – old wine in new bottles, or new wine in old bottles, whichever is chosen, a sorry rent is often the result.

Frustrated Freddie eventually took us to his flat, a beautiful home with all mod cons. Since his English wife was in Australia with their eldest daughter, who was a fine swimmer of international standard and due to take part in the Commonwealth Games, and his other daughter and son were out, Freddie felt unable to cook us a meal. However, he found the address of the young Chinese girl who had helped Greta with our children when they were young (twenty five years previously!). He then took us by car to her home which was on the 13th floor of a new skyscraper apartment block in Queens Road West. He left us there and we had the joy of meeting Ah Lin who wept to see us again. With her were her older sister Ah Chieh, and her two younger brothers Pak San and Wei San.

What a gathering of scattered friendships that was. Another relative was with them who spoke good English and was due to take his honeymoon very shortly, visiting San Francisco and Hawaii. How modern youngsters do get about, whether from England, Europe, the Americas or the Far East, with the exception perhaps of those in China and those in Soviet Russia. How we should rejoice in and encourage such travelling. Perhaps, as they meet each other, the young of the world may learn to appreciate and understand each other better and avoid a cataclysmic third world war and a nuclear holocaust.

Ah Lin and her sister showed us their family photographs, including those taken on a recent visit to Peking (Beijing). Greta had brought our family album and great were the acclamations when they saw photographs of our three boys now grown up and married, especially when they saw those of Philip, our youngest. Ah Lin had taken care of him from birth. “Baby Tiger” she exclaimed in delight : so named because, when the older boys heard that they were to have a baby sister or brother, one of them exclaimed “I’d like a baby tiger”, and that became and remained his nickname.

Eventually, after much excited remembrances, the family took us down to the ground floor of their block of flats to the Restaurant, where they gave us an excellent and late lunch. Although the dishes seemed to us to be very expensive, with typical Chinese hospitality they were only too pleased to entertain us.

The group also included Wei San's wife, a charming young girl, and their small and mischievous son. (When young, Chinese children are dealt with very leniently and with much good humour, but when they reach school age, discipline in the home really begins and the old Confucian family standards are observed, especially 'Honour your father and your mother', which appears written in four Chinese characters on the walls of the Confucian temples. The relationships between older and younger generations hold sway, certainly in Hong Kong, and probably still in mainland China – but that is to anticipate).

In due time, but without any sense of hurry, the meal and the conversational stories ended, and the whole family escorted us to the tram which would take us to the ferry and to Kwun Tong. Like St. Paul on the beach at Miletus, our friends almost wept as they embraced us and said farewell. However, they did it in the Chinese way, hiding their emotions under a smile or a laugh.

Sunday having come round once more, we decided to visit St. Andrew's Church to meet Freddie Wong again and seek out some other old friends. It was Harvest Festival and the service, not inappropriately, included a baptism. A number of church members from Christ Church, Kowloon Tong, had come to the service and there was a full church. The Vicar, the Rev. Ken Coleman, asked me to give the final blessing. As I did so, I saw Mrs. Priscilla Tse, my secretary at the time I was myself vicar, and a good friend of my wife and me. Twenty-five years seemed to have altered me, for she did not recognise me, but she had not changed in appearance. When I greeted her she was quite excited.

Freddie Wong was present and introduced us to a number of others who remembered us. Priscilla invited us and Freddie to lunch at the YMCA, near the Peninsula Hotel. Here we enjoyed our meal but also a long discussion about St. Andrew's, where our two friends felt that things were not the same as before.

Priscilla now gently asked Freddie if he would kindly leave us whilst she talked with us on personal matters, in particular the break-up of her marriage. She confessed that now the Lord had given her strength to persevere in living alone. Moreover, she had come back again to the church. It was all quite strange and very moving.

After this long confession, Priscilla took us over to Hong Kong Island in her Japanese air-controlled car. The only device it seemed to lack was an automatic pilot! We were very impressed with Japanese technology. At the formerly very well known Helena May Institute we waited for Joyce Bennett who arrived only a few minutes late along with her friend and so called adopted daughter Mary Wong. The latter was a very charming willow-like Chinese girl, who still suffered a little from being involved in a Hong Kong landslide as a child. Typhoons have over the years caused many such landslides. I well remember such a typhoon lasting for eight days and producing a rainfall of sixty inches, causing much damage including a landslide involving a block of flats.

After a pleasant tea in very English surroundings and atmosphere, we all went to the Cathedral for the installation of the new Dean, our new friend the American Dr. Paul Caspar, who, from the citation, proved to be an ex-scholar theologian and professor at Chung Chi, the Chinese University where I myself had once lectured, in its earliest days, in religious philosophy for which I had had really no qualifications. Chung Chi was the brain child of that remarkable Bishop of Hong Kong, R. O. Hall. With his fascinating persuasiveness and one of his sudden inspirations he had cajoled me into accepting the honorary lectureship.

The institution was a lovely liturgical improvisation in which Bishop Peter Kwok and Dean Caspar each preached for seven and a half minutes (I timed them) but at different points. Part of the service was in English, part in Cantonese. There was a very good congregation, including the Governor of Hong Kong, Sir Edward Youde, and his charming and literary wife. At the conclusion of the service and in the general casual retreat, we met more of our former acquaintances, one of them, a very old Hong Kong resident of the old school, inviting us to lunch the next day at the Peninsula Hotel. Eventually we set off for 'home' with Joyce in her car. Our woman

Jehu made short and expert work of the normally arduous journey, arduous normally however one does it. London traffic has nothing on cosmopolitan Hong Kong in this respect.

Monday saw us sampling once again the adventure of the MTR, which was just as crowded as usual. It is said in the guide books that in the Colony every day, seven million journeys take place, probably two journeys for every inhabitant. Quite a large proportion of the seven million passengers seemed to crowd into the trains in which we ourselves travelled!

On arrival at the CITS we duly received our flight tickets for Kunming, the first city of our five weeks itinerary. The flight was to be next day at 12.55pm. With a caring thought for our English friend Margaret Wake, teaching English in the Oceanography department of the Shandong University, China, and whom we planned to visit, we went shopping for food supplies at the Dairy Farm, where Greta was able to buy supplies of everything Margaret had asked for, except instant soups. Batchelors Foods Ltd. ought certainly to take note and gain an instant market! We also bought films for our two cameras, one for transparencies, one for prints – both of course colour. They were not cheap, in spite of every Hong Kong Chinese seeming to be photo-maniacs.

We continued to wander around the shops in the heat, getting more and more tired. Greta was determined to get some instant soups, but without success. Arriving eventually at the Peninsula Hotel – not one of those very up-to-date skyscrapers, but a homely and dignified colonial building like one of the older and better class London hotels – we duly met our friend Mrs. F. who also brought another former and kindly friend, widow of my former organist at the church.

Mrs. F. proved to be a very forceful and interesting individual. She had been in Stanley Camp under the Japanese during the last war, which would have been no picnic.

She gave us a lovely lunch, with the Roast of the Day (beef) and a salad – with all sorts of mixed things like poppy seeds, sesame seeds and a variety of creams. Finally ice cream and coffee and all for a large price – I should guess about $100 each, or £10 sterling.

Leaving our hostess, with many grateful thanks, we crossed the Harbour in one of the Star Ferry boats (at 40 cents each), and then on to the MTR and home finally on that roaring No. 19 bus from Kwun Tong. Exhausted with our journeying and trudging in the burning heat, we sat down to a refreshing 'cuppa'. Then after supper with Joyce, we began to pack for China and the Red Dragon's Lair, getting thankfully to bed about 10.30 pm.

Dongfeng Avenue

Da Guan Park

Chapter 6

Entering the Red Dragon's Den

"Bend Your Head When The Eaves Are Low"
(Chinese Proverb)

Departure day dawned. We were up early and zipping up our two lightweight cases, coloured bright red and brown for easy identification. We weighed them to find that each was under the 20 kilos free limit, although containing all necessary clothing and some books as presents for the friends whom we might meet.

The plane departure time was 12.55pm (noon) and we ordered a taxi for 11.00am. It cost us HK$16.50 (or £1.65) for the 5 mile journey to the airport.

At the check-in all went smoothly. Going through the Hong Kong customs without trouble, our baggage was taken to load on the plane. Beyond the customs' barrier, our passports were examined and we were searched electronically. My metal armbands which I had left in my trousers pocket were 'discovered', and perhaps my money coinage. However, all was well, and we proceeded through to the Waiting Bay, Gate No.7, about 12.15pm. The Chinese girl steward, announcing the time for boarding and the destination, got it wrong, saying : "The plane for Nanning" instead of Kunming. When I called her attention to the mistake, she smiled and giggled, and then corrected it. That was a welcome human touch!

After a short wait on the tarmac, the Chinese Government airline plane began to move along the runway at 1.07 pm. We breathed a sigh of relief and sat back to enjoy the flight into the Red Dragon's Lair. Outside was glorious sunshine and heat. Inside the plane it was pleasantly cool, with no need to use the gift fans we had been given on entering. After about half an hour, the stewardesses brought round hot, wet hand-towels – a lovely old Chinese custom for guests – followed by plastic trays with beef slices, fried shrimps, crisps, mantoe (or spiced meat-filled bun), various cakes and a proper cup of green tea (continually refilled at request) and two biscuits. Greta kept the biscuits and the gift-set of plastic knife, fork and spoon and two toothpicks, for later use.

The stewardesses were very polite and attractive. One of them sported a pigtail hanging forward over her shoulder, with a jewelled hair-clasp at the back. She looked just like a Chinese calendar picture. Four girls, one man steward and the pilot (or pilots?) comprised the crew. By 2.15pm we were above the clouds and heading over China's mainland in bright sunshine.

We were the only Britishers. All the Chinese passengers seemed to be taking the plane flight as a matter of course, as did a number of Japanese folk who seemed to form a China Travel Service group tour.

The plane was a two engine aircraft, a small counterpart of the big jumbo jet of British Airways. Our section had eleven seats, three on each side and we had two seats next to a porthole. It was difficult to see what the forward part of the plane was like, maybe it was first and not economy class, which we were enjoying. Over the public address system, a voice commented in Cantonese, Mandarin and English that the flight would take one hour and forty minutes, and that we were due in Kunming at 14.55 hours. If the plane was flying at, say 500 mph, the distance must have been 900/1000 miles.

From a guide book written by the wife of the Governor of Hong Kong, and called *China through the Eyes of Pamela Youde* – an excellent illustrated volume – I had made a note in my diary of places to visit as recommended by Lady Youde, an experienced China traveller:

> Kunming – old route to Burma. One million population.
> Hotel: Green Lake Park near Yuan-tong Hill.
> Temple of the Tang Dynasty, the only remaining Buddhist temple.
> The narrow streets to the temple – restored after 1966-76 (Cultural Revolution). Note the main hall with dragons, reputed to bring rain.

Kunming Lake, east of the City : the largest in Yunnan Province, being about 200 sq. miles in area, with Tower (Da Guan Lou) built in 1696 AD. Note the inscriptions in pairs.
The Dragon Gate in Western Hills, not far from the City. Splendid vista over the lake. Note the Sanqing Pavilion 1200 AD, Daoist in origin.
The Tai-hua temple of Yuan dynasty, 1271-1368 AD.
The Huo-ting monastery – 1670 AD, with its Hall of Bronze.
The Black Dragon Pool (Hei-shui-si) of Manchu dynasty.
The Yunnan Botanical Research Institute in the Park.
The Bamboo Temple (Quong zhu Si) – 8 miles North West of the City.
The Painted Clay Sculptures of 500 Yohan and 4 Guardian Kings by Li Guangden.
The 500 years old Peacock Cedar in the Courtyard.
The Anning Hot Springs, 30 miles from the City.
The Stone Forest in Yi Nationality Autonomous District – 3 hours away.
The Yunnan Provincial Museum, with bronzes from the First Century BC.

On arrival at Kunming Airport, we passed through Customs very quickly and without hindrance. A Mr. Gwang of China International Travel Service met us, observing our CITS badges on our coats. His small bus took us into the City and from the Airline Office, Mr. Gwang took us in his bus to the Kunming Hotel – where we duly registered and were given, not a double bedroom, but a treble bedroom. It was possibly the only available room and may have cost no more. It was No. 2418 – 2 being the number of the building; 4 being the fourth floor; and 18 the room number. It was a huge modern building with twelve floors and a flat roof for viewing the landscape. We tried to look like seasoned travellers but felt rather inexperienced inside ourselves.

We settled in first. Our room was quite large, with a desk-table on which lay a Kunming Hotel blotter, a flick-page daily calendar, a bottle of gum for sticking stamps and envelopes, a table lamp, airmail letter paper and envelopes in the blotter and a telephone.

Not yet having any Chinese currency, we went to the small branch office of the Bank of China on the ground floor of the main (No.1) building at 'Reception'. The Bank only opened in the mornings and in the afternoon from 5-7. So we returned to our room for a rest on our beds. These were complete with two pillows (at which I said 'Hurrah', one pillow never being enough for me abroad or at home), cotton twill sheets, and a warm thick blanket covering the bed. Yunnan Province consists mainly of an 8,000 feet plateau, I think, and therefore has a very pleasant temperate climate. Its name 'Yunnan' means South of the Clouds, and it is therefore sunny, and renowned for its healthy climate.

Our room had an attached bathroom and loo, with very hot water, towels in place, loo paper western style, and a paper printed red strip saying 'disinfected' across the toilet seat – an encouraging detail. The bath was of good medium size and there was an electric point for an electric razor if needed. We were duly impressed.

Greta went right off to sleep as soon as her head touched the pillow. I discovered later that she had had a headache, possibly due to journey stress such as jet-lag. Only at 5.15pm did I wake her, and both of us went out to find the Bank again, and to get our money. Foreigners were not given Chinese currency, but a special currency, just like travellers' cheques but printed like bank notes. We also tried to find a letter post box to mail two letters given to us in Hong Kong by friends. The search proved hazardous. Going to ask for directions, I stepped up to two men at a small enquiry place in the hotel grounds. Then, unknowingly, I stepped backwards on to some soft concrete in process of hardening! Therefore, I left my mark in China!

We now went on to the street, to try to find the old Christian Hospital called Hui Tien or Heavenly Mercy, which Greta's father had built somewhere about 1917 AD. He had been a doctor missionary with the Church Missionary Society. We also wished to find the local church. When we reached Beijing Lu (Peking Road), at the wide crossroads, we wondered which way to go. I should think we also said a quiet prayer asking for help. The help came in the shape of a charming young German couple, also touring alone, and also staying at the Kunming Hotel. She was Dr Monica Motsch, a teacher of Chinese at Bonn University, in Germany, where her father was a Professor. She was spending six months, centred at Beijing and writing a translation of a famous modern novel by a Chinese author, 80+ years old, who lives in Beijing and is helping her in the task. With her was her husband Richard, who knew no Chinese and was a lawyer especially concerned with East and West Germany relationships.

Monica spoke very good Mandarin and when we asked her help to find the hospital and the church, she pulled our her large map of the City with the roads marked in Chinese. We soon discovered the church, and found it to be situated near to the hospital now called the Children's Hospital (in Chinese 'Erh-tong Yi-yuan').

We all went along together. Monica and Richard had never thought of investigating the state of the churches in China but now became quite enthusiastic about it. The first church we found proved to be the Catholic Church on Beijing Lu (in this present era the Chinese government will not allow the use of the name 'Roman' Catholic because of Chinese insistence on the church being self-governing, self-supporting and self-propagating, and also patriotic or 'love-China' – so there is in China the Catholic Three Self Patriotic Church and the Protestant Three Self Patriotic Church only; all the Protestant former denominations now being united into one 'Christian' or 'Protestant' Church).

At this Catholic Church, we went inside the compound and met the Catechist – the priest being out. He told us where to find the Protestant church. This was quite near, as also the former Hui Tien Hospital, which he remembered by name even after these many years.

It was easy now to find the Protestant church and we found it open. It was very like the Chinese country churches of our day, thirty-three years earlier. And it seemed to be, indeed, the church where Greta had been baptised in 1917 AD!

A number of Christians already gathered in the church were intrigued and excited to meet four foreigners. They told us that they were gathering for a Prayer Meeting at 7pm and also sent for the pastor. When he arrived he welcomed us most sincerely and showed us round the building. There were some copies of the Bible about, and also a locally or Shanghai printed small hymn book. Some hymns, written out by hand on large sheets of paper were also hanging up at the front on the platform or chancel. Against the back or west wall there was a Communion Table with a cross above it, and at the front of the platform a reading-desk pulpit. Greta, my wife, also believed it was the church where, as a babe, she had been baptised or christened.

Remembering the old Chinese habit of arriving for a meeting perhaps an hour or thirty minutes early, we suggested that it might be wise for us to get a simple meal on the street at a restaurant. The Pastor understood and took us himself to a fairly clean-looking restaurant nearby and introduced us. It was already dark. The lao-ban or restaurateur welcomed us and we all sat round a table. Mine host put a 'huo-guo' on the table at which we were all quite cheered. 'Huo-guo' is Chinese for fire-cooking pot and is a metal pot centred round a short central chimney burning charcoal. The outer container contained soup, rice noodles, vegetables, elephant-ears mushrooms, pieces of pork and chicken and pieces of soya-bean curd (usually called 'do fu'), some meatballs and steamed rice in a large bowl.

Each of us had a small bowl, china spoon and chopsticks. Nothing could have tasted better, the four of us all eating a very good supper for 3.60 Yuan (or £1.20), which was very reasonable.

Not having change with which to pay our share, and the lao-ban already having been paid by Richard, I tried to change some of our 'foreigners' money. This seemed to be quite the wrong thing. The lao-ban and others there looked rather shocked and offended. Perhaps they thought I was trying a 'black market' deal. However, Monica in impeccable Mandarin, explained, I laughed, and we all departed with mutual smiles.

Arriving back at the church we discovered a woman preacher taking the meeting. She had already begun a Bible discourse on Jesus, with illustrations from David in the Psalms, Jacob, and Peter's three-fold denial of Jesus at the Lord's arrest. This led to a word about forgiveness, and the need to trust in Jesus and be saved, with a continuing readiness to say "Hallelujah. Thank God". She illustrated her talk with stories of a doctor or priest who was healed – vigorously acting each part, along with others who were healed after much suffering. No doubt she was referring to the suffering of Christians in the Cultural Revolution of 1966-76, or the earlier days of the Communist Revolution. So vividly and graphically did the preacher portray her characters by gestures and smiles, that the listeners broke into laughter – as did the speaker herself! She very amusingly imitated a person bent of back and walking with a stick: and from time to time the listeners joined in with comments and answers.

After having spoken from the time we had arrived, for some thirty-five minutes, she drew her discourse to a conclusion and announced a prayer time. All now knelt down towards their benches, on small mats of weaved straw. Each one began to pray his or her own prayers out loud, whilst the preacher seemed to give suggestions for prayer and some names of people present and their ailments. There was a quiet hum then of continuous prayer for about twenty-five minutes until, at the preacher's request, all ended up saying the Lord's Prayer together.

By now it was after 9 pm and everyone began to leave. There seemed to be over one hundred people present. Men and women were not segregated on either side, as would have happened in earlier days.

The majority were older people but some younger adults and young ones were present, with one or two small children. One little boy kept going up and down, walking along the seat in front of us to look at us, sometimes retrained quietly by mama or the Pastor who was present. They gave us a good and happy welcome and farewell, also inviting us to Thursday's afternoon and evening Bible Study or to the Services held on Saturdays and Sundays. Obviously there was an active church life going on. For the Thursday meetings, more than one hundred attended, whilst on Sundays over two hundred came. Up until two years ago, they had been a House church, with over two hundred people attending, but when the government allowed them to open and use the church building again, on condition that they became part of the Protestant Three-Self Patriotic Church, they were glad to do so and, apparently, have remained just as keen and active.

Their pastor was formerly in Canton, as also was the woman preacher. She was less drably, or perhaps more neatly dressed than the church members, with hair well done and an open and happy face.

We four all returned to our hotel very thrilled, if a little weary. Monica was singularly moved and very thankful that we had asked her how to find the church, and grateful to have heard the preacher's address, although she had not totally understood it because of the dialect. Richard, her husband, who knew no Chinese, had been very moved by the whole service nevertheless, especially the sincerity of the prayers.

Greta and I invited both of them to have a glass of tea up in our hotel room. They preferred just to drink hot boiled water from the inevitable thermos flask – tea would only keep them awake, they explained. After further discussion of the evening, they finally took their leave and returned to their own room. Greta and I went thankfully to bed but were both awake at 3am with headache and unease, probably exhaustion rather than the tea. After taking a tablet of Disprin, however, we were soon asleep.

Come 7.30am next morning, Greta was still sound asleep but suddenly I heard the sound of what seemed to be the Chinese National Anthem (pitched in a minor key, I noticed), sung over some public radio system, and she awoke. After a very good hot bath, in our own private bathroom, we both felt more refreshed. About 8.30am we went out to seek our CITS friend Mr. Guang.

With some difficulty we found him in his office in the main lounge and at the Reception desk of our building. Here I paid the fee for his yesterday's meeting us at the plane and bringing us to the hotel – 20 yuan (about £7), also the cost of our air tickets for the next day's flight to Nanning.

Leaving the CITS office, we met Monica and her husband Richard, who directed us to the hotel dining room. Although we were late, since it was past 9am, and there was only a French couple still eating, the waitress eventually and kindly relented and gave us breakfast of coffee (good and strong in a pot equal to three cups each), with milk and sugar, plus two pieces of toast each, jam and butter.

Returning to our room to rest and write up our diaries, we decided to go out once again to find the hospital where Greta had been born and brought up. We had discovered its whereabouts, near the church, the night before.

The sower sows the seeds

Chapter 7

I Remember, I Remember, The House Where I Was Born
(Thomas Hood)

Greta and I found our way to the old Hui Tien Hospital, now the Erh-Tong or Children's Hospital, without difficulty. We were alone. Going inside, Greta asked to see the doctor or Superintendent, but there was no one on duty until 1pm. We therefore asked and received permission to go around the hospital and to look about us. Some staff, to whom we spoke, remembered the old hospital and its name, and were quite excited to meet us. They even gave us each a cup of tea in old mugs, rather the worse for much use.

Remarkably, the house where Greta had lived with her parents was still standing and looked a little dilapidated, the verandas having been bricked up to make extra rooms. But the house where her uncle, Dr. Neville Bradley, and her Aunt Daisy (nee Cadbury) had lived, was now no more, a new modern western style seven-storey hospital block having been built on the site, and not yet quite completed. Other buildings also occupied the place where formerly there were tennis courts and flower gardens. The inevitable process of demolition and rebuilding had evidently been put in hand by the local government some little time ago. The seven storey block would soon house more than three hundred beds. At present there were between 800 and 1,000 patients visiting the hospital each day.

Our enquiries elicited the fact that the one old nurse who worked in the hospital was at that time ill and we were not able to see her. Greta did, however, see the doctor-superintendent, eventually. He was in charge of the present staff and had studied at Yunnan University. Other doctors were on call and available at the hospital but were, apparently, not resident. The superintendent kindly showed us round a few wards and some of the operating rooms in the new block, which seemed much like the facilities in the old hospital but more extensive.

Whilst looking around the grounds, we noticed a man carrying a canary or other bird in a cage. Chinese men seem very fond of this pastime still, as in the olden days. However, when we asked if we could take his photograph, he hurried away, rather embarrassed.

Having seen as much as seemed possible, or as little, owing to the reconstruction, we went into the street outside to visit the old Pagoda, with the figures of cocks on the top, which Greta remembered from her childhood days. It had twelve or thirteen stories with small Buddha figures at each level. I dimly remembered the Pagoda myself from the time I entered China during the Second World War in 1943. At that time, with the Japanese armies occupying all the coastlands of China from Korea to Burma, it had been the only way in, from Calcutta, India, by plane 'over the hump', as the Himalayan mountains were amusingly, and perhaps aptly, called. At that time, and no doubt when my wife lived there as a child, there had been a brook, acting as an open drain, along the street, and which, for obvious reasons, the missionaries and the personnel in the Friends Ambulance Unit (commonly styled the FAU), and other foreigners, called the 'stinking brook'. There was nothing stinking about it now. However, there was a lot of new building work, and the road seemed equally as rough as in those former days.

We now decided to visit the famous Da Guan Tower Park, and to make our way on foot. We walked through streets with all kinds of shops. There was a Tailors, with an old lady sewing with her sewing machine; watch-mending shops; a radio-TV shop; cake shops; sweet shops; little factories; a charcoal shop (to supply cooking fires I suppose); toy shops; tea selling shops; a bicycle park (equivalent to a car park at home and stacked with hundreds of bicycles, perhaps belonging to the workers of a nearby factory). China proclaimed, even boasted, that she has a bicycle owning, not car owning, economy; and there must be more than 500 million bicycles in that great country. Certainly we encountered many thousands of them on the roads of Kunming alone, and quite a hazard they proved to be to pedestrians like us! We saw, however, and contrary to our expectations, only a few restaurants. A bowl of noodles, or a glass of green tea, would have proved most acceptable just at that moment.

Eventually we realised that we had strayed from the road to

the Park. On enquiry, we were told to try a No.4 bus, for the Park was too far way to walk. With a feeling of relief, we made our way to the nearest main road – although all the roads seemed wide and long like main roads really – and there we got on a No.4 bus and travelled on to the terminus and the Park.

To enter the Park cost a few mao (pence) in money and we gladly paid and wandered around. The many paths led to a great lake and many Chinese, both individuals and families were out enjoying it. They included the Tribes People, mostly women but also one man wearing a turban. Their clothes were very colourful indeed, and seemed like Scottish tartan and rather hot for the weather. They were shy, especially of foreigners possibly, and tried to hide or turn away. However, Greta persuaded some to stand still for a photo. The man with them actually encouraged them!

The other women and girls in China now wear trouser suits – Chairman Mao type – but recently in different colours, although blue still predominates as far as we saw. Red, pink, purple, yellow and green blouses and tunics were now worn and altogether enlivened the scene. Men also were wearing occasionally brown and grey as well as blue jacket and suits in Mao style. I remarked to my wife that she was probably the only woman in China wearing a skirt, at times her more colourful Indian skirt, and sometimes her Scottish kilt, which the tribeswomens clothes resembled, but to which they added colourful puttees about their legs.

There were crowds of people in the streets and we saw one Kunming brochure giving the population of the City as 1,900,000. The crowds were nothing like as dense as Hong Kong, but then Hong Kong must have over 5 million inhabitants. The large number of people riding bicycles in the Kunming streets seemed at times to fill the roadway. Along the main dual-carriageways were sections 10 feet wide, reserved for cyclists, whilst buses, often single-deckers linked together in twos, lorries or trucks, carts – some pulled by horses or mules – taxis, jeeps, small buses and pedal or motor driven rickshaws, and a few official private cars for officials of one kind or another, all filled the other three lanes on each side of the dual-carriageways. The horse or mule drawn carts were quite plentiful, carrying merchandise or passengers, as were the rickshaws. The No. 4 bus on which we travelled had both a woman driver and woman ticket collector, and both were expert at their task, whilst, as elsewhere in China, the ticket collectors were most polite, likewise the other passengers.

After our afternoon trek, we had a cup of tea back at the hotel, and a siesta. Greta had wanted to buy a few presents, but being uncertain as yet how much we could afford to spend, I discouraged her for the time being. It was early days too. After our rest, we went to the Hotel restaurant and enjoyed an excellent Chinese meal, with a chicken and vegetable dish, pork and vegetable, mushroom and vegetable, soup of egg and tomato, rice and green tea. For the two of us, it cost only 7.40 Yuan (£2.47) and not having had an afternoon meal, kept us within our planned price range. It was good too, to eat in a well-lit restaurant, at tables with white cloths, served by nicely dressed waitresses. The Chinese certainly show 'style' in all they do – but then their civilisation and culture does go back some four thousand years or more.

After our evening meal, we suddenly discovered we had only a little ready money left, in spite of careful budgeting and spending, and cashing some Barclays Bank Travellers Cheques. The Hotel Bank of China had closed at 7.30pm to open the next day only at 11 am, too late for us to get the airfield bus. The nearest Bank of China was about twenty minutes walk away so we walked out to find where it was situated, so that I could make a hurried dash there next morning, for their 9am opening.

Returning to the Hotel after a pleasant night walk, Greta found the weather still rather warm and had to carry her warm coat. At 9.15pm, we went up to the Hotel Roof Restaurant. The lift only operated as far as Floor 12 and we had to walk up to the next floor which was numbered 14. We supposed that 13 was considered unlucky even in China! Or was it simply a concession to Western travellers? The roof restaurant also proved to be rather warm, although attractively decorated and set out. We returned to our room after a good look round at the restaurant and the great City far below, and to our relief we found that I had left enough extra cash in my small bag, for our next day's journey by plane to Nanning. We praised the Lord and retired to bed, glad we would not have to rush to the bank the next morning.

At 7am we were awakened again by stirring music over the street public address system and a strong message for the people. Greta had not slept too well again and took a Disprin about 4am after which she slept better. I had a fair night coloured by curious dreams which I cannot now recall. Greta too had dreams.

Breakfast in the hotel dining room was toast, butter, jam and coffee. Greta persuaded me to let her buy an illustrated Kunming brochure and two silk and cotton kerchiefs and two table mats for presents.

After breakfast, we walked along Dung Chang Dung road – very interesting with its new buildings, quite imposing, and others in course of construction, whilst the road itself was being repaired or remade by men with pickaxes and a motorised light roller. We also saw a mother and father, or possibly grandparents, with a lovely child, nicely dressed, being pushed along in a modern metal pushchair, whereas others were made of the ubiquitous bamboo.

Now we had adventures! After resting in our room at the hotel, we made our way to ground level, only to find the lift out of operation. Almost running down the staircase, lugging our bags, we found our good guide Mr. Guang waiting. He urged us to hurry to catch the CTIS bus waiting in the adjoining compound. As we arrived at the entrance to the car park, the bus was just leaving, without us! However, two Chinese gentlemen in a small motorised van stopped and invited us to ride with them with our luggage too. They were going to the airfield to meet a friend. We crammed ourselves and our luggage into the back of the tiny truck. Our Chincse good Samaritans turned out to be geologists, one of them having taken his degree at Chengtu University in the North, and both of them able to speak English. Quite a conversation occurred as both Greta and I had, at different times, lived in Chengtu and the University ourselves.

At the airport, the driver of the van obviously wanted some extra fare for taking us on board, but the two young Chinese men went into a long debate with him in very Chinese fashion and out of earshot for us to hear. It took some ten minutes for them to persuade the driver, and ever so courteously and without raising their voices, to leave without extra payment. Presumably, they urged that we were their guests and foreign visitors at that, who ought to be treated with consideration and kindness. We were very grateful indeed.

At the customs office inspection, we were allowed through without any trouble. Suddenly, I remembered about our passports, which we had not shown, and was afraid that we had not recovered them from the Kunming Hotel Office. After a moment or two's panic search, we found them in my larger handbag, to our utter relief.

Panic now over we adjourned to the waiting room and awaited the arrival of the plane. Looking at our plane tickets, we found that we had been given seats away from each other! Perhaps once on board the matter could be arranged. It was so arranged! The Lord seemed to be looking after his slightly wayward sheep. Praise Him.

The flight to Nanning took about one hour. Presumably it must have been a distance of 500 miles or so. On arrival, the bus journey into the City took at least forty five minutes. At the City office of the Chinese Civil Air Administration (called CAAC), we contacted the China Travel Service (the word 'International' now seemed to have been dropped from their title) concerning our hotel. Kunming had contacted them and after some interesting and somewhat confusing conversation over the 'phone, a CTS courier soon arrived in a taxi, and took us to a 'not first-class' hotel (i.e. a cheaper kind), but nevertheless quite good, and near the river. It was very large with at least three great twelve-storey buildings. This would cost us 30 Yuan per day (or £10 sterling). The clerk at the hotel desk fixed us up with room 1306. He also agreed to arrange for our further passport visas, to continue our journeys to Guilin, Lingling, Hangzhou, Shanghai, Beijing, Qingdao and Canton. This would cost us a fee of 2 Yuan, or the equivalent of two men's work.

Chapter 8

After the Red Dragon's Fiery Breath Ceased

We now reached our next destination called 'Southern Peace', Nanning. It is a fine City with probably almost a million inhabitants. It is also now the capital of Guangxi Province and also the hub of the Provincial Three Self Patriotic Christian (Protestant) Church.

The journey from the airport was long and had been rough at first, but quite wide so that two buses easily passed. Nearer the City it was properly surfaced. En route we saw water buffalo with some baby calves. Many people were wearing large brimmed white straw hats, attractive and possibly a modern style. Many of the fields were cultivated for rice, sweetcorn and sugar cane. All kinds of pony carts and bicycle-carts drove by. The road was very long and without ribbon building development. Eventually houses and factories appeared, then blocks of flats. The roads became very wide and, as in Kunming, the outside lanes were separated off for the use of cycles only.

The taxi in which we travelled to the hotel was quite new and most comfortable – in fact 'posh'! It cost us the usual fare of 6 Yuan.

Having settled into Room 1306, I wrote a letter asking the Hotel Manager kindly to arrange for our visas to the other cities we wished to visit. The lift was not working. "The man is having a rest", said one of the 'maids' – after all, it was about lunch time! So we walked down and delivered our request. We also bought a road map of the City for a few cents, and returning to our room, decided to rest until 6pm when dinner was due.

Our room was large, with two single beds, a table fan, and windows covered with mosquito gauze protection. The beds also had mosquito nets fitted, and we immediately realised that the climate here, in the southern sector of the province, was much hotter and more humid than in temperate Kunming. The usual large thermos stood on a cupboard, with cups and glasses and packets of green tea; the usual two cane chairs, a desk; and of course, the inevitable 'phone.

Greta now dozed off to sleep on her bed, and I followed suit. Awakening about 6 pm., we visited the top floor, the 8th, and went into the pleasant dining room, ordering two bowls of chicken mien (or broad noodles) and a pot of tea. The meal was both tasty and adequate. Thus fortified, we descended to the ground level and ventured out into the dark to look for the Christian Church, which our local map showed to be in the near vicinity of our hotel. Our friends in Hong Kong had given us the address – Jong Shan Road No.63.

The CTS had fixed our hotel for us, and might well have sent us to other hotels on the other side of the City. Nevertheless, here we were, settled in near at hand, and we thanked the Lord, in our hearts, for having directed our steps. It was an experience which was to prove common for us during our whole journey.

In the darkness, we found the address with a little difficulty. However, a Chinese gentleman on his bicycle, dismounted and came to our aid. He took us directly to No.63, which proved to be indeed the local Three Self Christian Church, as their notice board clearly stated. After knocking loudly on the great doors of the building, our bicycle friend departed with a smile, whilst from inside there was a great unbolting of doors, and a figure saw us and invited us in. His face was familiar, and he introduced himself. We recognised him as one of the young students I used to know well, who had been in charge of the Young People in Guilin in pre-liberation days.

It was a moving and deeply happy meeting. He brought in his wife who was from Gwangdong. He had been to Theological College and was now ordained as a Pastor, and was now in charge of this Church. He also confirmed that my old friend and former colleague, the Rev. Stephen Shen or Brilliant Flame, also lived in the City. He was retired and had a pension and was the equivalent of a bishop in the new Three Self Patriotic Church.

This local Church (important because it was in the Provincial capital City) had over one hundred people attending service on Sundays, and about thirty attending the Saturday night service. Later we learned that Saturday services were held to enable those working on Sundays to come on the Saturday, and to accommodate former Seventh Day Adventist Christians, who now belonged to the united Protestant Christian Church, along with the former mainline denominations.

Until recently, the Sunday offerings (which were not allowed to be collected at the services but had to be put in the offertory box in the foyer of the church) came weekly to about 50 Yuan (£17) but had now increased to 100 Yuan (£33). Since the Pastor's salary was 70 Yuan (£23) a month, the church now had money to spare, not only for repairs, but also for other necessities, such as hymn books, stationery and printing, and Bibles. Apparently many of the church members brought their own Bibles printed in the old Mandarin version, and bought from Shanghai, where one million Bibles had now already been produced. We saw quite a number of these Bibles in the church itself and presumable the property of the church and available to church members who had not yet a copy of their own.

The new version of the Bible and New Testament, printed in the modern script or characters (initiated for all modern means of communication by the Communist Chinese Government) were not so popular, because the older generations cannot read the new and abbreviated characters. On the other hand, the young, brought up in schools to read the new script or characters, do not easily understand the old characters. In addition the church office in Shanghai cannot yet print enough copies of the new modern version, whilst also producing the old version, which is still very much in demand.

The church also had a revised edition of the old large hymn book used all over China in earlier days, with new hymns added, and, like the Bible, nicely bound. They also use a smaller, so cheaper, hymn book of modern and older hymns, bound in paperback, many hymns of which I knew personally. These latter printed the tune system above the words where the tonic sol-fa is represented by the numbers 1-7 and was always very simple and easy to follow.

The ground floor seemed to be used as a guest-room and also the pastor's house and home. Upstairs, on the first floor, was the church worship room. This was large and wide, well furnished with wooden pews, and well lit by electrical tubular neon, or fluorescent, lighting. At one end of the church was a raised platform, with a simple table with a cross, a pulpit and a reading desk at either side, and a piano recently bought in Canton. (The inside lid of the keyboard was marked with the name 'Pearl River', presumably therefore, made in China.) The piano was in good 'tune' and our old friend the Pastor played it well. At the pulpit and the reading desk, there was a microphone, and the loudspeakers worked well. Beneath the platform and easily available by moving the floorboards, was a baptism pool. New Christians were given the choice of baptism by immersion or sprinkling ('finger baptism' as they called it) as they themselves chose.

Our dear friend the Pastor looked well and very cheerful and happy, much as I remembered him in his youth. He was now between 45 and 55 years of age, and had two or three children (my memory is faulty) who were now grown up and working. He had no complaints of any kind to make, although we heard privately from other sources later, that in the Cultural (Red Guards) Revolution of 1966-76, he had been arrested. He was treated very severely, and wounded by sword, knife, or other weapon. Of this, as a good Christian, and no doubt a good and loyal Chinese, he said nothing.

The Pastor was able to give us good news of some other of our old Guilin friends. The eldest son of our former, and now deceased, Chinese bishop, was still alive with his wife and children. His younger brother lived and worked in some other city. The young woman doctor, who once helped Greta in Guilin hospital, was now doing Pathology in Sian but had recently been in Kunming. The old Chinese pastor in Guilin who had been the first Chinese ordained in that city and in our church, had died and there was no news about his two sons.

The church buildings in Guilin, our former home city, St. John's and St. Peter's, were now pulled down, but a new church was open, and partly rebuilt and redecorated, on the main street near the old site. It was evidently the former Baptist church. Over one hundred Christians worshipped there on Sundays but they had no pastor.

The former Way of Life Hospital, where Greta had worked, was still there, considerably enlarged and was now a government hospital for mothers and babies. Other friends had now moved to other parts of China, to Beijing and Shanghai and elsewhere.

On our way back to the hotel in the dark, there were many cyclists. Suddenly a group rode right to us. One young girl missed me but rode into Greta, knocking her down. They helped her up – she was somewhat shaken, but with apologies all round, we ourselves went on our way. Back at the hotel, Greta found she had gashed her knee and some blood spilt. Like a good doctor, however, she cleansed and bandaged up the wound, whilst I went out to get a Coca-Cola from the desk. After prayer and Bible reading and a Disprin for Greta, we went to bed.

Sunrise was just before 7am, and we were up, had a bath, and were dressed just as my former colleague, the Rev Brilliant Flame and another former student friend, whom we called Barnabas, arrived to greet us. The latter immediately went out and bought some 'bao-dz' (dumplings) and cakes, so that we need not go down to the dining room for breakfast but could stay and talk with them.

As we talked the telephone rang, and the hotel clerk at the desk asked me to go down and see him. Barnabas went with me and helped to fill in our visa form correctly, and to pay the visa and service fees. As I anticipated, the desk clerk would only accept the foreigner's money, which I had in my pocket.

The hotel service clerk explained that Lingling in Hunan Province (where Greta and I had first met and I had worked for some time) was not yet open to foreign visitors. Neither was Pak-Hoi (or Bei Hai) on the Gwang Dong coast (where Greta's father had been doctor at the Leprosy colony and hospital).

Both places were poor and not yet built up, said Barnabas. He most probably meant that neither place had yet a modern hotel where foreigners might stay, although there was also a suggestion that Pak Hoi was rather too near the Chinese border and Vietnam, where the situation was 'delicate'.

Leaving a 10-Yuan currency note with the service clerk, Barnabas and I returned to the hotel room. Here a long and excited conversation began as we looked at photographs of the by gone days. Brilliant Flame gave us news of many old friends of ours and of other missionaries whose names we had written down. He also gave us the addresses of many of these, so that we might seek them.

Brilliant Flame had now to return home, whilst Barnabas took us to the Middle School ('secondary school' to English folk) where he was Senior Physics and Chemistry Master. This school was most famous for its teaching of English, and most of the communist cadres (officials) and teachers, sent their children there. Some ten teachers of English were awaiting us in the staff room, and after the usual courteous introductions, we all relaxed with the inevitable cup of tea, and they all enjoyed the opportunity to speak English and listen to us. What they especially valued was to listen to English English (an experience they had not yet had) rather than American English or Chinese English. There is a considerable difference!

We now asked them to use their English by telling us a little about themselves. One who had been educated in the Hwa Yan R. C. College in Hong Kong spoke excellent English. A young woman teacher, about 29 years old – she looked more like a girl of 19 – taught the younger children in the school. She had been a Red Guard in the Cultural Revolution (1966-76) and had had to work in the fields and in a factory commune, before being able to go to a 'normal' (or teacher training) college. Here she met a young man whom she married when they were both 27 years old (the Chinese government had forbidden marriage before this age).

Another man teacher spoke excellent English in telling us how he had been born into a peasant family. The natural leader of this group of teachers, whose command of English was undoubtedly the best, who was also a close friend of our Barnabas, had been born into a very poor family.

His father had been a peddler and shopkeeper who had died of TB. The mother had then had the task of bringing up the family, and our teacher friend used to help her with the vegetable garden and the housework. He became the favourite of her eight children and was enabled to go to Middle School (Secondary School) and then to University and on to Teacher Training College, where he graduated in English and became a teacher of English. His use of the language was excellent and clear. Amongst other things, he told us that people in China now were, on the whole, equal in terms of wages. Teachers were paid 70-Yuan (£23) per month, but food and clothing were very cheap, and rent, since all buildings were Government owned, was very low. Those people, including teachers, who had better qualifications earned a little more, but no one could possibly afford a car (even if the Government was to allow private ownership, which they do not). Our new friend himself had also been a Red Guard in the Cultural Revolution, but he was now ashamed of this. He incidentally, although not a declared Christian, had had a copy of the Bible, but this had been burned in that 'terrible era' (as all Chinese we met called it).

Yet another young man, rather good looking and with a very open, expressive face, who also had good English, had been brought up in Indonesia, and had been caught up in the revolution there, eventually returning to his family home.

All this free account of their experiences was more remarkable and encouraging in that the Communist Party Secretary or Government Political Cadre was present. He knew only a little English but seemed very kind, since we had tea and cakes, pears and bananas, of which there was a good supply for all.

Before we had gone to the school, our friend Barnabas had told us to speak freely but to avoid mentioning the word 'God'. So now, with this proviso in mind we said we would like to tell them, in English, something of our own background and experience, to their obvious delight. I suggested that Greta begin and give a short account of her childhood in Kunming, where she was born (this greatly intrigued them) and her growing-up years in Hangzhou and Shanghai, and then her university life in Cambridge. The teachers became most attentive.

Very carefully and excellently, Greta told of her early years in Kunming with her doctor father and her missionary mother. She included a story of a bandit robber chief, a sort of bad Robin Hood, who had been severely wounded, brought to her father's hospital, and who, after long weeks of treatment had been healed. During those weeks he had listened to Christian teaching given by nurses and doctors, noticed their quality of life and loving care of him, and heard their prayers. The day he left the hospital, the bandit chief took out a parcel, which he had kept under his pillow and allowed no one to touch. He gave it to Greta's father, saying that he wished to give it as a present to the doctor, and that he himself had no more need of it. The parcel contained a steel dagger, beautifully ornamented in silver, held in a beautiful sheath, likewise ornamented in silver, and hung with various silver coins (including one with Queen Victoria's likeness) on silver chains.

Then I told my story, mentioning my worker's family background and upbringing, my father being a foreman in a Liverpool factory (they all seemed to have heard of Liverpool Football Team!): my own youth in a Government school, my work in a shipping company, how I became a Christian and later a missionary, being invited to work in the Chinese Christian Church: additionally, my work in charge of a Refugee Camp in Guilin after the Japanese war. Just about this point, the Government Party Secretary or Political Cadre, left to do something else, but apparently as I had been speaking, he had given the thumbs up sign and said quietly to the teachers, 'He is one of us'. Perhaps, my one passport to fame!

Once the Party Secretary had left, however, the others did seem to feel freer to speak, but all said he was a kindly man. They themselves had appeared most interested, and even if sometimes one of them would get up and hand out more food and tea, it was a courtesy gesture, and maybe perhaps a slight relief from the necessary hard attention they paid, or had to pay, in listening to a foreign language continuously for a long time.

They now told us that their school/college had 1,500 pupils, and inferred,, naturally and without any apparent conceit, that it was the best school in the City and perhaps in the County or Province. It seemed to be a school for the intelligentsia, if indeed they ever thought in those categories.

Later, whilst we were having lunch with some of them in a very beautiful People's Park, and some other visitors to the park and restaurant were enjoying a very noisy meal, with some game that involved the losers having to drink a cup of wine, one of our new friends said that these others were ordinary or country people and that the intelligentsia would not behave in that way.

Continuing the story of our first morning visit to the school, we were now given a tour of the school and its facilities, including the library and a closed circuit television and radio control room, both of which were good. The buildings themselves would not compare well with modern British schools, however. They were old wooden structures, which had survived the traumatic years of the Japanese War, the Civil War, and the Communist Revolution. Nevertheless, the campus had beautifully laid out gardens and trees, a recreation area, which easily accommodated their 1,500 students, all exercising together, as they did to music at least once, if not twice daily. The spirit of the school and of the boys and girls was excellent. They would also have liked to be linked with say a Hong Kong school, or one in Britain, Europe or America, so that exchange visits might be made, and their horizons widened.

Our visit to the People's Park with some of the teachers, who invited us to share lunch with them, was most enjoyable. They were able to take us in the small school bus. We gazed at the hundreds of goldfish reared in pools and lakes, crossed lovely decorative bridges, saw an amusement lake with pedal driven pleasure boats which had awnings to keep off the strong sunlight, and finally, the piece de resistance, shared a sumptuous meal of various Chinese dishes, not only delicious but much more than we could possibly eat. After which, pleasantly at ease and perhaps a little sleepy, we all returned, they to their school, and we to the hotel for a snooze.

Good Barnabas, who had brought us back, promised to return at 3pm to take us to the school once more. The teachers all seemed most pleased to see us again, and Mr. Z asked me to attend his English class to hear them study *A Tale of Two Cities*, of course, by Charles Dickens. It was that memorable tale of Paris and London during the French Revolution, in an abbreviated form.

It seemed to be a curious and perhaps a salutary choice of reading for the students of a nation that had, within recent years, gone through their own bloody revolution. Mr. Z certainly handled the class and taught with great expertise and some panache. He had half a dozen alternatives for every adjective or noun used in the text. The students read well. Greta, for her part, was asked to talk to the class of the 'girl' teacher, which she also enjoyed. As he took us home at the end of the afternoon, Barnabas said he would call for us again at 8am the next day. The Chinese have an expressive word for reaction. It is 'Ayah'. We had had a most enjoyable and rather tiring day.

However, we had yet to meet, not only the school and the teachers, but also the Church, in the person of my old colleague, the retired but active bishop-equivalent. Our dear 'Brilliant Flame' had arranged with me to be at his humble home at 4 pm. However, dear Barnabas had told us we were expected at 5 pm. The usual and delightful courtesies and explanations were duly made and received. Communist China does not seem to have lost this excellence.

We now met all Brilliant Flame's family, in his home – a great privilege even in the earlier more relaxed China. His wife, now aged 75, was there, looking little different from our memories of her thirty-three years ago. Three of their sons, Paul, John and Peter (a biblical trio indeed) had come for the occasion, and towards the end, the son who was epileptic. Two of the sons' wives were also there, with their young children, one of which was very good and healthy looking, whilst the other who was only 8 months old had an obvious birthmark. Greta encouraged them about the birthmark, which might disappear later.

Again, we had a meal, of fruit and cakes and deliciously soft noodles prepared by our friend's wife. Of course, we had to look at all Brilliant Flame's photographs and remember old friends and old times.

We were also able to look at TV from Peking (Beijing) in black and white, which gave the national and then world news, including sporting occasions like the European Games, which was a relaxing joy.

Finally, after fond farewells, it was back to the hotel and to a rest, after a first writing up of our diaries. There, we also found our Visas had arrived, enabling us to go on further to Guilin, Hangzhou, Shanghai, Qindao, Beijing and Gwangzhou. This was all at a cost of only 2-Yuan (66p) to the Government and a like sum to the hotel man, which is very cheap indeed.

Barnabas, our fairy godfather, had in the meantime obtained some medicines for Greta's gashed leg and her headaches. How kind and good he is, a fine Christian in thought, word and deed.

It was 10pm, Greta was asleep, and I was soon to follow.

Pastors invite us for a meal

Speaking to the whole school

Guilin Church members

Elephant Hill and River Li

Chapter 9

Some Bread for the Red Dragon's Seed and Some of China's Christian Pastors

It was Saturday 16th October 1982. Early that morning, Barnabas arrived. He was a man of many gifts, having been an engineer for some twenty years before becoming a teacher. We had first met in our first home in Guilin many years before where, pastor and doctor, we had cared for the bodies and souls of our adopted Chinese people. Barnabas remembered our meeting, and even the scrolls that decorated our home in those adventurous days. Now he came like morning dew to our hotel room at 7.45am, bearing gifts of apples and bananas to supplement our breakfast.

"I would like to take you to our school to meet the English teachers, and maybe to help a little in their English classes," he said with a smile.

So early did we arrive that Mr. Z, our loquacious friend, in some ways the leader of the others, was not yet ready to take us to his class. Then we visited Mr. W's class. He had spent some years working in the countryside among the peasants during that crisis called the 'Cultural Revolution'.

Mr. W. was in the process of teaching his students two stories, printed in their text books, of two great Americans – Abraham Lincoln who freed the slaves; and George Washington who 'did it with my little hatchet'. There were many such stories in their language lesson book, given in simplified language. We had a vision of 500 million children throughout China learning these pleasant stories of these two American folk heroes, as well as others.

Asked to address the class, I spoke about Lincoln's life from 'Log Cabin to White House', recalling what I remembered of my own childhood reading of this folk hero.

> "Abraham Lincoln as a boy was only able to study now and then, in between working hard for his father, and

only really enjoying one full year at school", I said. "Nevertheless, he became President of the United States of America. Perhaps before me there is a boy, or girl!, who may in future rise to similar heights and become a future Chairman of the Chinese People's Republic!".

Mentally, I bowed to such a one. As for George Washington cutting down his father's tree with his little hatchet, I decided to tell them a Chinese legend entitled Bamboo. I had first heard this from the lips of a beloved Chinese friend some thirty-three years ago. I later translated it into English for use at home in England. It became a famous legend there. Here it is:

> In the land of the Western Kingdom, the King had a beautiful garden. In it he planted specimens of all the most beautiful trees and shrubs and flowers which grew throughout his whole kingdom. Of all these, there was one which was most beloved of the King, and, as he walked each day in the cool of the evening through his garden, he would pause before it, a young, tall and graceful bamboo. As the King stood admiringly before him, Bamboo would greet his king with joyous and cheerful delight, tossing his graceful head to the sky in utter abandon. Then there came a day when, as he paused before his beloved Bamboo, the King said, "Bamboo, beloved Bamboo, I wish to use you".
>
> Bamboo bowed his noble head to the ground and then lifted it high into the air. The day of days had come, the day for which he had been grown, the day when his king would use him. Cheerfully, he replied "O King, do with me whatever you will, if only you will use me!"
>
> Gravely the King replied, "Bamboo, to use you I must first cut you down and lay you in the dust". Bamboo grew silent and still. "Cut me down, O King? Me, the loveliest thing in all your garden? Cut me down?"
>
> And the King continued quietly "Bamboo, beloved

Bamboo, not only must I cut you down and lay you in the dust, but I must strip off your delicate leaves and beautiful branches, cleave you in twain from top to bottom, and dig out your heart. Only then can I use you".

Bamboo bowed himself to the ground. A listening butterfly flew fearfully away; wind grew still; sun hid his face; the birds and beasts hid themselves. All was silent. Slowly Bamboo lifted himself up, tall and noble, and replied "Then, O King ... cut away!"

The King called his gardener. Bamboo was hewn to the ground and laid in the dust. A great knife stripped off all his beautiful branches and delicate leaves, and then cleaved him in twain, and dug out his heart.

"Now take Bamboo to yonder corner of my garden", commanded the King. In the corner of the garden was a sparkling spring and a flowing stream. "Put one end of Bamboo into the spring, and the other end into my dry waiting fields", cried the King. Soon the sparkling water of life flowed down Bamboo's broken body into the dry brown fields. Soon, the rice shoots were planted, the days went by, the rains came, the sun shone, the winds blew, the seasons passed, until at last there was a bountiful and golden harvest. Then was Bamboo, in all his broken-ness, much more glorious than he had been in his youthful splendour.

"And who", said I to the class, "who is Bamboo?"

They had no answer, and I repeated what my friend had said so long ago:

"Jesus. He is Bamboo. But Bamboo is also you and I".

When we had been asked to speak at the school, Barnabas had said that we should not use the word 'God'. Understandable in a communist-atheist-based school, but the historic Jesus seemed acceptable. At least no one passed any comment, certainly not the students. Bamboo's abound in China, and no doubt the story would be remembered by some, for the students listened with interest. At 'break' time we went on to Mr. L.'s class for the next lesson.

Mr. L., we learned, had grown up in the period called 'Let the 100 flowers bloom' and later in the Cultural Revolution, when his freedom of speech had been greatly curtailed. Now, however, he told his class about George Washington and about a certain Baashi, a boy who got lost in a crowd. This latter story was also in their English primer – and unknown to me. However, I could certainly speak about the boy who 'did it with his little hatchet'.

In her class, my wife Greta spoke about her medical work as a doctor in the old China, illustrating her talk with her stethoscope by taking the pulse of one or two students, and showing a medicine bottle. From these, she drew appropriate moral lessons. At my turn, I told a story of the Guilin refugee camp, which I had helped to manage after the surrender and retreat of the Japanese invaders. Using rather basic English I began:

> "In the Guilin camp there were some 1,300 refugees. Each day numbers of them left, walking east to reach their old homes, perhaps 500 or even 1,000 miles away. Others arrived daily to take their place, having already walked untold distances. Each week, at least 10 died from their hardships and disease.
>
> Once a week, a Chinese colleague and I held a meeting in the centre of the camp, in the open air, where we sang Christian songs and spoke about Jesus. This was to encourage them whilst we also provided them with a little rice and vegetables and medical treatment where possible.
>
> Another English friend now arrived at the camp and we asked him to speak to the refugees. He was very tall and had white hair. He spoke Chinese well and, in local Mandarin, simply told them the story of a father who had two sons. One son (he said) asked his father for his share of the family inheritance, and then ran away to a far country, where he wasted all his money.

> Therefore, he had to help a farmer by taking care of a herd of pigs, and he was so hungry that he even tried to eat the pigs' food. At last he decided to return home. It was a long way to walk. The boy grew tired and hungry and soon his clothes were all torn. However, his father saw him coming and ran to meet him, embraced him and brought him home, commanding the servants to bring clean clothes and some shoes, and to prepare a great feast of welcome. 'For this is my son', said the father, 'who was dead and is alive again. He was lost and is found'.

As the white-haired tall Englishman ended his story, all the listening refugees burst into applause, clapping joyously, for had they not also been lost and now found".

In this way, we were able to tell those Chinese students – and Chinese people love pigs – of some of the good news of the kingdom of God, without mentioning His name. At the break between lessons, we were invited to watch 1,000 students doing their 5 minute morning exercises to stirring music with vigour and enthusiasm in the warm sunshine – a splendid sight indeed. As we watched, we were introduced to the best English speaking student in the school, a girl named Niu Qing, 16 years old and very charming and attractive, who belonged to Mr. Z's class. She spoke to us in excellent English without any nervousness and with great poise.

We now went to Mr. Z's senior class. They were reading and discussing a shortened version of *A Tale of Two Cities* by Charles Dickens. The day's section described how Doctor Manette discovered two young people in Paris, in the Bastille Prison. The boy had tried to avenge his sister whom a French nobleman had tried to abduct. In the ensuing duel, the nobleman severely wounded the young man. After having told his story to the Doctor, the boy died. Perhaps it was simply the human drama rather than any political reason, which justified this inclusion in the Government's schoolbook reader.

Mr. Z. now showed his skilful command of English by writing

on the blackboard the various adjectives used, comparing them with others of similar meaning, e.g. horrible, terrible, dreadful and awful. This would certainly increase the students' vocabularies.

When I was asked to speak, I also took up the Dickens' story and told the class of the hero of the plot, Charles Darnay, and the villain of the piece, Sidney Carton. Both men, I told them, loved the same beautiful heroine. However, in the end, the villain gave up his life for the hero, and accepted execution, since the lady loved the other man. Romantic fiction, or truth, still appeals to Chinese youth and takes a strong place alongside patriotism. So also does the strength and mutual love of family life. The students were very interested to hear us say that it was a lovely thing for us to bring up our three sons. Mr. Z. also referred to the recent Government edict allowing married couples to have only one child in view of the danger to the country of a rising birth rate.

We both continued to earn our privilege of teaching modern Chinese sons and daughters (Red Dragon seeds, as they are called). After the next lesson break we were invited to speak to Miss Y's class of first grade, first year students. She herself showed excellent technique and sensitiveness by using simple oral examples (like 'These cows are black') and then showing well drawn illustrations of three black cows. So, too, with pigs, goats and horses in white and black. She then showed them a pair of shoes, neither black nor white, but brown.

Greta and I followed up with a double act, one of us as teacher asking questions, the other giving answers. Greta taught them to sing an old familiar song from home 'I am H.A.P.P.Y'. The children took it up with great delight.

We now went to lunch with Mr. Z. in his flat in the school premises; an unusual privilege. His father, a water conservancy expert, joined us. Although over 60 years of age and thus able to retire on pension (which at 80% of his former wages was worth 50 Yuan a month). He chose to continue working. Mr. Z's two children were there too. The little daughter, who was rather pretty, wanted her father to feed her (either out of shyness or to attract attention!) Mother was out working (but I do not recall what work she did) and a fellow teacher cooked the meal so that Mr. Z. could eat with us. Chinese men are, in fact, very willing and very able cooks.

Having enjoyed lunch, we said farewell and returned to find our friend Barnabas. We all walked to the church some 8 minutes away. The sun was strong, the weather hot. Being Saturday, there was a midday service at 12.30, held to meet the needs of those who worked Sundays, and to suit Seventh Day Adventists. We arrived late, in the middle of the sermon, given by the Rev. Y, Chairman of the Provincial Three Self Church, and a Cantonese. His sermon was based on Psalm 133, and its theme, 'Unity of the Brethren'. His Cantonese was very clear, yet neither Greta nor I could understand very much, but caught his reference to Jesus' words on unity in John's Gospel, Chapter 17. A hymn followed with us singing in Mandarin from the Chinese characters. We also found that we remembered the Lord's Prayer, even after 33 years. At the end of the service, we were able to meet and talk with the thirty or so members present.

We now returned to the school and were taken by three teachers in the school bus to see a famous cave some 33 kilometres away. Unfortunately, about half way, we found the road blocked by three crashed trucks, and were forced to turn back. Therefore, our friends took us to visit a lake, famous for its feeding tanks and pools for fish farming, and its famous garden of Chinese medicinal plants and herbs, used in traditional Chinese medicine. The lake was very pleasant with many beautiful bridges, around which we could see large groups of fish, including goldfish of a variety of colour and sizes. The breeding tanks supplied a large restaurant in the park, noted for its meals of all varieties of fish.

We then journeyed into the City to find a restaurant to have a meal together. It was not a particularly attractive place, but under pressure from the teachers (class or rank will tell, even in today's China!), the staff provided us with some excellent food – meat dumplings, three common meat dishes, an egg dish and two bowls of delicious soup. However, being late in the day, the establishment had no tea to offer and we drank boiling water from bowls instead!

Next morning our Barnabas came early again, bearing some yu-tiao (lengths of deep fried dough, an inch in diameter and twisted into a plait), some chestnuts and hot milk in a thermos – and all for breakfast! The hot milk made good coffee. All very appetising.

Barnabas also brought, as promised, an outline speech which I had been invited to give to 200 teachers of English from the area. We went over the speech together, especially the Chinese introduction, with the lecture itself in English and the subject 'Methods of Teaching English'. Barnabas' suggested script was excellent. All I had to do was to correct the English. His grasp of the subject was obvious.

Barnabas returned an hour later with his wife and two daughters, aged 27 and 23. Both were married but we did not ask how the younger could be married before the Government set age limit of 27 years. She may have been married before the date of the edict itself.

The elder daughter was a hairdresser and sported a lovely modern style haircut. The young one's husband was a baker and she helped him in the business. Our breakfast and other food gifts probably came from their shop. Both girls were very good looking.

After some pleasant talk together, Barnabas took them home and then returned. We were beginning to feel ourselves to be regular teachers by now, and we learned that the Headmaster had asked Mr. B. to invite us to the school for one week. In the meantime, I was busy preparing and rehearsing my tomorrow's speech. This made us late for the Sunday church service.

Leading the service was my old student and friend the Rev. L. Another pastor played the piano – excellently. Another pastor, the preacher Pastor Y, and the Rev. S. were also present. The preached sermon was the same as that on the previous day and to our surprise we understood quite a lot of it. The theme of 'unity' was illustrated by the presence of five ministers, formerly of different denominations but now of one.

Pastor Y applied his text firstly to family life. This was bold, considering the Government policy of former years when family life and solidarity was deliberately broken up to strengthen patriotic and national consciousness. Had not Sun Yat-sen, father of the Revolution which overthrew the Imperial Rule, said that China was like a heap of sand. It was fast becoming quite a solid body indeed.

His next point applied to the oneness of the Chinese church as fulfilling the prayer of Jesus in John's Gospel Chapter 17, and achieved under the leadership of the Communist Government. He had an interesting but curious story illustration of two quarrelling sons of a family who had a horse race. After one had won, they had a fight. Was this a pointer to the Communist and the Nationalist sections of the country, and that competition leads only to conflict? Whatever he meant, he now applied the text to the politically achieved unity of the nation.

Over 100 people were present, including many young people. These stayed for a hearty music practice after the service in which we were allowed to join, they singing in Cantonese, we in Mandarin. We sang old favourites like "Blessed Assurance", "Crown him with many crowns" and "All hail the power of Jesus' name" to the Welsh tune!

Service over, indefatigable Barnabas took us on a slow tour of the City, through some very dusty lanes and broken down buildings, until he found a really 'local' eating house, where we tasted local cooking. The noodles and pork were not quite so appetising, however. Returning us to the hotel, Mr. B. left us to snatch a quick, short nap in Greta's case, whilst I practised my 'lecture'. We had learned from Barnabas that teachers earned about 70 Yuan (£23) a month, with better-qualified teachers earning a little more. This made his generosity and that of his friends, who refused to let us pay for anything, seem all the greater and we were quite humbled.

Finally, in the evening, our teacher friends invited us to an Acrobatic Display at one of the City's auditoriums. It was the final of the national competition between Provinces. It was magnificent and there was tremendous vocal support from the local provincials for their team, which was the host Province. Led by the cheerful and dignified Mr Z, taken there in the school bus, having reserved seats, we felt rather like Royalty, or the Communist equivalent! Three thousand or more people packed the auditorium, and had I closed my eyes, I might well have been in my home town Liverpool's football ground, so great was the enthusiasm; or alternatively, at Liverpool's splendid Philharmonic Hall attending a popular concert. We returned to our hotel about 10 pm.

Next morning, whilst eating our breakfast of shi-fan (or rice porridge) with peanuts, we were surprised in the act by Mr. B's arrival at 7 am., with more shi-fan, more yu-tiao and more hot milk. What hospitality. Once again, the school bus arrived to take us to the school, there to address the whole student body of over 1,000. They were assembled, in the sunshine, in the grounds surrounding the school building, which included pleasant gardens. Fortunately, they also provided the school's public address system, and an interpreter, who was no other than our amazing Mr. Z.

Chapter 10

Small and Large Dragon Ears are Pricked, as St. George Addresses the Red Dragon's Youth and their Teachers

The 1,000 students of No.2 Middle School lifted gleaming eyes and cheerful faces from every corner of the school campus as they squatted elegantly on the ground. They gazed at the first English visitors they had ever seen. Microphone and loudspeakers carried the voices of the speakers and the interpreter to every near and distant corner and around every flower-bed and clump of well-tended bushes. Those hundreds of excited and well behaved boys and girls, having listened to the gracious and courteous welcome given to the visitors by a senior teacher of the school, now applauded vigorously as the two speakers came slowly to the microphone. The 'Professor' from London University (who was in fact but a graduate of that esteemed institution) on being invited to speak first, said, with a dignified twinkle in his eye and the wisp of a smile round his mouth,

"In England we always say 'Ladies first'" and let his gracious doctor-wife take the rostrum. The students and teachers settled down to listen and perhaps to learn, whilst Mr. Z, the interpreter settled with considerable animation to his task for which he proved eminently suited.

Speaking in English and in her exceedingly clear voice, Doctor Greta spoke first about the importance of living together in unity (taking a leaf or two from the Sunday's sermon delivered by one of the church pastors).

"This idea comes from a poem written by a Jewish King of long ago called David, a famous scholar-warrior", she said.

The words and sentences were excellently interpreted in Mandarin (which we both understood) for the sake of the students, some of whom had only just begun the study of English.

"Unity is important for me also", she added, "for I am a wife who must understand what her husband likes and dislikes. He also must do the same".

(This was excellent Confucian teaching, although I would be uncertain about its Communist appeal!)

"As a doctor, too, I realise its importance, and also as a world citizen, since as the Chinese proverb says "Within the four seas, all are brothers (and sisters)".

Greta then went on to tell the story of a Chinese girl-nurse in Guilin, named Miss Tang Yu, and of how a mortal illness she had contracted was healed by getting the nurses and staff, including even the gateman at the hospital, to visit Tang Yu each day, to say 'Hello', and to take flowers to her and to love her. Love conquered that mortal illness. Greta's talk had a most enthusiastic reception.

The 'Professor of London University' now came to the microphone. My head of white hair (and dark eyebrows!) must have given me a certain advantage, for the Chinese generally, and even communist-trained boys and girls, show great respect to their old people and listen to their wisdom. And so I began:

"A great man said, 'We must become like little children to enter the Kingdom of Truth'. So we must become like little children to enter the kingdom of English or Chinese language. Children learn at their mother's knee: and your English teacher is like a mother or father.

We can learn English nouns more easily through using pictures, like Miss Yang did the other day. We see and we hear at the same time, through eyegate and eargate. For example, we see a lion etc. and read or hear the noun "lion", "dog", "cow", "bicycle" or "car". The teacher-mother says "This is a bus. That is a cat. This is the Sun. That is the Moon. That is a boy. That is a girl."

Now learn short sentences like "This is a house." "My house is a home". We learn these short sentences to begin to THINK in English.

Then we can learn longer sentences by adding adjectives to nouns, and adverbs to adjectives, e.g.

(1) I have a boyfriend. I have a good boyfriend. I have a very good boyfriend.

(2) My father has many books. My mother has much patience.

(3) I have an interesting English story-book.

Next try to learn simple English poems, such as Nursery Rhymes, by heart, e.g.

Mary had a little lamb,
its fleece was white like snow,
and everywhere that Mary went,
the lamb was sure to go.
It followed her to school one day,
it was against the rule.
It made the children laugh and play
to see a lamb at school.

Then learn longer poems, like this one by Thomas Hood:

"I remember, I remember the house where I was born,
The little windows where the sun came peeping in at morn,
It never came a wink too soon nor brought too long a day,
But now I often wish the night had borne my breath away."

We can also learn short stories, real stories about real people, like Abraham Lincoln or George Washington. It is good to learn them by heart (or memory), and to say them aloud. In this way we learn history too.

So let me tell you a real story about a British King and a man called Paulinus.

Paulinus (who was a monk – and not a monkey!) came from Italy to England about 620 AD. When he arrived in England, he went to the castle of an English King, who was only king of a small area of land. The King was feasting with his soldiers. A great fire burned in the hall. A knock came at the gate. The gateman came in and said, "There is a monk named Paulinus who wishes to speak to the King". The King said to his men, "Shall we receive him?" A wise man, and friend of the King, looked up and saw a bird fly through a window from the darkness outside. The bird flew round the hall two or three times and then flew out through another window into the darkness of the night and was gone.

The wise man said to the King, "My Lord King, look at that bird. We men are like that bird. We come from the darkness and stay in the light for about 50/60 years, and then go out into the darkness of death. If this man Paulinus can tell us where we come from and where we go when we go into the darkness of death, let him come and tell us, and we will listen."

Paulinus came in and spoke to them about birth, life and death, and life after death. The King and his men listened very carefully and asked Paulinus to stay and teach them more about these matters. And he did so.

It is a good thing to write out such stories in English in your own book and to read them aloud several times, and to memorise them. Also, it is good to tell them to other people and to other children. Then they will listen and both of you will enjoy it.

In this way you will, first, learn English and second, you will enjoy learning. Your English will improve and one day, perhaps, you will become a Professor of English like your teacher. But when you begin to dream in English, then you will have become a very good Professor, and perhaps you will come to England to visit us. You will be welcome."

It all seemed to hang together at the time and our words were excellently interpreted by the indefatigable and gifted Mr. Z. The whole school applauded us enthusiastically and with courtesy at the end. Inevitably we were duly thanked by one of the school staff, whilst some of the pupils came and presented us with gifts of flowers and Chinese pictures, and finally we were each honoured to receive the red scarf of the Chinese Young Pioneers!

The Chinese are certainly masters of ceremony and we were deeply moved.

These morning speeches over, Greta and I and our Chinese

teacher friends made our way through the crowds of animated young students to the teachers' common room, where we made our farewells. Returning to our hotel we had some lunch and, whilst Greta had a welcome snooze, I practised my requested speech on 'Teaching English' which I was to give that afternoon to 200 or more Chinese Middle School teachers of English.

I would have been at some loss to know what to say but dear Barnabas had come to my rescue. He had outlined and written out such a speech that included some classical quotations, including one from a famous Chinese poet and another, a well-known Chinese proverb, to be followed by the speech proper in English. After a little reflection, I prefaced the whole with a spoken Chinese introduction of my own, with the cheerful approval of dear Barnabas!

In due time, and with a certain understandable sense of trepidation on my part, the great occasion duly arrived. When the inevitable introductions had been made and the crowded school hall was quiet with expectancy, I began gathering courage and confidence as I proceeded. Here is what I said:

Introduction, spoken in Mandarin:

"Good friends, I would like to say first a few words in Chinese. During the last 33 years, I have had no opportunity to speak Chinese. So if I make mistakes, please excuse me. I welcome, today, Mr Wen Shu-ji's invitation to speak to you in English. In coming to China this time, my most important desire is to enjoy visiting the places in China where I used to work in times past. This is something I find difficult to forget. When I left China, I was still a young man. Now I am old. An old Chinese proverb says, 'A man's life has seventy old loose strand ends'. I am almost 70 years old. In the Songs of Tang (or Tang Poetry) there is a poem with a seven-characters metre (written by He Dz-dzang):

"Leaving home a young man, returning grown old,
Dialect unchanged, hair now white;
Children meet me, know me not,
Smiling ask, 'Sir, whence d'you come?'"

(In English):

“When I was a young man, I left my family in England to visit China. I was here for six years. I returned home after the ‘Liberation’ and then went to Hong Kong for five more years. Then, with my wife and three sons, I returned home again to England. I remained there until I grew old enough to return.

My speech and my attitude remained the same as before, but my hair gradually became white and I became old.

Now that I have returned to visit China in my old age, when children meet me, they do not know my family or me as formerly, so they ask me with a smile, ‘Where are you from, sir?’ At first, I felt I was a stranger, but a welcome stranger, especially since coming here to No.2 Middle School.

Today, Party Secretary Wen, and Mr. C., have invited me to address you about the work of teaching English. Incidentally, I am not really a qualified teacher of English. I am qualified in a different profession, but I do know and love the English language. There are hundreds of languages in the world and each language seems to be the most important to the people who speak it as their own native tongue. Of course, that is not a strange thing because it is the language they learned at their mother’s knee, and it may be the only language they will ever speak throughout their lives.

The importance of a language may be judged by a number of things. The first is the number of people that speak it as a native language. The second is, how widely are the native speakers distributed throughout the world. Thirdly, there are the cultural and the political influence of the people who speak and write this language as a mother tongue.

There is little doubt that English is one of the world’s most widely used languages today.

People use a language in two or three ways; as a native language, as a second language or as a foreign language.

English is spoken as a native language by nearly 300/400 million people, in Britain, the United States, Australia, Canada, New Zealand, and some Caribbean (or West Indian) countries and in South Africa.

As a second language, English is often necessary for official business, for education, in giving information, and in various other activities, e.g. this is so in India and Pakistan, in Nigeria, in Singapore and in the Philippines.

English is also one of the few 'working' languages of the United Nations, and it is used more frequently than the others are. So it is said that English has become the language of international trade, transport and also justice (at The Hague in Holland).

Most planes flying between countries use English to talk to passengers, and to airport air terminal personnel. Most and perhaps all ships sailing in the oceans use English to call for help by radio in emergencies. It has been said that 60% of the worlds radio broadcasts, and 70% of the world's mail, is also in English. In international sports meetings, and in meetings of world scientists, and in discussions between writers and artists of different nations, English is probably the most commonly used and most widely understood language. It has become, in fact, the language of international co-operation in science and technology. The most advanced results in space and nuclear and computer research are published in it. A scientist who is able to speak and write English is in closer touch with other scientists in other countries, compared with those who do not.

In learning a foreign language, like English, it is best first to learn to speak it. This becomes the groundwork of reading and writing. It is much better to try to *talk* first, even if one makes mistakes. However, it is also important not to let fluency of speech and ability to hear and understand another language prevent you from perfecting your reading and writing of that language.

It is a good help, say, to keep a diary in English, and to write notes, letters, and articles if you can. Get someone to go through what you have written and to tell you where there are mistakes. Do not be afraid to ask! Many mistakes made in talking may pass unnoticed, but they become obvious when you write them down.

Try to speak slowly at first. Do not worry about mistakes. 'The man who never made a mistake, never made anything!' To help to give you fluency read, read and read again, either to yourself or by reading aloud to yourself and then to others. However, it is important to choose something not too difficult for you but which is also interesting. At first, do not stop to look up words if you can guess their meaning, or if they are not the important words in the sentence. Do that later.

Many Chinese find it difficult to translate Chinese into English because phrases, word order and prepositions are difficult to grasp and to use correctly. For example, the English dictionary may say, 'Fame portends trouble for men just as fattening does for pigs!' First find the subject – 'Fame' – then the verb and predicate – 'portends trouble' – then the extension of the predicate – 'for men' – then the second subject – 'fattening' – then the verb – 'does' – then the predicate – 'pigs'.

However, the Chinese order is different.

Again, 'Distant water won't put out a fire near at hand'. In Chinese, the order is reversed. So, because the word order in English and Chinese sentences is often different, pay attention to this problem.

To translate Chinese poetry into English is especially difficult. There is a well-known Chinese poem, which reads in English:

The moonlight shining on my bed
Is like the frost upon the ground.
I raise my head to see the bright moon
I lower my head and recall my native home.

It is necessary also to work hard at prepositions and other grammatical forms. In examinations, there are many forms of this to be illustrated, e.g.

(1) Fill in the blanks with an 'a' or with 'the' where necessary.
(2) Fill in the blanks with prepositions.
(3) Supply the correct tense.
(4) Turn the following sentence into the Passive Voice.
(5) Combine the following 'simple sentences' to form complex ones.
(6) Translate the Chinese sentences into English.
(7) Translate the following paragraph in English into readable Chinese.

These are all good ways of learning English. It is probably due to shortcomings in our teaching that students sometimes fail in learning English. Reading and writing and mechanical memorising are so widely required that students are not interested in English and think it is a dry subject. So, try to make it interesting. Students' vocabulary and sentence patterns are very few at first. They forget them very easily. Some people ask 'Why are Middle School students not encouraged and helped to write short articles in English?' Teachers should also teach English by speaking, writing, translating and listening, so that book learning can make a deep impression on the students very quickly.

The day before yesterday, my wife Dr. Hague, and I were fortunate to listen to some open classes at No. 2 Middle School given by Mr. Dzen, Mr. W. and Miss Y. We heartily congratulate the teachers on their skill and ability. They were very clear indeed and the students answered with excellent pronunciation, whilst the teachers' handwriting on the blackboard was good and clear, and we enjoyed the use of pictures to illustrate words in the youngest class.

Now it is good and worthwhile to notice the following points:

(1) We should teach our students to pronounce *correctly*, because hearing and writing is mastered only by correct pronunciation. Tape recording can also help in this regard.

(2) In class, on the other hand, the teacher should stress the central subject, to help the students to pay attention to the teacher's lecture and understand it better. This method of bringing out the meaning should also proceed *from the easy to the difficult*, so as to help the student to get new knowledge systematically. In this way, the student's knowledge can be consolidated, given a good foundation, and the content of the new lesson can soon be mastered. The substance of the text can then be analysed more easily.

At the present time, we should help the students to be interested in English itself. In the past many teachers have been keen rather to point out their own opinions (of course, these are often correct and of value).

Now let me sum up and speak about *my own view* of lecturing in an English class. I think it is important that we are clear about both the *purpose* and *the methods* of teaching English. There are four aspects of such teaching:

(1) Listening; (2) Speaking; (3) Reading (4) Writing.

In addition, we must begin by realising the differences between English and Chinese. English words are, of course, alphabetical, using 26 different letters to form words; whereas Chinese words or characters are hieroglyphic or pictographic.

It is difficult for Chinese people to keep a lot of English words and sentences in their minds at first; English language usage may be mixed with Chinese language usage. This is natural and inevitable. So it is important that English words and sentences be fixed clearly in the mind of the student and teacher alike, and that we should use some memory aids. In teaching English, it is necessary to use the words and sentences in the textbook as much as possible. If some sentences are not clearly understood by the students, they may be translated into Chinese. Meanwhile, the teacher must analyse the grammar as simply as possible to help the students to master the basis of the language-form. *Drilling* the students in reciting and writing will soon achieve remarkable success – or as we say often in English, 'will soon bring dividends'.

I realise that each teacher will acquire or have his own various ways of teaching English, for as we say in England, 'Each will do his own thing'. I expect many of you will each have his own opinions. I would like to end my lecture with a Chinese saying which hangs on the wall of my house in England and which I constantly remember because it is also written in beautiful Chinese script. It is just four words and reads 'Neng-je do lao', meaning 'He who possesses ability will/must work harder'. Thank you for listening so attentively."

At the end of this 45 minute speech – probably the first all those Chinese teachers of English had ever heard spoken, not by Chinese, nor Americans, nor Europeans, but by a 'pukka' Englishman, - the whole assembly applauded with pleasure as well as with courtesy! However, not content with, or to be done out of, hearing only the male 'professor' of the species they enthusiastically invited Greta also to add a few words about 'Eye-gate', 'Ear-gate' and 'Acting Methods' of teaching a language. She duly did so in great style, and to further applause, not least, I surmise, because a woman's voice and articulation, and her own in particular, were exceedingly clear.

Somewhat exhausted although also a little elated, we returned to our hotel reflecting on the amazing talents of our dear Chinese brother Barnabas. Having enjoyed a bowl of hot noodles for supper we were again collected by our teacher friends. They took us, in the school bus, to a classical music concert, given by the Beijing National Symphony Orchestra. It was held in a second beautiful, newly built auditorium or concert hall, seating some 2,000 people (or so we were told), and every seat taken. Mr. Z., Mr. B., and the school bus driver, Greta and myself had seats on the front row, just below the conductor's rostrum, the seats bought for us by our Chinese friends, with no possibility of our sharing the cost! Such is the loveable hospitality of the Chinese.

The concert itself was inspiringly beautiful. Included in the excellent programme was the Overture to Mozart's 'Swan Lake'; a violin concerto, in which the Chinese soloist was quite brilliant; a Chinese composition put into western form (and lovely to listen to). There was also a romantic piece by the Austrian or German composer Brucke. After the interval came another Mozart Concerto as the finale – and again brilliantly played. Then, in answer to the tumultuous applause, the orchestra played, as encore, the opening part to Carmen and the Toreador's song. We were very moved by the whole evening's magnificent music and I could not but reflect inwardly that I had had to travel some 8,000 miles, and to China, to bc present at such a concert for the first time, although I had often listened to the London Promenade Concerts on both radio and television, on many occasions.

During the interval, we had left the auditorium and mingled with the crowds. As the only foreigners apparently present, we were the object of many quick glances and even some courteous questions, and not least my wife in her western dress, of course, and some glances also at my white hair! In talking with our Chinese friends, I asked how much salary the conductor would receive. He was also China's leading conductor, although I forget his name. They assured us that the conductor would receive a salary equal to that of the schoolteachers, i.e. about Y100 per month. This is certainly a 'People's Republic' and in my heart I applauded and even envied their belief in equality.

We returned to our hotel and to bed with joy in our hearts and sleep in our eyes.

Chapter 11

Fish Farms, Medicine Gardens and Church Community
We Meet More Dragon's Teeth and
Make Our First Railway Adventure

The day and the dawn come early in the City of Nanning, even in October, being on the edge of the tropics. It was 7am when our friend and ex-colleague the Rev. S. arrived to check if we had received his note left at the hotel desk last night. He had always been an early riser in the old days, needing only three or four hours sleep each night. Having made contact, he left to return later.

We had just begun breakfast in our room when, at 8am, Barnabas arrived, bringing more 'breakfast', including a flask of hot milk, and then left. At 8am the Rev. S returned with his gentle wife and Pastor L, my former student in bygone days. They took us by bus to South Lake and its Chinese Medicine Garden and its famous Fish Restaurant. It was a miniature garden of trees and herbs used in Chinese medicine. They were planted in pots of various sizes and looked most attractive. By chance, we met the woman caretaker who listened to us reading the notices and was very grateful when we pointed out one or two amusing mistakes and corrected them for her. Taking a courteous leave of the lady, we made our way to the famous Fish Restaurant.

This was built on the edge of the great lake, and cultivated its own fisheries in pens, and in the lake generally. Here we waited for the arrival of the five ministers of the local Chinese Christian (or Protestant) Church, as distinct from the Chinese Catholic Church. These ministers included a former Baptist, a Presbyterian, a Methodist and Episcopal ministers, who were working happily together as a united team in that area. In the united Protestant Church, the ministers varied their liturgical practice as each minister officiating would wish. The Catholic Church still used Latin but had no ties with Rome.

About noon, the pastors duly arrived and we all sat together at a large round table in the typical Chinese way (all are thus equal!). They ordered a lunch feast of a variety of fish dishes, which lasted one and a half-hours. It included two kinds of soup, with vegetables and fish; two other different fish dishes; a huge fish on a separate dish; a sweet-sour fish dish; and one chicken and one pork dish; and finally Chinese tea. Not surprisingly, we all refused a bowl of rice as well! Having finally finished feasting, our hosts paid the bill, refusing to allow us to pay a single cent. We then took a stroll round the park and eventually landed back at the hotel at 3pm.

By now we were both feeling rather exhausted, so taking leave of our companions, we decided to have a short sleep on our beds. The weather was still sticky and hot and Greta had contracted another headache. However, Barnabas was waiting for us to say that the school bus had arrived at the hotel at 2 pm and then returned a second time and finally left. He was very philosophical about it and not at all perturbed.

"God meant it to happen like that", he said, "because He knew you were tired".

Perhaps we had also eaten too much at the fish restaurant!

Barnabas stayed and talked, mainly with me, because Greta had stretched out on the bed and gone right off to sleep. He told us more about the troubles of the past after the departure of all foreigners from 1952, but especially about the 'ten terrible years' of the now infamous Cultural Revolution of the Red Guards from 1966-76. Our dear friend Bishop Xu had been very roughly handled and, on one occasion, had been tied up with a rope about his neck tied to his hands behind his back. In weariness or weakness, his hands would drop and the noose about his neck tighten. It seems to have been a common practice. Eventually the bishop, who had been imprisoned or under house arrest for some years, had died from ill treatment and ill health. The pastor of the local church had also suffered the same treatment and, in addition, had received a sword thrust. But possibly because he was younger, he had survived. However, the treatment had left him weak of body but he remained, nevertheless, cheerful and active. He had never once referred to his own treatment in our hearing. The Rev. S. had also been roughly treated, the Red Guard students having ransacked his whole house and examined and thrown out all his books and papers. Consequently, he had developed a persistent nervousness.

In my talks with other ministers, I was asked about the state of theological teaching and the views of theological teachers in England. They had heard some strange reports and assured us that they were praying for the church and the Christians in England.

"Some theological professors and teachers have become notable because of their odd and strange views". I replied. "Yet the majority of the ministers and church leaders and most teachers are still faithful, good Bible-based men, who were themselves grieved by these intellectual eccentrics".

The time of our farewell was now drawing near and the Rev. S. and his wife called at the hotel with lovely gifts. They included two locally made feather fans, some Chinese sweets, a lovely scroll written by the pastor himself. It was written in his beautiful Chinese script and a second scroll written by him in Beijing, quoting a famous Chinese scholar, who had given him permission to hand it on to us.

Miss Y, a teacher at the Middle School, where we had taught her class during a lesson, together with her sister, clerk in a foreign export department of a local firm, now called to say farewell and bearing gifts. They were not allowed to enter the hotel until they had telephoned to our room from the hotel gatehouse. Greta then went down to welcome them, at which they were allowed in. Their gift was a beautiful painting by a famous artist, a professor at the GwangXi Medical College in the City. Miss Y's father had heard from his daughter that, in my talk to the 200 teachers, I had commented on her excellent teaching method in English to the lowest class, which involved using pictures and drawings to help the young students. In gratitude, her father had obtained the painting from his artist friend and gave it to us. Their kindness covered us with some confusion, even accustomed as we were to this Chinese courtesy. Greta enjoyed looking after the two charming sisters and discussed some religious matters with them about which they were deeply interested.

Now, suddenly, a young Chinese man appeared at the door, greeting us with a shy smile. We recognised him immediately. He was John, son of our former bishop. John had graduated long ago in music and, not only taught it in schools, but was a composer as well. He said with a smile:

"You taught me to sing, pastor, and here is a gift reminder of my gratitude and your successful teaching".

He gave us a loving memento that we prize very highly, a song for which he himself had written both music and poem.

John had come by chance to the City for a music conference and hearing, via the grapevine, of our arrival, came to see us. It was a very moving reunion. Pastor and Mrs. S. looked on with joy and joined in our animated conversation. John had been our hope amongst our young Christian friends long ago. We had prayed that he might even assume his father's role and become another Shen I-fan, one of China's Christian leaders at this time. We hoped that he might also have news of former friends. However, he could tell us little, and even nothing about his foster sister, Beautiful Jade. He had lost touch with her altogether, not knowing even if she were still alive or not. The Revolution had scattered families to different corners of China.

"I don't think anyone in Guilin will remember you now", he said.

They all seemed strangely reluctant to talk about Guilin and the church there. Maybe memories were too painful to recall. However, they promised to introduce us to the leading Christians there. We already knew that his mother had also suffered and died in somewhat painful circumstances.

John and I gazed at each other with deep interest. I remembered the day when I had first met his father.

"You are very like your father, John", I said. "I would like to tell you of his very moving words to me on the day I first arrived in Guilin 33 years ago. You were very small. I was eating my first breakfast in the house where I was to live, a young man at one journey's end and a new journey's beginning. I was far from home. As if he knew what was in my heart, your father said with a welcoming smile, 'Mr. Hague, my home is your home. My family is your family.

My people are your people'. I have never forgotten".

John smiled and said nothing. I went on:

"Also, I once heard your father, in a sermon, tell a Chinese legend, a story about a Bamboo. I never forgot that either, and when I returned to England and wrote my first book called "In the Shadow of Nine Dragons", I included it as the sequel. Since then, it has been preached in innumerable sermons by me myself, and by many other people, and has been copied and printed in many books and magazines all over the world".

Eventually and regretfully, at about 10 pm., they all moved off home, wishing for us God's blessings on our further journeys. Greta looked rather drawn and tired. That headache was still there. I washed up and we both got to bed at 11 pm. Greta dropped off to sleep immediately whilst I tried to write up my diary until my eyelids would no longer keep open.

We awoke with the dawn. Departure day had arrived. Greta went to have her morning bath, and dear Barnabas arrived, like the wise men as usual, bearing gifts probably from his daughter's bakery. While we bathed and dressed, he went to the hotel enquiry desk to collect our Visas, to which the authorities had now added the city of Hangzhou on our list of places to be visited. As we ate our breakfast, I corrected for him a copy of a letter in English, to be written later and officially by the school, inviting us to be Guest Teachers. This was to be a keepsake and we might use it elsewhere. I corrected a second letter which he had written and which he would send to our Hong Kong friend's school, St. Catherine's College, and to the Secondary School in Chipping Norton where we lived. He was always a good man for the main chance.

Breakfast over, we gave Barnabas two devotional Bible books in Chinese for the two Misses Y, and a large music edition of a new Chinese hymnal for John. As Barnabas went out to get our train tickets for Guilin, the local Pastor L. and the Rev. S. called to take us to see their new communal church house, soon ready to be occupied by four of the local ministers. Barnabas returned to tell us that he had been unable to arrange a ship's passage for us to Qindao from Shanghai.

"Ships were small, crowded and old, and the Government did not like to let foreign tourists travel on them since they would lose face".

Barnabas suggested that we should try again when in Shanghai asking local Christians there to help us. As later transpired – and we duly took to heart the lesson – the simplest, quickest way to get sea passages or to make reliable travel arrangements, was to do it through the Government agency, the China Travel Service.

At last, we could set off to see 'Church House'. Barnabas joined us en route and handed over to us our railway tickets. Being foreign tourists, we were charged extra and had to pay Y32 (£11) but this would save us cash, compared with plane prices Y100 (£33). We were pleased.

The communal Church House proved to be nearly completed, was on a good site, and well built. The former Church House, or building, had originally been confiscated by the Government in the difficult early days, when all church buildings were closed. The new regime changed their attitude to the churches, allowed them to be opened and re-occupied. However, in this (and other) cases, the Government wished to continue using the building and in exchange gave the church a new site and the money to build on it. It was being well built. Walls were three bricks thick, each floor had two separate sections, one for the pastor's family, the other half for the second pastor. Each section had a bedroom, a sitting room, and a kitchen with electric cooker and sink with piped water, a bathroom/WC, and an outside veranda. Electric light and wall plugs for electric fans etc., were also fitted. The building was four storeys high, the flat room space was for communal use, and it held a large water tank against times of low water pressure. Along the new building, the old one-storey buildings, divided rather like horseboxes, were now freed to house church workers. These workers could help to lighten the workload of the pastors.

Having duly done the viewing, we all had lunch together, generously paid for by Barnabas. It consisted of jiao-dz (meat pies), soup, one meat and one fish dish, and tea. As usual, it was well prepared and very satisfying.

The afternoon saw us visiting yet another middle school, where Barnabas' wife taught. In an atmosphere of great fervour and excitement, 800 students and the school staff stood in the light rain to welcome the foreign English guests. An address of welcome to Professor and Mrs. Dr. Greta Hague was given by a staff member. Given in Chinese, it read as follows:

"Comrades,

Today the Professor of London University, Professor Hague and his wife, Mrs. Hague, come to visit our school. Let us first welcome them warmly" (Applause).

"The Chinese people and the British people have been good friends for a long time, and we are glad to find that in these recent years our two countries have made great progress in co-operation on the economy, trade, science, technology, culture and education. Today, Professor and Mrs. Hague's coming will give impetus to our English teaching. At this moment, we express heartfelt thanks to them both.

At present, things have taken on a new aspect in the construction of our socialist 'four modernisation's'. So we young people must try our best to study well in our knowledge of science and culture, especially in foreign languages, because we know that only in this way can we undertake the task given to us by history.

Finally, we hope with all our hearts and souls that Professor and Mrs. Hague will come to visit our school again if only they have time.

Thank you very much.

China GwangXi No.24 Middle School
Chwan Ben"

Greta, on the principle of 'Ladies first' again, gave the opening talk on 'unity', and I spoke on 'Learning English', just as at the former school. Two very nice girls were chosen to be our interpreters, but also a young man, presumably a teacher, who helped in the interpretation when the girls ran into difficulties of understanding.

Later in conversation, the young man told us that he wished to become a Christian and it seemed evident that we were known to be Christians ourselves.

The interpretation was surprisingly good but not quite up to the standard of our Mr. Z. at the other school. However, there they had not asked any pupil to help. At the end of the meeting – whether the rain ceased or not I forget – we were graciously thanked for coming and were presented with flowers and two gift boxes depicting in three dimensional form and in colour, scenery of the famous River Li, with its spectacular hills, in the Guilin area. These now hang in our home in England, a perpetual and nostalgic delight for us. The material is plastic, beautifully treated, and possibly a new art form. We were also presented with a red kerchief each, symbol that we were now Chinese Young Pioneers! We felt honoured. The kerchiefs are very like English scout neckerchiefs. Were they also a tribute to our youthful spirits albeit elderly bodies? As well as being a symbol of Chinese patriotism?

We were taken back in a rather pleasant school bus. The two girl interpreters very gaily sang English songs on the way, one a song from 'Sound of Music', another, 'Are you sleeping, Brother James?' (or Frere Jacques in French). Also, and curiously, 'Ten Green Bottles'. Culture has wide boundaries! One of the girls, whom her friends said looked like a Japanese girl – compliment? Perhaps slightly more sophisticated? – quoted Wordsworth's 'Daffodils' and Thomas Hood's 'I remember, I remember'. Greta and I joined in the singing with a smile. It was really an 'occasion'! We reached the hotel about 5pm and said a joyous and reluctant goodbye. In parting, we were given a copy in English, given above, of the address of welcome delivered in Mandarin by a member of the school.

Being Wednesday, we attended the evening Church Prayer Meeting. About 20 people were present, including some young people who were preparing for Baptism (this can only take place after the age of 17). My old colleague the Rev. S. said that the woman who gave the address, lasting 50 minutes, based on a passage from the 1st Book of Samuel in the Old Testament, was an excellent preacher, but I noticed that two of the ministers present had their eyes closed, whether sleeping or meditating it is difficult to say. However, since only the church pastor is paid by the church and the others earn their living by having a job outside in the world, it would not be surprising if they were tired. The preacher was an ordinary lay Christian with a very quiet voice, not helped greatly even by the microphone. However, she had a cheerful smile and at times became animated. At the end of her talk, we were all invited to pray together which we did aloud with a kind of quiet loudness, and in our own words, all at the same time. I reflected that, if the Lord can hear and understand his people from all over the world praying at the same time, in different languages too, it would not be difficult for him to hear twenty, or a hundred people praying all together in one place. Almighty and omniscient God indeed!

The local ministers attended the meeting but evidently let the lay people get on with it. I felt personally that a little less time on the speaking and more on the praying might have been better. However, the Lord understands and blesses both. After all, praying is a much more difficult spiritual exercise than listening.

Next morning we were up at 7am and ready to catch the Guilin train. Brother B. came at 7.15am as usual, bearing gifts. At 7.20am the school bus with Mr. Z., Mr. B., wife and daughter and the school driver aboard, took us to the railway station in good time for the 8.40am fast train. Our two faithful pastors were awaiting us too.

We were directed to the special Waiting Room, reserved for foreign tourists, women and children, and the halt and the lame! Presenting our tickets at the barriers, we found our train, coach and our numbered seats. When the doors were unlocked, we struggled in through the crowd of passengers waiting. Our dear friends found our seats but the numbers had fallen off so they secured two other places on another seat, after some excited conversation with other passengers. Finally, everyone seemed to be happy and Greta and I sat down. Our eager friends placed our two large suitcases and our small hand pieces on the luggage racks. Barnabas, Mr. Z. and Pastor S. all asked the attendants, and two young Chinese sitting opposite, to look after our luggage and us. It was a long open coach, and as the only foreigners travelling in it, we were objects of friendly curiosity for the hundred or so other passengers.

A voice over the radio-communication system announced our imminent departure. All our friends went out on to the platform. To Pastor S. and his wife, we gave the flowers we had received yesterday at the school. The diesel-driven engine struggled to eager motion and we were off, and ahead of us lay Guilin, our home of yesteryear, when we were very young and just married. We were due to arrive there at 5pm with some 8 hours and 20 minutes travelling and 400 miles to cover.

The cheerful, chattering, curiosity-filled people crowded around us, gazing uninhibitedly at the two foreign tourists, and probably saying to themselves:

"Why do these foreigners travel 'hard class' (meaning second class in our idiom) and not 'soft class' (first class in England)? Why are they not in a reserved sleeper compartment and not in this long, open, very public coach with its hassle and lack of comfort and possible secret police?"

"The old white haired stranger's bag says 'British Airways'," adds another who can read some English words, "so they must be English people, mustn't they?"

When we casually spoke a few words in Mandarin, their eyes opened wide and their interest grew. Above the babble of countless conversations, we were able to make ourselves heard and start some casual conversation with our neighbours.

Suddenly, a Chinese man made his way through the crowd with catlike tread. He had an intelligent face and piercing eyes and a strong aquiline nose like a northern Chinese. He sat down near us, pulled out from somewhere a drawing or sketching pad and a book, on the front of which I read 'Picasso', although the name was spelt differently, as if in Italian or other language.

"May I sketch both of you?" he asked politely, with gleaming eye and friendly gesture. "For free." He added!

"You may, you may" we replied in the Chinese way.

Pulling out a charcoal pencil, he drew with rapid strokes a likeness, first of Greta, and then another of me. Other travellers gathered round with interest and excitement. There was little doubt that he was a good artist. He would suddenly open his eyes wide, shoot a piercing glance at us, and with swift strokes put in lines and shadows. Many spectators began to comment audibly.

"The sketch of the foreign lady is good, more like her. The old gentleman's is not so good". "Not so, not so. The man's face is better."

The artist began to talk as he sketched, in a more northern accent not too clear to us.

"I am a travelling Art Teacher", he remarked. "I have been to Russia. My name is Jiang Men. I am of Gwangxi, and in the Education Department".

He wrote it down on a piece of paper and I noticed he wrote his name in English as 'Ching-men', although the Chinese surname character was certainly 'Jiang'. Handing the finished sketches with a polite bow, he made off as quickly as he came. We were sorry to see him go, he was a most interesting and intriguing character. From the remarks of those near us, we gathered that he was an artist who visited and taught in various schools in the province. He certainly had a vivid and artistic temperament.

As the journey progressed, a little more normally, we began to feel hungry. Seeing some food trolleys being pushed along the central passageway, we tried to buy something. For some reason the attendant refused to let us buy a ticket like the other passengers were doing, maybe because there were unwilling to accept our foreigners special money; or forbidden to do so. Later we were allowed to buy some 'do-fu' (soya bean food), whilst we found in our baggage some 'bao-dz' or dumplings, and some cakes, which no doubt Barnabas must have given us. We also had some pears and oranges.

The passing scenery was interesting. Fields were green with growing rice, and here and there, we saw ripening golden grain. Sugar cane and vegetables were plentiful. There were beds of flowering plants like hollyhocks, which we were told, was food for horses and water buffaloes and the yellow oxen. We saw only a few pigs and not many dogs. Fellow passengers said dogs were a delicacy in those parts! Peasants were to be seen herding ducks, and geese were a-plenty.

Occasionally we heard bird calls vaguely familiar from the past, such as the bulbul. Greta saw a kingfisher and I some mynah birds. There were small villages and larger commune-like villages and towns, with factories. Old type mud wall cottages, some thatched, as well as brick built buildings were to be seen. Some homes were built round courtyards as of old, but many in terraces. These were built with bricks, probably supplied by the many brick kilns we saw. Parallel with the railway a large river flowed, with many tributaries flowing into it and many newly built bridges and many good surfaced roads evident.

Our train, diesel engine drawn, pulled about 15 coaches, all very crowded. Over longer distances between stations, it built up a fair speed, perhaps 50mph or more. There seem to be three types of trains: the express, covering long distances with only a few stops; the 'fast train', like ours, stopping only at main town stations in every county, about seven or eight times in our case; and the slow trains, stopping at every station. We saw some splendid, rhythmic steam-driven engines, stimulating nostalgic memories in us, which seemed largely to pull the goods trains, but on later journeys we saw steam engines pulling the deluxe trains to and from the capital Beijing.

Between stations, music was broadcast over the loudspeaker train system, some in modern popular style but also the old Chinese operatic style. Continual conversational hubbub filled our coach, amidst which some folk put their heads on the small tables between facing seats and dreamed their journey away. Chinese people seem to be able to sleep anywhere and in any posture. Our fellow travellers had not lost the art.

From time to time, woman attendants brought round large cisterns of boiling water, pushed on narrow trolleys along the central passage of the coach and refilled passengers' cups. Most of them had their own cups, being hygienically minded; and we were loaned two porcelain cups by the woman attendant.

Soldiers were travelling, conspicuous in their green uniforms, but seemed to be ordinary passengers and not guards. One particular woman attendant went round putting straight and secure pieces of luggage on the overhead luggage racks, either to make more space or to make them safe or both. Another, from time to time, brought a mop and washed the floors, and put straight hand towels hanging on stretched out string lines, but whether these were public or private towels, we were uncertain. At journey's end, they all disappeared. First Class or Soft Class coaches, we discovered later, had a western style pedestal toilet at one end of the coach, and one of the Chinese style at the other. Everyone was friendly, cheerful and well behaved. At some stations food vendors appeared on the platforms, providing tasty steaming hot rice or noodle dishes. They were well patronised.

As we neared Liuchow (Liuzhou) area, the landscape changed to show large and smaller limestone hill formations in curious shapes, standing up from the flat plain, like those we remembered in Guilin. Some were complex and large in size and shape, often with small valleys, and sometimes groups of humped-back oxen and water buffalo were wandering through them. One buffalo would be ridden by some small boy, gently driving the beasts through the fields.

Generally, indeed altogether, the land looked prosperous and well farmed. Food indeed is so plentiful, it is quite cheap to buy. Although peasants earn only 50 Yuan a month, pastors of churches 75/80 Yuan, teachers 100 Yuan (if better qualified academically), it is apparently adequate to meet all needs, especially if both parents are employed. Since the Government owns all land, properties and houses, rents are very low.

People can sometimes save enough to buy extra luxury consumer goods, such as a bicycle, a watch, a radio, cassette-recorder and even sometimes a television set – all such goods being manufactured in China itself. A wide level of economic quality was evident. However, a few people, with special qualifications, or in special positions of responsibility (so it was said), could earn as much as 300 Yuan a month and be considered to be 'rich men'. What Government leaders and personnel, soldiers and other members of armed forces earn, we never discovered and indeed never asked!

Another interesting economic and social fact which we discovered was that all citizens, presumably both men and women, were able to retire at 60 years of age and were by law entitled to receive about 80% of the wages figure as pension. Old age is therefore provided for. The pension, apparently, has to be provided by their former employers, whether in industry, education or whatever. It is not therefore provided directly by the State as in England. With a population of one thousand million people (one billion United States parlance), this is an amazing social miracle. We were very impressed.

We were now approaching the beautiful city of Guilin, China's showpiece, and what better than to read of it in that song-poem of our young friend John, the music teacher.

Chapter 12

The Dragon's Most Beautiful Lair – Cassia Forest City

Rather tired by the train journey, we were glad to arrive at Guilin, reputably China's most beautiful city, and decided to alight at South Station, being uncertain about the old North Station, now possibly closed. Waiting for us was Mr. Luo Yu-feng, a former fellow student of Barnabas, who had telephoned or telegraphed details of our arrival. Our guide welcomed us most earnestly and joyously, and insisted on carrying one of our heavy bags. He was a very good looking man, with a lovely Christian character and a strong Christian faith and trust in God – or 'Our Father', as he described Him so often. Taking us to a bus stop, he insisted on paying our fares – a few 'fen' or maybe two 'mao' – and took us to the Li-jiang (or Li River) Hotel.

Being Autumn time, cool and colourful, hundreds, perhaps thousands of visitors thronged the City streets and the hotels – not only Chinese but many Japanese and Westerners too, from Germany, Switzerland and France, at least two Britons, and also Australians, Americans and New Zealanders. All the hotels (for tourists, both Chinese and foreigners) were fully booked up. Whilst at Nanning, we had left so much to our friend Barnabas including travel arrangements, that I had forgotten to book train tickets and hotel accommodation, through our friends the China Travel Service. We now learned our mistake and determined not to repeat it.

Since the Li-jiang Hotel was full, Mr. Luo left us in the hotel lounge and went out, presumably to contact the CTS, and eventually returned later along with two other Chinese, Mr. and Mrs. Bao Tsun-chuan, also leading Christians of the Guilin Church, and all three rather concerned on our behalf, since no hotel rooms were available. Going out again, they eventually found a room for us in the Osmanthus Hotel – the name being the Australian word for Cassia tree – as 'Gui' in Guilin is in Chinese. The one room available there was really for five people, and would cost us 72 Yuan (or £24) a night. We had to make the reservation immediately or lose it. Mr. Luo was so anxious for us, and we were so weary, that we gladly agreed to accept. Greta's headache had returned, and I felt ill enough to wonder whether or not we should continue our China journey. The long train journey sitting up in the crowded coach, the lugging about of our two larger bags (now filled with gifts from Nanning friends) had exhausted us. We were glad to move to the other hotel, get to sleep and just to trust the Lord to help and provide for us.

We awoke next morning still feeling exhausted and a little light-headed. It was very early, about 5.30am. After taking Disprins, which Greta had brought in a small bag of medical necessities, we went back to sleep. At 7am and after a good hot bath in a bath surely made for Japanese rather than large English folk, we began to feel better. While Greta freshened up, I went investigating and, at the hotel desk, found that they still had no other room available. The CTS representative, also, had not yet arrived. Breakfast, however, was available from 7am to 8.30am. Taking the lift back to room 602, I reported to my wife and we went downstairs, or 'down lift', to the hotel restaurant for breakfast. After consuming coffee with milk, toast, butter and jam, and scones – all for 3.50 Yuan – we felt restored and refreshed.

In better spirits now, we went to find the CTS representative, who had arrived, and arranged to visit the CTS office in town. At our hotel the desk-girl seemed a little brusque at first, on hearing that we wished to move out, but she agreed to hold the room for us for a little while to help us. Eventually we found the CTS office, away from the main road, up a nicely shaded road by one of the lakes. A great discussion ensued, but once they knew that we wished to buy a train ticket to Hangchow (Hangzhou) and to travel by sleeper-coach, and also wished them to telegraph ahead to the Hangzhou CTS, to book a hotel room and order a taxi there to deliver us, all was sweetness and light. They were most willing to help us. They telephoned the Jung-hu hotel, booked a room there at 25 Yuan (£8.33) a night, and asked us to return to Osmanthus, pay our bill, order a taxi and go as soon as possible to this new hotel. It was no sooner said than (almost) done. Returning to Osmanthus on foot, we packed up, brought down our luggage, paid our 72 Y bill, and booked a taxi at 5-Yuan (£1.83). Whilst waiting I took the precaution of selling some more British Travellers Cheques at the hotel bank counter. Four £50 cheques brought up 672 Yuan – quite a good rate of exchange – and no problems since we had passports.

Our taxi took us quickly through the pedestrian crowded streets to our new hotel, which was certainly cheaper and rather more simply furnished that the other. It might even have been called spartan, with its Chinese wood and rope beds but decent mattresses, non-carpeted floors, a desk with desk lamp that wouldn't work, a table and two easy chairs, a bathroom with a Western pedestal loo and a shower in place of a bath. Nor was the room and bathroom well lit, but all the hotels generally seemed to suffer in this way. However, with memories of old China behind us, it really seemed quite comfortable. So having asked the girl room-attendant to get the light fixed later, we set off to find our way to the former Way of Life Hospital, where Greta had been Hospital Superintendent and Doctor, but had to leave when the Communists took over 33 years ago.

After a long walk towards the old North Gate of the City, asking our way, and excitedly recognising various landmarks as we strode along, we came to the hospital. We were warmly welcomed by some nurses, and eventually the present Doctor Superintendent, who were all agog with curiosity. The old Cook, we learned, was still alive and retired, but suffering from old age, likewise the wife of the former Dispenser, Mr. Luke Shen. A couple of other hospital workers also remembered us.

The Doctor Superintendent was very kind to us, saying that she had first come to the hospital (now called the Mothers and Babies Gynaecological Hospital) some 31 years previously. During the Cultural Revolution 1966-76 AD, she had had to leave the hospital for some years and go to the countryside to help the peasants. She now took the two of us round the hospital which, to Greta, seemed to be much the same as before but much larger, with some 35 doctors, 170 nurses and nearly 100 in-patients, besides a great many outpatients. The operating theatres and the equipment, however, were better and more adequate. After a long tour around every department, we returned to the entrance to say 'goodbye'.

The hospital statistics were rather disturbing : between 20 and 40 abortions every day, and of course many babies delivered safely. In the Nursery, we saw rows of new-born babies, wrapped up tightly in the Chinese way. As we came down to the ground floor again, a hospital trolley carrying about a dozen babies like sardines in a tin, sped past us – no doubt en route to the nursery. It was rather an amusing sight in an odd sort of way. However, our hearts ached to see a mother weeping or wailing or groaning for her new baby, who seemed to be needing special treatment from life-support equipment. The hospital, the doctor told us, had many ante and post-natal clinics for mothers, and many outpatients, whilst doctors and nurses also visited outpatients at home.

The recent Government decision to enforce newly married couples in the future to have only one child (or two in the case of peasant farmers living in the country) was creating many problems for the hospitals and the community. If one small hospital had up to 40 abortions a day, what must be the total number for all the hospitals throughout China? It is, of course, the Government's attempt to deal with the problems of controlling the staggering rise in population of a country with over 1,000 million people, according to a recent census.

After having seen the hospital, we retraced our steps to look for our old home in Feng Peh Road. En route a certain Tu Se-fu met us and took us there. It looked most dilapidated; Greta took a photograph. Bishop Xu, and the Pastor Mr. Shen in turn had lived there. Now, two Christian families live there. The garden had disappeared, but other smaller dwellings had been build on the land.

From there, we went on further, past the Ba-guo-tang, where our New Zealand colleague Miss Blanche Tobin used to live, and on to the great rocky molar tooth hill called the Fu-Bo Hill (or Buddha Hill). We climbed the 305 steps to the top, where there were some 'tea-houses' or Ting-dz, where folk could rest. Whilst at the summit we rejoiced in the panoramic view of the winding River Li, with the Seven Star Cave on the opposite shore. In the distance, some 5 to 7 miles away, the Tien-dz-tien (or the Field of Heaven), a 'proper' mountain covered with flowering azaleas. At the Spring Moon Festival, the local people used to process out to this place, climb the mountain to the temple on the summit and then return carrying bouquets of red, white and yellow azaleas – a most colourful sight.

Climbing the 305 steps were two old Chinese ladies, who were most interested to meet us and exchanged greetings most courteously. An old man with a long straggly beard sat in the rest house playing Chinese chess with his friends, who showed no resistance to being photographed. On our descent, we caught up with a young man and his wife (or was she his girlfriend?) spending a holiday in Guilin. She came from Hunan Province and had a relative living near Lingling in Hunan Province, where Greta and I had first met thirty-five years ago. He kindly presented us with two persimmons from a carrier bag when we admired the fruit – the first of that kind we had seen for many years. We were moved by the courteous gesture, typically Chinese.

We now wandered along the rather pleasant promenade by the riverside. On the river, we saw quite a number of sampans, large and small, some motorised and some large two-decker junks in the old style. Some of them advertised as restaurants, while others, painted rather better, took passengers down river to Liangshuo, a famous beauty spot. There were rafts of bamboo logs tied together, some with many logs, others with only three or four lengths of bamboo. Fishermen used these for poling up and down the river, some fishing with a single line, others using nets held by a pole. These were immersed from time to time below the river surface and brought up to see if there was a catch. Some of these rafts, and sampans too, had cormorants sitting on the gunwales, held captive by a string leash. The fisherman would tip the birds into the river – or perhaps they would dive in on seeing a fish. They would come to the surface with a fish in their beaks, but a tight ring round their necks prevented them from swallowing the fish, which would be taken by the fisherman and thrown into the boat.

Making our way back to the hotel, we came across a street café and called in to buy a bowl of rice noodles – the wheat noodles were not yet ready. Joining the queue, we gradually came to the sales counter where we bought a ticket for 8 Mao. This obtained us each a bowl of noodles at the nearby serving hatch. An oldish woman waitress or cook gave us a bowl of steaming noodles in soup, to which she added chopped up meat and vegetables from another large cooking pan. The noodles were delicious.

We also found and visited the local Christian church nearby; not the old St. John's Church, where I had formerly acted as pastor, for the roof of that had fallen in earlier and could not be used. This one was the former Baptist Church, but now known as the Christian Patriotic Church. Inside the Church, we met the minister-in-charge, who was not ordained, along with the two Christians we had met on our arrival the previous evening. Here we drew out some photographs taken 33 or more years ago, and there was great excitement as different persons were recognised. One of them was a young man who had cooked for me in 1945 on my return to Guilin after the Japanese Army had surrendered. I had met him in the Guilin Refugee Camp, set up at that time, which I had helped to organise and run for about six months. Later we had found work for him at the hospital, but after the Chinese Communist liberation, he had become a teacher of music and art. Saying goodbye, we returned to the hotel for a rest and to have an early night. The mosquito nets had to be fixed and the beds, albeit having string or rope mattresses and being rather hard, were quite comfortable.

In the early morning of Saturday, Greta had some cramp and a slightly husky throat. After a pleasant and warm shower on rising, she seemed somewhat better. Indeed, the shower was more acceptable than the bath arrangements in other hotels. For breakfast in the hotel dining room we had rice porridge (called 'wet rice' in Chinese), peanuts, some Szechuan vegetable in vinegar (which I did not care for), toast and butter, coffee with hot milk in a jug, and scrambled egg. At the adjoining table, a young Chinese was eating a Chinese pancake, not unlike Yorkshire pudding. Noticing our interest, he kindly shared some of it with us and then asked the waitress to bring some for us. What courtesy! A nice gesture in every way. We enjoyed that and the pancake, and the fact that the whole cost us only 2-Yuan (£0.67p).

At the enquiry desk, we asked about out tickets for the Tuesday midnight train and sleeper accommodation to Hangzhou. We learned later that the tickets can only be obtained the day before departure. So buying a couple of Chinese pears, we set off to visit the famous Seven Star Cave. A path along a stream led us towards the river proper and, in passing a large lake, we were interested to see, presumable for hire, pleasure boats with prows shaped like swans (or geese!) and a great crowd of excited school children about to use them. We soon arrived at the embankment promenade and watched people washing themselves and their clothes in the clear water of the River Li. Some young men were swimming, whilst craft of various shapes and sizes sailed up and down the gently flowing waters. Crossing a new and excellent bridge built in concrete and stone, we made our way along the opposite shore and up through little shop-lined streets until we came to the entrance of the Seven Star Cave and a public garden. Entrance tickets to the garden cost 5 cents each and those to the Cave 40 cents (about 33 pence sterling in total for the two of us).

In the Garden there were some beautiful walks lined with fine trees and colourful flowers and the curious Guilin-style craggy cliffs. One of them looked very like a camel and was so called. At the entrance to the Cave, we waited for a large enough crowd to gather (between 60-100 people) and the group was then taken inside by a guide, who was armed with an electric torch. In the series of caves and connecting passages, the young woman guide switched on coloured lights in the roof or walls. These revealed some fantastic stalactite and stalagmite formations, one like a colourful waterfall, another like a lion, one amazingly resembling a harvest field, another like a seaside scene with boats and figures; here a lizard shape, there a large-sized peanut, now a giant turtle or tortoise, then another resembling a school with teachers and students. Many scenes illustrated well-known Chinese stories or fables.

The cave tour took at least an hour and all was beautifully arranged, both artistically, unobtrusive and sometimes startlingly beautiful, and practically, with concrete paths and steps and balustrades for the benefit of visiting tourists. Every cave in the whole complex was different and quite exciting. For us, at the same time, it was also tiring physically. When we emerged, the exit seemed to be situated on the other side of the mountain. However, we sat on a nearby stone wall and each ate a Chinese pear – interesting fruit, sweet and juicy and yet slightly woody in texture – excellent for satisfying both hunger and thirst. Wandering slowly back through more lovely trees and gardens, giant rocky formations and resting-places, we eventually found our way out and back towards our hotel. Near the Li River Hotel, we met two American women tourists, one a medical doctor, the other an employee from the US Tax Office. They belonged to a party of thirteen who were making a study of the position of women in today's China. As we talked together, they were deeply interested in Greta's report about the Women and Babies Hospital with its numerous abortions and births by Caesarean section, during which prevention of further pregnancies was often the practice. They urged us to have supper with them but we declined.

Arriving back at our hotel, we rested and wrote up our diaries until 6pm supper in the dining room. Here we enjoyed rice, a roast chicken dish, pork with bamboo and mushrooms, a fish dish, soya bean curd with vegetables, soup, two mandarin oranges and Chinese jasmine tea. It was delicious; we ate almost everything and it cost only 4-Yuan (£1.33), possibly (we decided) because we were wearing the school teachers' badges presented to us by the Nanning Middle School where we taught. Teachers are granted special cheaper rates. Barnabas' influence was still at work!

Taking the mandarin oranges with us, we retired to our rooms, wrote up our diaries again, and marvelled at the Lord's provision of our needs. We prayed, too, for His help concerning a hotel in Hangzhou, which might be cheaper. The CTS could not telegraph about the hotel until we had bought our tickets.

Chapter 13

Between the Claws of the Red Dragon
The Christians in Guilin

Sunday dawned much cooler. I had to wear a warmer jacket and trousers whilst Greta put on a woolly cardigan. After a good breakfast costing 2 Yuan (66p) we wrote and posted a family letter to our No.2 son John (to be copy-typed and sent around the family) and another to No.3 son Philip, and some dozen cards to friends.

At noon, we set out to go to the church on East Hill East Road. Being early, we made a detour to walk to the large rocky bluff, which dominated the City Centre and was called the Peak of Solitary Beauty. At its foot nestled the not so new Government Buildings, erected after the end of the Sino Japanese War by the Guomindang or Nationalist Government in a modern Chinese architectural style. It was difficult to decide what they were now used for. Since there were basketball and volleyball courts in the surrounding gardens, we thought they might now be used as schools. There also seemed to be remnants of the ancient City walls still standing.

Continuing our walk back to the church, we found people arriving for the worship service, perhaps some sixty in number, including half a dozen young people, some of whom afterwards attended a teaching session. There was no ordained minister at the church – it was not clear to us why. The person who took the service and preached was old in years but strong in voice and he used good sermon illustrations. It was a simple Biblical sermon, forty minutes in length. The subject was the Good Shepherd, and based on St. John's Gospel, Chapter 10. The Shepherd's voice was known to the sheep that would not listen to any stranger. Here the preacher imitated both sheep and false shepherd or thief. Jesus was also the door to the sheepfold.

Some of his illustrations were from the Old Testament. There was the story of Samuel hearing God's voice and not at first recognising it. Then, he continued, what happens when (as in Isaiah,

Chapter 6) we do hear God's voice speaking from glory? Our reaction also ought to be, "Woe is me, for I am a man of unclean lips".

God sends his messenger – an angel or one of the seraphim angels came to Isaiah, but Jesus comes to us – to cleanse our lips and our hearts. When God's voice cries out "Whom shall I send?", we must also reply, "Send me". The preacher seemed to suggest that the Christians should let God send them, especially when the Guilin Christians get their new church (now almost completed) to seek out others and tell them the Gospel Good News. The preacher went on to quote from St. Mark's Gospel, Chapter 3, Verses 22 f.f. and referring to the casting out of Beelzebub and binding the strong man and Satan's kingdom.

There was no mention, as far as I can recollect, of the Three Self Patriotic Movement at all —but then the subject did not necessarily require it. The new church building, the preacher explained (possibly for our benefit as strangers, although it might have been an updated report for all the Chinese members) was the former Baptist Church which, until the previous year, was used for housing (Government?) printing presses. These had now been removed, and the building returned to the Christians by Government. It was now almost completely repaired and decorated, and would soon be ready for use, perhaps for Christmas. As the building was right on the street, if they were able to leave the doors open, passers-by might hear and be drawn in, and so the church would grow in numbers.

The place in which we were sitting was a rear hall, small yet large enough to hold the sixty who were present, or the one hundred who sometimes attend. Such a building might well become a pastor's residence in future, we thought. Everyone received us warmly as individuals, but no-one mentioned us publicly in the service. One of the four laymen who were in charge of the believers was an old student of mine from former days. He was Mr. Jou, the youngest of the four, now retired, at over 60 years of age, from the factory (I think) where he used to work, and which pays him his pension. He told us that he had enough to get by, apparently without difficulty. He also said that he remembered me preaching at the Way of Life Hospital in former times, and that I spoke Chinese better in those days than now! In those days, I would have used Guilin dialect, and besides, I realised that my mind was quite tired after concentrating on the service and the sermon, at least, so I comforted my dented pride! He also recalled how I used to teach them to sing.

The small hall had no piano and so we sang our hymns with a 'cantor' to guide us (rather like the Wee Frees in Scotland). The new church, however, already had a new piano, purchased in Canton, and kept safe in a wooden crate until the opening of the building. In conversation, some of the Christians, including my old friend, wondered why Nanning had so many resident pastors at their church – at least six – whilst Guilin had none. One young person spoke to me, suggesting (perhaps only in fun) that as they had no ordained minister, perhaps I could come!

The two leading laymen, whom we had met on arrival at the station, spoke very good English and were well dressed – in modern Chinese fashion. One of them took the 'Small Learners Class' after the service. He had studied earlier at Nanjing Theological College, along with our friend in Nanning. When he retires shortly, he may be ordained; whether immediately or after further study, he did not say. We hoped to learn more later in the evening when they both hoped to come to see us in the hotel before we went by train to Hangzhou. It was interesting to see which hymns were chosen for the service in church: 'Holy, Holy, Holy', 'Praise God from Whom all Blessings Flow' and 'I know who I have Believed', all good Western hymns of the missionary era.

At the hotel we had a light lunch meal – milk for me, a cup of tea using the hot water in the thermos for Greta, a piece of cake, some roasted chestnuts (still left over from Nanning) and an orange each.

There seemed little more to do in Guilin other than sightseeing, and feeling it better to travel on to Hangzhou (Hangchow), we called at the Hotel Travel Service Bureau and booked tickets for the Guilin-Hangzhou midnight train the next day, instead of waiting until Tuesday. It was soon arranged by telephone and they promised to deliver the tickets next morning at 10am. That done, we retired to our room for a short siesta. I looked at the note which a friend had given me: in Chinese it said Matthew 26, 1-16 and Psalm 53, 1-5. The first was the story of the plot against Jesus and His betrayal by Judas, as well as the anointing of the feet of Jesus by a woman with an alabaster jar of very expensive perfume.

The second, Psalm 53, begins: "The fool hath said in his heart, there is no God. They are corrupt and their ways are vile; there is no-one who does good." They might both have been comments on the China scene – either about the Christian Church or the new regime. We were both moved by such courageous convictions.

Supper at the hotel consisted of frogs' legs in batter, pork pieces, chicken, mushrooms, white cabbage, egg soup and tea. It cost only 3.5-Yuan (£1.17). We both enjoyed that too! At 8pm our three men from the church arrived – Mr. Bao Tsuan, together with a lady (his wife, we presumed), Mr. Luo Y. F. and Mr. Jou Shih-ming – my former student and now retired on pension. Going to our room, we welcomed them, and then began long discussions about the Church in China. They all spoke very quickly – or perhaps they seemed to speak quickly, since we had mentally to interpret into English all that they said. They seemed excited, and deeply interested in all our comments. We understood about half of what they said.

When we asked why, when at Nanning there were four and sometimes six ordained men, Guilin had not even one. Only a sort of Catechist from the former Baptist Church, or the Alliance Church. They explained that, at Nanning, the Rev. Shen Ming-sui, who was now retired anyway, was also Chairman or the Representative of the Provincial (GuangXi) Three Self Patriotic Church in the area. The Rev. Lian was pastor at Nanning, and the others were honorary or non-stipendiary clergy who had their daily work in Nanning and so were unable to come to Guilin.

Then we talked about the Pearl Project in which the Brother Andrew Organisation had delivered one million Bibles to China in a secret mission. Our three, or rather four, friends, vigorously disapproved, calling it illegal smuggling or stealing in by stealth. We said that in England and the West, we understood that the Bibles had been requested by Chinese Christians in China, whilst the Project was the work of Chinese Christians outside China, and not necessarily foreigners. Our friends, speaking for the Three Self Church, disliked it as interference in the task of the Chinese Patriotic Church in China, and as anti-Self Governing and anti-Self Providing. In reply they stated that the Three Self Church had themselves already printed one million Bibles in Shanghai, and were to print a further million copies.

At the time, we were unaware that the Shanghai printed Bibles were in the old Chinese language characters which the older people, but not the younger people, could read, whereas the 'smuggled' Bibles were printed in the modern script which the young could read but the older people would find very difficult.

In talking about the names and addresses of Churches and Christian clergy and leaders in Shanghai (which we were due to visit), they mentioned the name of Bishop Shen Dz-gao's young son, aged 34 or 36 years, and pastor of one of a number of churches now open there, who would be glad to help us. We also talked about John, the son of the late Bishop Xu of Guilin, and who, with his wife and two children, was living at the house in North Phoenix Street which was our old home. We had met John's wife and the children at the church earlier. John's gift of music and singing, and his gift to us of a song he had composed about Guilin's beautiful scenery, obviously moved them too. Their faces lit up with agreement when we said we were hoping that John might develop like Bishop Shen's son. In the course of conversation, I told them that I was a worker's son, my father having been foreman in a Liverpool factory, and my elder brother being a carpenter-joiner (like Mr. Jou Shih-ming). There was no visible reaction to this. Archbishop Runcie, of Canterbury, and his recent visit to China, albeit very short, interested our guests. As far as we could understand, one or more of them had gone up to Beijing to meet the Archbishop, as local representatives. They had obviously been pleased to meet him and, although the visit was not very long, had been encouraged by it. They were most interested to hear that I had brought a letter of greeting from the Archbishop to the Chinese Church, in which he hoped to make a second and longer visit. I added that I had given this letter to the Rev. Brilliant Flame who would later be telling them all about it.

A very vigorous discussion now ensued about the Three Self Churches and House Churches. It seems that they felt some of the House Churches to be a little heretical. Mr. Jou Shih-ming waxed eloquently fervent about them, quoting from the Epistle of Titus, Chapter 1, Verses 10-14, which says *inter alia*, "For there are many rebellious people, mere talkers and deceivers ... They must be silenced, because they are ruining whole households by teaching things they ought not to teach ... Both their minds and consciences are corrupted. They claim to know God, but by their actions they deny Him ..."

Mr. Jou quoted from memory and did not include Verse 12, which speaks about Cretans and liars; but obviously he applied it to these Chinese non-conformists. Our friends wanted the House Church Christians to show solidarity and to keep theologically and biblically straight by joining the Three Self Church. They readily acknowledged that some Christians, both inside and outside China, thought that the Three Self Church was under the thumb of the Chinese Communist Government, but they were most emphatic that "We do not fear Communism or Communists".

Regarding preaching outside church walls, they said that the Government had given freedom of belief to both Christians and atheists. If the Christians were to begin to preach outside, they would only arouse fierce opposition from atheist believers. My old student friend, Mr. Jou, mentioned in course of discussion an outside mission in which we had shared in the days before the Communist Revolution, nearly 30 years earlier. He may even have been the young student to whose house I was invited, along with the Chinese pastor, where we were able to speak to some 120 people, who comprised the whole household, including servants. What a different situation that had been. However, there was no opportunity to ask him more about it.

When we asked them about the words of Jesus – "Go into all the world and preach the Gospel to all people" – and how the Three Self Church regarded that command, they seemed to be uncertain and made little comment. We asked if, in the future, Chinese

Christians of the Three Self Church might visit England, and stay there to help in a church, and vice versa, foreigners might come to help in Chinese churches, but again their replies were uncertain and unclear. Perhaps they did not understand our question. "But how can the English Church", I asked, "help the Chinese Church today, and the Chinese Church help the English Church?" Their reply seemed to be simply, by regular prayer, but by nothing else, except perhaps keeping in touch by letter We shared with them that some Chinese Christians had told us that they were praying for Christians in England and the West, that their churches would be saved from the dangers of economic security, wealth and self-sufficiency. We also testified that in England many House Churches had arisen, that many young people preferred them because they were more fervent in belief and in regular Bible teaching, and were less bound by the structures of the Church. They were interested but made no comment.

Finally, about 10pm we ended our most interesting and animated talking and had prayer together in Chinese. Mr. Luo Yu-feng, in his beautiful and fervent way, prayed for God's help to us on our journeys and our continual trusting in Jesus and the Holy Spirit. We thanked the Lord for letting us meet them and the Guilin Church, and asked for their increase in faith and service. So, with much hand-shaking and hopes for meeting again, either in China or in Heaven, we separated to go our different way. My friend Mr Jou, with laughter and joy, said in parting "Another thirty-three years and we shall all be meeting in Heaven and not here!" So they left us, commending us to the Lord, and our Heavenly Father's blessing and continued guidance, 'in peace the whole way' (as Chinese Christians constantly say in parting).

One interesting matter struck me. Our lady visitor, whom I presumed was Mr. Bao Tsuen's wife, had spoken very little. However, she had made copious notes about all our conversation; yet just as I also did after they had left, continuing my diary's record. Next morning we went on to the street looking for simple gifts to take home. Two Chinese-made biros and a Chinese Chess set caught our eyes, together with a Chinese one-string fiddle, which we admired but did not buy. To lug a Chinese fiddle across China would only have been a nuisance. At 11am we returned to the hotel CTS and purchased our train tickets. The fare, including sleeper accommodation, and handling charges, came to a total of 161.80-Yuan. They arranged by telephone for us to be met at Hangzhou and to be taken to a cheap hotel.

The train was due to come into Guilin just after midnight, at 0.16am Tuesday and to leave at 0.24am. It would arrive at Hangzhou at 2pm on the Wednesday afternoon, a day and a half's travel. The Travel Service insisted that we should leave the hotel by taxi at not later than 11.40pm. The taxi fare would be 4-Yuan (£1.33). At the hotel, we met an American businessman who often stayed at Beijing. His card read Mr. Stephen Mulder of the Cummings Engine Corporation. He told us that he always stayed at the Beijing Cultural Palace, 3 Floor East, Room 305, which seemed to be his business address too. With him, was a Chinese friend who gave us the names of four other hotels in Beijing, the Ho-ping (Peace), the Hwa Chiao (Flower Bridge), the Min Tsa (The International or Minorities Hotel) and the Shin-chiao (New Bridge).

With time on our hands, we decided to walk out to the other famous Reed Flute Cave (Lu-Li-An), outside the City and near the Pearl Blossom River. It took us just over an hour, walking through pleasant countryside. It was not the time of the 'Pearl Blossom' however, but the river was quite picturesque. At the Cave, we paid 20p to go in. There was a large party of people waiting. The cave was certainly very beautiful indeed, with remarkable limestone rock formations. In some places stalagmites seemed to hold up the roof. One large cave had some lovely rock formations right round the edges, about 2 feet in height, and was lit up from behind by many coloured electric lights. It could have held some 600 or more people easily. It even seemed more beautiful than the Seven Star Cave, whilst the different caves were nearer together and were all beautifully illuminated. It took us some 40 minutes from entrance to exit. The way to the cave had followed the Pearl Blossom River and we passed one large Restaurant, called I think the Jia Shan (probably meaning Turtle Hill), which was very inviting, and in the open compound were a number of coaches, no doubt for tourist visitors. The road itself was lined with trees bearing beautiful red-purple flowers, probably Cassia trees, or cinnamon, from which Guilin gets it name. Gui is also the ancient name for GuangXi Province, of which Guilin was formerly the capital. We also noticed some neat factories and communes en route.

Having seen the cave, we chose to return to the hotel by an available bus. Greta had a slightly sore throat and was not feeling a hundred percent well. The bus conductor seemed quite ready to accept our 'foreigners' money, and the fare for the two of us was 8 Mao (20p). At the hotel, we refreshed ourselves with some hot 'glass-tea' (otherwise boiled water) and ate an orange each.

Two visitors now called to see us at the hotel, a Mr. Jang Gwo-jen, the former architect-builder of the Way of Life Hospital, rebuilt after the surrender of the Japanese in 1946-47, where Greta had been Superintendent. He was now an artist, selling his paintings and other artistic articles in a shop in the City. He came with his daughter aged 14 years, who was being taught music in school by our former friend (whom I had 'christened' Brother Juniper). We spent quite a long time together, recalling old times.

We were not clear why he had ceased being a builder. It is possible – but mere speculation – that he had also rebuilt the former St. John's Church after the Japanese War, and this church had subsequently suffered the collapse of its roof, but at midday when there was no-one there, fortunately. Whatever the reason, he ceased being a builder and became an artist. The Chinese are certainly a very versatile race.

His children did not seem to be Christians. The youngest daughter who accompanied him was possibly too young, and under the official age fixed by Government, to begin attendance at church or be taught the Christian faith. Brother Juniper, her music teacher, had become my cook after I had found him in the Guilin Refugee Camp following the end of the Japanese War in 1946. He had not attended the church on Sunday, so we sent him a photograph of us both, with our granddaughter, her mother and their dog! Mr. Jang's elder daughter had gone to the USA and had married an American.

They had a child who is now an American citizen. Perhaps, he said, after his daughter and son-in-law visit China next year, Mr. Jang himself may be allowed to visit the USA. He was very interested in the Christian calendar pictures which the Rev. Shen Mingsui had given us as a gift from the Nanning Christians (this had been their only copy, and so for us a real gift of love). We suggested to Mr. Jang that he try to paint other pictures like that, and sell them in his shop near the Guilin Crossroad or Circus. He has had a good sale of pictures in the Chinese style, depicting the beauties of the Guilin landscape scenery. He also knew the two artists who painted the pictures given to us in Nanning by Mr. Change Dzung-te and Miss Yang. We also showed him the poem, which the Rev. Shen Mingsui had written, which he translated for us. It spoke about Archbishop Runcie's visit to China.

We were now joined in our room by two young Canadians, Philip and Jannetta Vanden Berg, of Willowdale, Ontario. They were very interested to hear us talk to Mr. Jang and his daughter in Chinese – parts of our conversation we translated for their benefit – and then to hear our prayer with them in Chinese. Mr. Jang and his rather pretty daughter had specially enjoyed looking at our old photographs of China and Guilin in particular, and our family photos, which included so many places and people that they recognised and remembered. However, now they had to take their leave, and I took them both down to the hotel entrance. They waved goodbye right until they turned a corner and disappeared from sight. As Shakespeare so beautifully expressed it, "Parting is such sweet sorrow".

Philip and Jannetta Vanden Berg were still talking to my wife when I returned to our room. They had come to see us to talk about Chinese Christian affairs. They had guessed we were formerly missionaries, and proved to be friends also of the Chinese Christian Research Centre in Kowloon, Hong Kong. They were very interested as we told them of our long talk the previous evening with our three Chinese Christian friends about the official Chinese Church and the House Churches. They had both taken a six months' holiday from their work in Canada. Philip was a representative nurse working in an intensive care unit in Toronto. They had not mentioned to their parents yet about their venture into China.

They were both very attractive young Christians, about 28 years of age, and belonged to a church in Toronto (possibly a House Church) and were considering missionary work, but waiting for the Holy Spirit's guidance in the matter. They were visiting the Philippines, Thailand, Hong Kong, China and England. We invited them to visit and stay with us in Chipping Norton, and they hoped to do so. After prayer together, they left us to allow us to get ready for our Hangzhou train journey.

Once our guests had left, we speedily packed our bags and, at 11.30pm went to the hotel entrance. There we were met by two of the hotel staff who made sure we had paid our bill by seeing the receipt – which was four days at 25-Yuan, or 100-Yuan (£33) – and then called our taxi. The fare was 4-Yuan (£1.33).

Arriving at the station in good time, we had to wait until officials opened the locked gate to the Soft Class Waiting Room. There were no problems in getting on the train when it arrived, on time, or in finding No. 6 coach and bed numbers 31 and 32. The woman guard took good care of us and kindly put us in a different compartment next to numbers, 31 and 32, which was empty and where we could be alone. The train soon moved off and we were, at last, on the next leg of our venture into the interior of the Red Dragon's country, and headed for the City of the Willow Pattern China, beautiful Hangzhou.

Willow Pattern Island

Temple in honour of Yueh Fe

Chapter 14

The City of the Willow Pattern – Hangzhou

The shunting movement and stopping of the train woke us up after a fair sleep. It was 7am and we were at Henyang Station. Quite a crowd of passengers alighted to get breakfast at the station café. We visited the train's loo – it was Western style and a Chinese style at the other end – and then after a brief walkabout, we returned to our compartment. A number of Chinese joined us for some conversation in English. The first person to greet us was a Chinese doctor of Traditional Chinese medicine, who practised in Kunming and, with four other friends, was making a visit to a meeting on Chinese medicine being held in Nanjing; they were all delegates. He was joined by a young woman delegate, who was studying Pharmacology in Kunming. She was a perfect example of young China such as can be seen today on the front cover or inside colour illustrations of Chinese magazines. She was travelling with her father, a Professor in Chinese Medicine. Yet another man joined us. The latter's English was quite good. One of the others spoke a Chinese English; using English phrases in their Chinese word order. I imagine we do the same in reverse! They all just came in to sit down and talk. We liked that.

About 7.50am we were called to breakfast by a steward or porter, and proceeded to the Restaurant Car to sample wet noodles and scrambled egg (Chinese style). We ourselves quite enjoyed it and gratefully paid only 1.60-Yuan (55p) for the two of us. Returning to our compartment, we each took a Panadol – anti-Malaria pills – which we had decided to take once per week, usually on Sundays – and then wrote up our diaries in comparative peace. It was cold enough now, as we were journeying North, to put on warmer coats. Hearing that we were not due in Hangzhou until 2am the next morning, we settled down to enjoy the passing scenes. On the small table by the window we found the usual Chinese cups with lids (to keep the tea hot), the thermos filled with very hot water, and some tea-bags. We had noticed in the restaurant car, where we sat at individual tables, that the tablecloths were white and clean, and that on the walls were some very good paintings of Chinese scenery and well-known places, such as the Great Wall, Hangzhou Lake, and Beijing (Peking). On each table had been placed a pot of growing flowers.

Greta was a little 'under the weather', having a throat infection and a low fever, but she bore up bravely. My own throat had also begun to feel a little sore. It had been raining all morning when we were called to lunch, and we tried to enjoy the curried chicken, scrambled egg (probably cooked in some oil which tastes a little unpalatable), a bowl of fresh vegetable soup, eggs and rice. One bowl each was enough. The cost was 2.70-Yuan (90p), quite cheap, for the two of us. We noticed that the train was now travelling at a fast speed, and the engine driver seemed to enjoy blowing his whistle quite often, sometimes every 30 seconds. The train was being pulled by a steam engine and occasionally we heard the 'chuff-chuff', reminding us of the old British 'puffers'. The scenery was uninteresting, mile upon mile of flat fields of ripening rice-grain, whilst rivers abounded everywhere. Hunan and GiangXi are in China's rice bowl. There were many new houses build with new bricks. Many people were carrying umbrellas even in the fields. Roof tiles seemed to be smaller. Where we came to stations, there were two sets of railways lines and the train kept to the left track, unlike road driving, which was to the right. Little stacks of rice occasionally covered the small fields, like chessmen. Small, low hills began to break up the flat contours of land. The continual rain made it difficult to see the countryside. We both dozed off for a while.

On the long journeys, meals helped to break up the monotony. About 6pm we were called to supper, which consisted simply of noodle soup. It was not very appetising. Taller hills and some mountains began to make the landscape more interesting and we had been climbing steadily to higher ground. Anticipating our arrival at Hangzhou in the early hours of the morning, we relaxed and slept, and were duly called about 1.30am. Eventually, the train arrived at Hangzhou about 2.30am and a little late.

As we alighted at the station, even at that early hour, many pedal rickshaw boys offered to take us into the town -—or where-ever – but having asked the CTS at Guilin to telegraph instructions ahead, we waited for some official car. No such vehicle or taxi arrived, but the station police were very kind to us, and let us rest in the waiting room for women, children and the disabled! I was not sure into which category I came, but my wife was safe enough. They tried without success to telephone the Hangzhou CTS and told us they must be closed for the night. Eventually a taxi did appear, called in fact very thoughtfully by the police, from some hotel. So, after a tiring delay of three hours, at 5.30am we found ourselves being taken to an hotel. At the hotel, almost all the staff were asleep, but one active clerk fixed us up with a room for two, at a cost of 60-Yuan (£20) per night. We said vigorously that it was too expensive and eventually they offered us a room at 40-Yuan (£13.30) a night, which we gratefully accepted. The room was large, and had an adjoining and very nice bathroom, with loo, towels and soap, and in the room itself a TV set, radio controlled from the bed. As we discovered later, it also overlooked the famous West Lake.

After one and a half hours sleep, we went down to breakfast in one of the hotel dining rooms. Scrambled egg, toast, butter and coffee cost us each 4-Yuan (£2.70) – not cheap, but we did not mind. It was certainly a palatial hotel, and we were rested and hungry too. After breakfast, we called at the CITS office in the hotel, to find out what had gone wrong yesterday. A telephone call to the CITS central office elicited the fact that they had got the time of the train wrong, and had expected us in the afternoon. Hence no taxi or courier. They half apologised and asked us to pay the taxi fare. In seeking to arrange our next journey to Shanghai by train, we found that they could not, or would not, arrange for us to travel 'Hard Class'. Moreover, unless we agreed to travel 'Soft Class' they would not arrange our journey nor collect our rail tickets. We accepted the inevitable, having had enough for the moment of being stranded and of lugging around our two heavy pieces of hand luggage.

When all had been amicably arranged, we went out into the City to find the Christian Church. According to the girl clerk at the hotel post office, the church building was a long distance away, but lay on the Third Route public bus. To get to the nearest Third Route bus stop, we had to take the No.7 bus route, from a nearby stop. Needing a cheap city road map – printed in Chinese, of course – we asked directions of two Chinese girl students. "Please follow us", they said, most charmingly, and we all crowded on to the next bus, a No.7. One of the girls told us that she came from Beijing and was a student at Shanghai University. She was visiting Hangzhou and returning to Beijing on the morrow. With an attractive smile, she handed us her large street map of Hangzhou, saying she would not need it any more, and that we should get off the bus at the stop following that at which she and her friend would alight. We felt warmed by such genuine Chinese courtesy from two young students.

The No. 7 bus took us half way round West Lake to the No. 3 Route. Here we decided to walk the rest of the way to the church. A passer-by told us to walk the next four stages of No. 3 bus. Having walked beyond three stages, it began to rain and we stopped to put on raincoats. Two women were looking out from the window of a shop where we were standing, and smiled at us, so we asked them if they knew the street and the Christian Church, which we were seeking. They pointed across the road and we soon found the church.

Thanking the Lord for having directed us so wonderfully, we turned into a short lane, to discover the church set back inside a walled compound and a locked gateway. On the old style church wall was written the Chinese name for church "worship hall". A man came out and let us into the compound through a side gate and invited us into a waiting room, in which hung a copy of the Chinese Christian Calendar, similar to that which our friend the Rev. Shen Mingsui had given us.

After a few moments, the pastor of this "Three Self Church" came in and apologised for being indisposed. His kind face smiled welcome to us. He seemed to be about 72 years old. Having introduced ourselves, we all sat down and began to talk. We discovered that he remembered many missionaries known to us, such as Dr. Stephen Sturton, a Miss Marion, the Rev. W. R. Taylor and a Miss Tindall (whom I had met some thirty eight years earlier in

Kunming). We also discovered mutual friends in Bishop Michael Chiang, Bishop Maloney, Bishop Curtis and Miss Moule. As regards the local church, the pastor, the Rev. Mark E. Chen, told us that there was a very active spiritual life. There was a second church near where we had alighted from the No. 7 bus, and near it was the hospital in which Greta's father had once worked, and where Greta herself had lived for a year. In their two churches each Sunday morning, there were congregations of 900 and 500 people, whilst in the evening some 1,000 people gathered for worship, many of them young people.

As Greta spoke of the hospital and her father's work, and we told the pastor our own history, he grew increasingly interested. There to hand, he showed us some of the one million Bibles and New Testaments in Chinese which the Three Self Church had had printed in Shanghai in the old translation. A new modern translation would, it seemed, take a long time, and in any case, the teachers at the re-opened Nanjing Theological College were really too busy to attempt it. There was the promise of a new hymn book, but local or provincial churches tended to make and print their own. As regards House Churches in the Hangzhou area, the pastor said that their members, and those of the Three Self Churches, came together on a Sunday and there seemed to be no friction between them. As for the numbers of Christians, he said there were three to four hundred "wan" (a "wan" is 10,000), but whether this was in the Province or in the whole of China, we were uncertain. Three to four million is rather like the numbers given publicly by the leaders of the Three Self Church.

Finally, the pastor took us in to show us the church interior. It was an old large building, seating 800 people but not, he said, sufficient seats for their Sunday congregations. As we entered, a young girl about 18 years old was playing classical music. She told Greta that she was not the Sunday pianist, and added that she was a Christian. The Church Secretary was there with us, and posed with the girl and me while Greta took a photograph. The Pastor, the Rev. Mark E. Chen, told us he hoped that the church would have some young men studying theology and preparing for ordination before long. However, because of the problem raised by such young men having to work for a living, the church would probably begin evening classes for theological students. At Nanjing Theological College, they were not able to have many such students yet.

Mark Chen, also, was a former pastor of the Chinese Sheng Kung Hui (or Episcopal Church) which helped to confirm what we had been told in both Nanning and Guilin, that former members of that church were predominant in the Three Self Protestant Church. However, it seemed that the former different Protestant denominations have really become one and were now accustomed to each other's different ways and belief. At least they were learning to become one on this level. After the Pastor and I had each prayed in Chinese, we said a cheerful and nostalgic goodbye, realising that we might never see each other's face again. The Rev. Mark Chen said with great hope that we might still see each other again in this life as well as in Heaven. Having taken our farewells, Greta and I went back on foot, to try to find the other church and the hospital where her father had worked. This did not prove too difficult, being indeed just beyond the point where we had alighted from the No.7 bus.

This other church was not open to visitors but we were told that there would be a service there the next day at 2pm. A little further on, we found the hospital. One or two old type buildings were still standing, but nothing that Greta recognised. There was also a very large new building, eight storeys high. Each storey was given over to one particular department of the hospital. A passing member of the hospital staff – perhaps a trainee doctor – gave us some staff figures. He said there were 300 doctors and over 700 nurses and hospital workers, over 1,000 in all. There were 500 beds in the hospital and there was the usual outpatients' department.

Greta, at this point, met an older doctor and his wife, also a doctor. This man remembered all the former doctors, like Sturton, Duncan Main and others. Both people had such lovely faces that we felt they must be Christians. After some animated conversation, they had to take their leave, since they had to return home for supper, whilst we also had to return to our hotel.

We found our way back quite easily. Having bought some tangerines and pears at a street fruit shop for 8 Mao we caught a

No.7 bus and arrived back at the hotel at 5.45pm and in good time for supper. A chicken dish, soup, rice and an apple each cost us 6-Yuan (£2). We enjoyed it – we were hungry. We had gone down to the dining room at 6.30pm after a short rest and a writing up of diaries, and found it almost full to capacity. Probably all were eating early because there was to be a film show that evening in the large cinema of the hotel. The film was a story of an ancient Chinese Robin Hood, a Maid Marian, a Mayor of Nottingham, bad soldiers and good bandits. Some of the good bandits seemed to be Buddhist Priests (Friars Tuck?). The film was brilliantly produced, full of battles and pursuits on horseback (Chinese cowboys?), and interspersed with fierce kung-fu battles. The commentary was in beautiful Mandarin with captions in English. The scenes amidst mountains and tall reed grass, a Chinese maze and a Buddhist monastery were most artistically and astoundingly beautiful. The blood shedding was perhaps, too dramatic to be true to life, and it made many in the audience, and us, laugh. The story portrayed a reluctant Buddhist priesthood indulging in most un-Buddhist activity. One of the words most used on both sides was the word "sha" – meaning "kill". Yet the film portrayed some good Buddhist behaviour and teaching at the same time, but with an ironic side-glance at the religion as a whole. The film was the Chinese version of the Japanese film on Chinese history called the Water Margin, which we had seen back home. Ultimately, the goodies defeated the baddies, of course, as in the Western films. The Chinese version seemed to us to be better than the Japanese version done with the Japanese actors.

We had gone to see the film along with two young Australians who were also hotel guests, and who came from the Sydney area. They also proved to be earnest Christians, Presbyterians originally but now in a United Church. We all enjoyed the film immensely, and laughed heartily at many scenes. They were Robert and Megan McPherson, of "PAX", 10 Essington Lewis Avenue, Whyalla, South Australia. At the 7.30am breakfast in the hotel the next morning – consisting of wet rice, egg, toast and butter and coffee, which was very nice and cost us only 4.70-Yuan (£1.60) – we exchanged addresses, said goodbye and hoped to meet each other again when they visited England later.

The T.S.P.M. Moore Church, Shanghai

Rev. Shen Yi-fan at the T.S.P.M. Community Church

Chapter 15

We Meet Strangers on Willow Pattern Bridge

Mr Gwang-Fu was a young art student aged 23. We met him on our way to a well known pagoda not far from the hotel. It is specially noteworthy for the calligraphy of its past masters or other writers who studied and taught there. They had also carved stones, which were used to make rubbings for decorative scrolls common in Chinese homes or institutions.

The young man was studying at Hangzhou Art College, and he told us he hoped eventually to be an art teacher. Interested in meeting two foreigners attracted to the temple and pagoda, he took us round and explained the historic and artistic significance of the place, which was built on a rocky site. Since he spoke very good English, we were able to converse in both Mandarin and English. Altogether he was a most courteous and attractive young Chinese. Eventually, coming down from the pagoda site, we asked him if he knew anything about Jesus and Christians. Indeed he did know and was very interested, and from his pocket he produced a Bible given him by an Australian acquaintance. He had also, on one occasion, visited one of the Hangzhou churches. "If people were like Jesus", he remarked, "the world would be better and wars would cease". He quoted a saying of Jesus : "If someone strike you on one cheek, turn to him the other also", and he thought that Jesus did not only mean just that physical response but also meant – "Love your enemies as well as your friends", and if that could be done, the world would be a better place.

He was very interested to hear that Greta was a medical doctor, and that she was born in Kunming, whilst her father had worked as a doctor in Hangzhou No.2 hospital, and that I was a Christian pastor formerly working in Guilin but now retired. Our Middle School visit intrigued him and he wished we could have come to Hangzhou to teach. However, he thought that the Government would first want us to go to a University to teach, since Chinese universities were short of English teachers.

Our conversation then turned to Christian beliefs. "Was it not true that if people became Christians and lived a good life, then after death they could go to a new, heavenly life?" We replied that Jesus, when we believe in Him, would give us eternal life now by His Holy Spirit in us, and that after death, he had prepared a place for us in the Heavenly Father's House. There was so much he wanted to say, and so much more he wanted to know about Christianity and about Jesus. However, alas, we had to return to the hotel to arrange our Shanghai rail tickets that afternoon, and for lunch. It was clear that Jesus had touched his heart already and aroused in him some measure of faith, at which we inwardly rejoiced. He also knew something about St. Paul, and we reminded him that Paul had once written "Rejoice in the Lord always". He was further interested to learn that, as individuals, we prayed regularly and sometimes in Chinese. He knew, he said, that in the Hangzhou church they read the Bible, said prayers, listened to sermons and sang songs.

Inevitably we all felt regret in having to say goodbye. We gave him, in parting, a booklet in Chinese and English, which was the testimony story of a scientist who was also a Christian, and which could be of some help to him. He took it gladly. At the hotel China Travel Service Office, we learned that our Shanghai train tickets would arrive later in the afternoon. These would cost 25-Yuan for the two of us, and we paid a service charge of 7-Yuan also. As regards our further journeys from Shanghai there was a 'phone service to Qingdao in Shandung on Mondays, Wednesdays, Thursdays and Saturdays, but there was uncertainty about return flights. It was also possible to go by train, first to Beijing and then from there to Qingdao, and then we could fly back to Shanghai or Nanjing. However, we would do better to enquire at Shanghai.

We took the opportunity to enquire about a cheaper hotel in Hangzhou and near the CITS office, but were told that we could do this at the hotel service counter. However, the CITS clerk agreed to book rooms in a Shanghai hotel, which was not too expensive, and which was also near the CITS Shanghai office.

There was still some time to wait before we could pick up our train tickets, so we wrote some six postcards to England, which cost us in total 4.20-Yuan (£1.40), posted them at the hotel desk, and returned once more to the City Centre, walking half way and going the other half by bus (which only cost us 12 cents (3p). We were just in time for the church service which began at 2 pm.

As we entered the church, we were immediately welcomed and were taken right up to the front row of seats. Every other seat seemed taken and there were about 600 people present, to our astonishment. Those present were mostly women, and we were intrigued to hear an announcement of a meeting of the Mothers' Union! The meeting seemed to be more in the nature of a Bible Study and Prayer Meeting, rather than a church service as such, and everyone seemed to have a Bible as well as a hymn book, and they kindly provided us with a copy of each.

As we sat down, a leader or pastor was leading the congregation in singing some hymns, and then he taught them to sing a new music version of Psalm 23. The leader first sang each line of the psalm-hymn and then had the people repeat it two or three times. Finally, he sang the complete song, which they all sang together quite easily. The version was taken from the Bible, and was sung to a very effective and lovely irregular tune, which I thought might be local. When the meeting or service began, they sang from their own hymn book, the hymn "Since Jesus came into my heart". I remember it was number 91.

Prayer, led by the pastor, followed and then came the Bible Study or exposition. This lasted one hour and five minutes and consisted of certain passages of scripture, illustrated by stories with local colour and spoken in two local dialects, including Southern Mandarin (which is what we had spoken those 33 years ago in Guilin). The scripture passages expounded were from Paul's second letter to the Corinthians: James' Epistle, Chapter 4, Verse 8; and Proverbs, Chapter 6, Verses 16-18.

The pastor used the figure of two oxen, one young and the other old, and suggested that our walk with Jesus, or each other, must be equal, if it were to be properly accomplished. He used also a local story, illustrating the parable of the Prodigal Son. The pastor, who was an oldish man, spoke forcibly and yet with humour, and an occasional smile and some gestures, some of his words making the congregation laugh and smile. They quite obviously enjoyed the one hour and five minute address. The lady who lent me her Chinese Bible might well have been a worker, for the Bible contained many bookmarks, including one, which was a picture of former Chairman Mao! Another lady lent Greta her own Chinese New Testament, partly because, she said, she could not read it without her glasses, which she seemed to have left at home.

After the meeting ended, we talked with another pastor or minister, who had formerly been a Presbyterian. He told us that on Sunday evenings, 1,000 people attended the service and half of them were young people. There were also, he said, over 500 House Groups (House Churches?) in Hangzhou, who now join with the Three Self Church services, although some, like the Brethren, refused to join in. He added that there were about 14 ministers or pastors in the local Hangzhou churches, with a total of between two and three thousand members, whilst in the Zhejiang Fujien areas there were some 900,000 to 1 million Christians. As regards China as a whole, there were three to four million (registered?) members. We guessed that this was indeed the official figure for the Three Self Church, and did not include the numbers attending the unofficial House Churches.

Returning quite astonished and elated by this experience, we boarded the No.7 bus, which took us back to the hotel in time for tea and a cake. We were both feeling a little tired by this time, and after a short rest, we went to the hotel dining room for supper. It was sweet-sour pork, sliced chicken, a vegetable dish and China tea, which depleted our funds by 6.70-Yuan (£2.24) but it put some new vigour into our veins and gave us a comfortable feeling inside!

Having had supper, we visited the hotel shop, which was well supplied with quite a variety of goods, and bought some presents for those at home, including some scissors, some paper and some biro pens, all made in China. They were not at all expensive. We then walked to the West Lake. It was nearly dusk and another young Chinese student spoke to us. He proved to be a student of Computerised Engineering at Hangzhou University. He was obviously delighted to try out his English on two real English folk. We soon found ourselves talking in both English and Mandarin, about Jesus, His birth, teaching, death and resurrection. The young man confessed that he did not believe in the Christmas story, although some of his family and friends did. Soon, we were discussing some of the teaching of Jesus – e.g. "Do unto others as you want them to do unto you", and he compared this with the saying of Confucius, "Don't do unto others what you don't want them to do unto you". From this we progressed to "Love your family, your friends and even your enemies". He asked, to our astonishment, if this love included the homosexual relations of men and lesbianism among women. We replied that the love, which Jesus speaks about, is spiritual rather than physical, and is really God's love in our hearts.

From this, we turned to Creation – where and how did it originate? He mentioned Darwin and Einstein. We asked him where did computers from? A mind, we suggested, and a mind created the universe. This Mind, we explained, is Jesus. Jesus is God, or the Son of God, who gives love to those who believe in Him, and gives also joy, peace, patience, gentleness, faith and self control. Our young man seemed interested and a little astonished in his turn. His English was excellent and he struggled to express himself clearly. He had evidently only read a little of the Bible or New Testament, but he knew the names of Matthew (a businessman, we added), Mark (a young man), Luke (a doctor) and John (man of wisdom). He was obviously much attracted, and so attractive. Alas, we had nothing to hand to give him to read. His name was Yu-yu. We left him with real regret in our hearts, and with an assurance that the living Jesus loved him, and would not forget him.

I recall another matter about which he asked, "You say", he said, "that if I believe in Jesus, then after death I can go to live forever with Him, with God. But what if I do not?" "Then you cannot be with Jesus. But if you do, He has prepared a place for us with Him in the Father's home in heaven".

The student then mentioned the story, told in the Gospels, of the woman whose husband died, and whose seven brothers then married her in turn, as each died. "The Chinese Buddhists", he remarked "would say that in heaven, she would have to share her body with all seven". At which we were able to quote to him the words of Jesus, that in heaven there is no marrying or giving in marriage, but we are spiritual (I thought "angels" would confuse the issue, but on reflection I think I was wrong) that there were heavenly beings as well as Jesus, and the Holy Spirit. (Angels would, in fact, probably have helped his understanding rather than otherwise.) Greta and I also suggested that, like the caterpillar that develops into the butterfly, the heavenly life is freer and more wonderful than our earthly life.

Our new found friend now mentioned Buddhist teaching – that, if a man or woman is good, in his next earthly life or reincarnation, he would become a person or being of higher rank. If a man were bad, he might become an animal – at which the student himself began to laugh in disbelief. We replied that Jesus and the New Testament taught that, after death, we would become spiritual beings with spiritual bodies, not tied to time and space.

This seemed to solve one of his problems – where, after 2,000 years, or since man began – could all the dead beings live? Where would there be enough space? For now he saw that if "spiritual" means not bound by space or time, then many could live together in a different space and time existence.

We asked Yu-yu to come back to our hotel with us, but he said that the hotel authorities would not allow him into the hotel. With regretful smiles, we said farewell and he disappeared into the darkness. If only we could have talked with him still more! There was certainly a spiritual hunger in his mind and heart. However, we could only return to the hotel and prepare for bed. On arrival back, I went to the desk to get our hotel bill. They had charged us only 40-Yuan per night and not 44-Yuan as I had feared, and charged us only for two days and not two and a half days. So, only 80-Yuan. Good. We felt that the Lord was continuing to guide us and meet our needs.

As we prepared for bed, the TV showed another interesting Buddhist-based Chinese film about "Treasure and Murder". The story in itself was interesting – a secret rhyme, a secret treasure; a golden Buddha, a secret killer skilled in Kung Fu; a hero who solves the mystery. There was a heroine who had been trained in the circus to use a whip as the South Americans do – a bolero; plenty of full-blooded Kung Fu fighting; the usual involvement of Buddhist monks and the quoting of Buddhist aphorisms (possibly scripture sayings); and the final success of the hero and heroine. It was all splendidly produced.

One wondered what the Chinese Communists thought about these things. However, against the old background of a Chinese Buddhist society, it is no doubt as natural as the involvement of Christian pastors and priests and the church generally, in Western society. What an excellent thing it would be, I thought to myself, to get space on TV for Chinese Christian writers and stories.

Both the Chinese and the Buddhist element in their films seem to be "romantic" in the classical sense, and contain elements of magic. Christian themes and elements are, I think, more natural, or real, as well as 'spiritual'. In the Chinese films, Buddhism seems to be part of a long lived cultural tradition – and even in this communist era. Just so, very often, Christian elements in Western films (as distinct from Biblical films) are also largely cultural, although films about Jesus Himself and about the Bible, are only indirectly cultural and are more directly evangelistic or religious and even historically based. Having seen the TV film to its interesting end, we retired to bed and sleep at 11.35pm.

A slight rise in blood temperature prevented me having a very good night's sleep. Greta, however, seemed to be well. After breakfasting on wet-rice or congee, scrambled egg, toast, marmalade, butter and coffee for 4.20-Yuan (£1.40), we went out for a long walk on the causeway across the West Lake. It was beautiful, with willows lining the banks almost the whole way, and with attractive shelters of colourfully curved roofs in the Chinese style every so often, for resting. Many Chinese visitors were also making the walk, including parties of school children who marched along joyously, faces smiling, in formations of four with a leader in front. All wore colourful clothes and sported the red neckerchief of the Young Pioneers. All smiled at us and some greeted us courteously and cheerfully. We crossed a number of decorative bridges, and even those built in modern concrete materials had beautiful carvings on them of dragons and fish.

Eventually we arrived at the end of the causeway where there was a park area with many lovely flowers such as chrysanthemums, including miniature species, michaelmas daisies, cannas, hollyhocks, flowering cherry trees and magnolia bushes (not in flower). This garden jutted out into the lake, and there was a large play area for children, with crowds of them eating buns, mandarin oranges and tangerines. At a number of bridges, the water below was thronged with hundreds of goldfish, many with dark red patches and a few white in colour, some almost a foot long, all threshing about excitedly (perhaps fed by the children). All the fish, we were told, would mature and become bright red in colour.

Here we also met an old Chinese gentleman, 71 years old on his own confession (as I would be eight months later), who had been a worker on the railway. He told us he had met many English men in his work, from which he had learned English. In spite of that being years ago, probably before the Revolution, he still remembered words like 'eyes', 'nose', 'hair', 'hands' and 'feet' etc. We had an interesting conversation with him and then took our leave, as usual, rather reluctantly.

A slight misty rain now began to fall, so we hurried home but even so got a little wet in the process. Greta still seemed to be the only woman in China wearing a skirt instead of trousers, and arousing not a little curiosity. Back at the hotel, we rested a while and then took up our bags, left our room, and called at the hotel desk to await a taxi that we had ordered the previous evening. The bill having been paid, the taxi took us to the station, where we were due to catch the 12.50pm train to Shanghai.

At the First Class (or rather 'Soft Class') waiting room, we met an American traveller from Boston whose speech was very British, with little trace of accent. He knew no Chinese and was spending a holiday in China with a friend who had formerly been at "Yale in China" in Changsha. Our conversation turned to the Church in Hangzhou, with its large congregations. Both he, and his friend, also an American and formerly a Professor at Yale, were deeply interested. As they heard our account of the Chinese Church today, the Professor remarked that he felt all his past labours in China had been worthwhile after all.

Chapter 16

Gateway to the Four Seas

Our American friends had left to go to their Hangzhou hotel, just as some other passengers for the Shanghai train entered the waiting room. They proved to be fellow travellers on the same coach and in the same compartment. One was an American, Mr. John Green from Dallas, Texas. His friend was Chinese, married to a Chinese girl also travelling with them. With their two children she normally lived in Dallas also. The husband's name was Shang Yueh-ming, which means Brightness of the Moon. He had work in Hong Kong, but Shanghai had been his original home. He now had British citizenship. He disliked the Communist regime but loved China, earnestly desiring her to become completely capitalistic as the only way to a better future. In conversation, he remarked that China should have said long ago "We want Hong Kong tomorrow, and we will take it". As regards Margaret Thatcher, the British Prime Minister, and her China visit, he felt that she had been badly advised by the Governor of Hong Kong to say what she did. He also expected the Governor to be replaced before long!

Mr. Shang seemed to be a young man of considerable ability. He often went to China as an interpreter with various United States groups and seemed to be a man of some influence also in Hong Kong. If China were to say that she wanted Hong Kong tomorrow, and if Britain agreed to hand over the colony peacefully, he asserted, everything would be better. China would let Hong Kong carry on as usual, and China and Taiwan would also be able to meet there about trade, and all would be happy.

However, he was utterly pessimistic about the present China authorities, and spoke very bitterly about the treatment Chinese received in the United States of America, along with Negroes and other coloureds. His friend from Dallas, whilst not understanding some or all of the Chinese part of the conversation, did understand the English. He told us that he was a Roman Catholic, but criticised many Christians in the US who were cultural Christians only and were prejudiced, and also did not live according to Christian teaching. Mr. Shang proceeded to expiate about everyone and everything in his own half-jocular, half-angry way; an angry young man of the East, criticising everyone but himself. We decided to turn the conversation round. "How," we asked "could our difficult world be put right?"

Sitting opposite me and next to my wife, was another young Chinese, who lived in Hangzhou and was a script writer for the radio station there. "I have written a number of plays", he told us. "I travel 'Soft Class' on the railway so as to get opportunities to talk to other people, especially foreigners, and get copy for my plays. In Hard (or Second) Class, it would be impossible. It might arouse suspicion and questioning from Party Members." He was, he told us, twenty three years of age, loved China, loved his work, and was not yet married. He had a real dignity of bearing very common to the Chinese, and was attractive in person and speech. A quiet man.

Greta now pulled out of her bag a Chinese chess set. The young dramatist kindly helped her to write down the names and positions of the various pieces. Greta and I prepared to play each other.

"I will show you how to play", said the young playwright to my wife with a smile. "I will help you" said the dashing Mr. Shang to me. "Do not make me lose face, will you?" I said to our Hong Kong friend. "I am a Hong Kong Chinese," he replied with a big smile, "I will not lose!"

The result was a real, serious contest between the two men, the capitalist versus the communist. We all watched the battle with amusement and interest. After a great struggle, the quiet young man won. My secret personal but not political wish was fulfilled!

Another contest began between my wife and me, with help from all round. My wife, possibly helped by a natural chivalry, won. Having now forged and forwarded links of friendship, we all began to discuss how to put the world to rights. After much discussion, and flying quotes from Confucius and Mao and other great men, I tentatively suggested that if only people could love one another, and even their enemies, there would be peace. Mr. Hong Kong leapt into the debating arena, saying somewhat extravagant things like "You can't make the world right just by getting everyone going to Church, or by reading the Bible, or by praying! That is no use". Young Mr. Hangzhou, in his quiet, convincing and sincere way, agreed that we had to get people right. "I love my country, and our people. I just want to do my bit to help China. I also try to reflect other opinions in my plays".

Mr. Hong Kong attacked the present Chinese Government policies on 'one family, one child':

"This is rubbish, and will not work. It will make these single children terribly spoilt and selfish. In our family we have two daughters. I love my wife," – she was listening to him without altering her expression and without comment – "Our two girls are very obedient". He turned to Mr. Hangzhou, "Now you are a young unmarried man. What will you do?"

Our attractive Communist friend said that he liked the idea of marriage and of having a home, and he hoped to find an attractive young girl who would become his wife, and for the sake of China, he would accept the one family, one child policy.

Mr. Hong Kong butted in "He can't have girl friends. If he has a girl friend and then is attracted by another, the first would make trouble!.

Firmly and with dignity, Mr. Hangzhou replied, "I may have a number of girl friends without their expecting me to marry them."

On went the discussion in a most animated fashion. The idea of 'loving one's enemies', let out strong criticism from Mr. Shang of the present situation in China. Only four years ago, Yunnan Province in the South West had turned against the Central Government, since Yunnanese are very independent and orientated towards Moscow. Yunnan had all the planes and equipment left by the United States, and more, sent by the USSR. When the Central Government prepared to act again Yunnan, they suffered serious setbacks. When Peking looked like using their planes against the Yunnanese, rumbles from Moscow, and a threat by Vietnamese Communists to invade China, made the Central Government draw back.

By this time, we were drawing very near to Shanghai, so our conversations had to cease. Alas, we all had to say 'Goodbye' too soon. Greta and I remained most impressed by Mr Hangzhou's lack of bombast and his quiet dignity, plus his ability to smile. Even Mr. Shang and his wife smiled farewell.

The train drew in to Shanghai station and came to a gentle stop. We already had our luggage ready. Waiting outside the carriage door stood a very charming Chinese girl who spoke excellent English. We were not difficult to identify, being the only foreigners, and she introduced herself as our CITS guide. Later we learned that she was a member of the Shanghai Community Church, whose pastor was the Rev. Shen Yi-fan, son of former Bishop Shen Dz-gao, one of my wife's old friends. Our guide had just graduated at the University in Foreign Languages and had immediately been offered a job with CITS. Leading us out of the station, we found she had a taxi waiting to take us to the Park Hotel. After paying for the taxi (the usual 6-Yuan fee), she took us into the hotel and left us at the visitors' desk, whilst she herself departed.

The hotel had booked us a room at 52-Yuan per night, which seemed to us a little excessive, since we had asked the Travel Service to find us a "cheaper" hotel. When I asked about this, the desk clerk told us it was a cheaper hotel, and that although the room had three beds, they were reckoning it as only a double-bedded room. We accepted the inevitable. After all, this was Shanghai.

Our room was on the eleventh floor. The hotel had eighteen floors, with a roof garden. Gratefully, we settled into our room and rested on the beds whilst writing up our diaries. Supper was in the large hotel dining room, and we enjoyed meeting two old friends, the Australian couple, who were at a table enjoying a vast spread, since they were on an official tour, with meals included. They found it impossible to eat all that the menu provided, and very kindly invited us to help them eat it! We cheerily accepted their offer, and ordered an extra pork dish and vegetable dish, which only cost us 1.50-Yuan (50p)! The young couple were most pleased to invite us to join them.

Returning to our room after supper feeling pleasantly at ease, we turned on the colour TV set in the room and, lying on our beds, and in the pleasantly warm atmosphere, we watched in succession two contrasting film plays. Both were very interesting and well produced.

The first play was gently political propaganda, backed up by lovely scenic photography. A young man and a charming young girl meet on a famous mountain in a sacred temple beauty spot, and fall in love. It was acted most beautifully and delicately. The boy, however, turned out to be the son of a Gwomindang (nationalist) general or senior officer, who had gone to the USA with his wife. The girl's father, a former close friend of the other father, had remained in China under, and a convert to, the Communist Government. The young man's parents were opposed to his friendship with a girl in China, but the girl's parents, after much thought and debate, decided to accept the situation and allow the two to marry. Both parents contrive a meeting and become reconciled and all ended very happily, indeed 'happy ever after'! The film had been made by a mainland China film company. It was not only good propaganda but also good cinema.

The second film was in the old style, and situated in Hong Kong. A Chinese father has to leave his wife on the birth of their baby, going away to get work. He builds up a circus team. The wife, the baby's mother, dies and leaves with the child a peculiar hairpin, which may help the child to find her father. A man, passing by, finds the child and becomes her self-appointed guardian. He joins a circus team to get work. The circus manager is merely a money spinner who strives to make a fortune and get a position in Hong Kong society. Eventually, through the hairpin, he discovers that the girl is his daughter. The girl, now grown up, also discovers that the circus manager is her father, whom she hates for having abandoned her mother. She leaves him and the circus for good. It was perhaps excessively 'tears and sadness, sadness and tears', and a showing of Hong Kong society at its worst. Probably made in China, too, this was also, and less successfully, a propaganda film.

There was, however, one curious element common to both films. Both included scenes of the heroine concerned praying for help to God (using the Chinese term 'Shang-di'). How odd, in two mainland China films and presumably allowed by the atheist Government of the mainland.

Nicely relaxed after these two films, and after a piping hot bath in our own bathroom, we had our Bible reading and prayers, and so to bed, to sleep, but not (as far as I remember) to dream.

The next day was Saturday 30th October. We were up betimes, had breakfast in the hotel dining room at 8am (for 4.36-Yuan (£1.45)), sent some clothes to the hotel 'take-away' laundry service in the bag supplied (it was returned that evening at 8.30pm) and cost only 2.35-Yuan (78p), and then made our usual way to the Travel Service Office. The office was in the Peace Hotel, some distance along the Nanjing Road towards and near the Bund or Waterfront.

For about half an hour, we walked at a good pace along the thronged pavements of the main road, where hundreds of people were shopping in the well-stocked and attractive shops and more hundreds seemed to be just walking and shop viewing. Many of them also took sideways glances at the only woman in Shanghai wearing a skirt, or rather, dress. The wide road was crammed with traffic, trolley buses, petrol buses, taxis, pedicabs, lorries, vans and bicycles galore. It was quite an adventure to cross the road, but there were traffic signals and crossing points.

We duly found the Peace Hotel, and the Travel Office, and booked our tickets for the soft sleeper express to Beijing (Peking), leaving Sunday evening about 6.15 pm. The total fare cost, for of us 292.00-Yuan (£97.40) and was made up as follows:

2 Passengers	121.20
Excess for express	27.40
2 'soft' bunk sleepers	142.80
	291.40
CITS handling charge	80
	292.20
Telegram to Beijing CITS	10.00
	Y 302.20

Thus achieved and relieved, Greta and I sat down in the palatial hotel lounge and ate a Chinese pear. Feeling more relaxed, we visited the Hotel Information Service, where we pinpointed the sites of the City churches on our maps, and then sallied forth to find two of them.

We made our way via the Bund or Waterfront, a scene as famous as the London Embankment or the Liverpool Pier Head in its heyday. Perhaps more famous. The river was full of liners, and beautiful new cargo boats, all with Chinese names and registration ports, obviously built in China, and including a local trip ferry boat of truly grand proportions, with three decks, carrying at least 500 or more passengers. We walked along the Bund, which was a veritable hive or ants' nest of activity, turning off to find a local Buddhist temple, which had now become a splendid arcade of shops. It had a beautiful, decorated roof, with great beams, also decorated, and tall wooden pillars in deep red, and hung with many lanterns. It no longer served as a temple, however, truly a sign of the times.

On we wandered, buying some fruit at a pavement fruit stall. Beginning to feel tired, we found a childrens' play centre, with slides, sea-saws and roundabouts operated by hand, and a few seats scattered around. Many parents accompanied their children, whilst some left their children in the charge of a middle-aged man and woman. These latter welcomed us to one of the vacant seats, where we rested and watched the children, and ate our persimmons and tangerines. We had bought these at that pavement fruit stall, to the great interest of the gathered crowd, who listened in surprise to our Mandarin speech, especially when we bargained with the shopkeeper to buy them at a cheaper price – in fact for the remainder of the small change in my purse.

Having rested, we went on, not quite so wearily, to find the first of the churches on our map, the former Moore memorial Church. The Rev. Lee Wen-tsai was the minister in charge, whilst his fellow minister was a woman, the Rev. Tai Li-tsung. They welcomed us gladly and graciously to this former, and famous, Methodist Church, and talked to us at some length about their present situation in China. The Rev. Mr. Lee had formerly been ordained into the Sheng Kung Hui (Anglican or Episcopal Church), whilst the Rev. Mrs. Tai was an ex-Methodist minister.

There were, they said, already ten churches opened in Shanghai, and three more were then being repaired for opening. Some 20,000 Christians at least attended these churches. At the Moore Church, at their 7 am. Sunday morning early service, there were usually 2,000/2,500 people present and at the 9am service (at which the earlier service was repeated in every detail, including the sermon) there would generally be between 1,700/1,800 people. Six pastors were attached to this one church alone and, in Shanghai as a whole, there were 40 ministers and a number of retired ministers.

There were very few House Churches in the City, since most Christians had now joined the official Three Self Churches. There were local Christian radio programmes, taken by individual persons, and not just using tapes. A number of Bible Schools had opened and four students were now studying to be ministers. In Nanjing Road there was a Short Term Bible School also.

Very encouraged by this news of the Church in China, we returned to the hotel for a cup of tea and a brief rest. Then, out again to find the Community Church on the other side of the City, where former Bishop Shen Tz-gao's son, the Rev. Shen Yi-fan, was in charge. We boarded our first trolley bus, No. 27, and at the terminus, made our way on foot, consulting our road map. The way took us through a Peoples' Park (entrance fee 30 cents (10p)), where it was a pleasant sight to see all the elderly people and younger ones alike enjoying the park and the sunshine, talking, walking, doing "Chinese Boxing", sitting watching the goldfish in the ponds, admiring the flower beds and the many varieties of trees and the stretches of green lawns nicely mown.

At 53 Hengshan Road, in the old former French concession area, near General Joffe Road and Le Roi Albert, we duly found the Community Church and the Rev. Shen Yi-fan. He invited us into his home and talked with us for over an hour. Regretfully, his father, Bishop Shen Dz-gao, who had once travelled from England to China on the same boat as Greta and taught her some Chinese and became a good friend, had died a week previously. A memorial service for his father had recently taken place.

Shen Yi-fan had a slender figure, a fascinating face and a clear light voice. His English was excellent. He told us a great deal about his church, the Chinese Church generally, and about China. At the Community Church, of which he was the chief pastor, he had now five assistant ministers and a woman worker, Mrs. Peng En-mai, had just joined them. She was not yet ordained as a minister but was an evangelist. The early morning Sunday service at 7.30am, usually had some 1,500 people attending in the main church and 300 in a nearby church building, to which the service was relayed. At the 10 am. Sunday service, they usually had another 1,300 people.

He knew many of our old colleagues, like Bishop Xu, of Gwangsi-Hunan, Bishop Curtis of Chekiang, Dr. Sturton in Hangzhou, Bishop Maxwell in Szechuan and others. In 1957/58, the Rev. Shen said that he went as the only Chinese Christian on a delegation to England, when this Chinese Communist group met the Red Dean of Canterbury, Hewlett Johnson. During the Cultural Revolution, 1966/76, his church had been closed. It used to be called the International Church, he said, with a congregation of Chinese senior officials and of foreigners. He did not say what he himself had done during the cultural revolution – whether or not he had had to go to the countryside, like many others.

With the liberalisation of Chinese politics, he continued, the church was reopened two years previously, at Christmas 1980. The Community Church was now part of the Three Self Church, and up to that time, some nine or ten churches were open in Shanghai, with three more about to open. As the churches opened, the Christians in the House Churches began to join them and so the number of House Churches had decreased. However, there were still many House Churches in the countryside, and indeed, they had recently been allowed and had actually built two large churches themselves. The Rev. Shen Yi-fen seemed to bear no animosity towards the House Churches. In the Community Church, he went on, one of the previous ministers, who had formerly been an Anglican, had slightly reshaped the church interior. It now has an altar or holy table, with a cross on it (during Sunday services), and two lighted candles, together with a pulpit and reading desk. A robed choir sat behind the minister's desk, facing the people.

Mr. Shen had also known the Henry Lester Institute in which Greta's father had worked in pre-revolution days. His wife was a worker-helper in the Young Women's Christian Association (YWCA), and one of their two children, the son, was vice-principal of a school. The other, a daughter, I think, taught in kindergarten school. Both children were now grown up, and Mr. Shen himself was 41 years old.

The old Anglican Cathedral, it seemed, had lost its spire, and had been taken over by a Government department, and was not (yet) returned to the church. The church was now running Youth Groups, Choir Groups, etc. and more young people were coming to the church, but work duties prevented many attending. However, there was, as yet, no scheme by which young men could study, say, at Nanjing College, due to lack of money and of Government permission.

Our stimulating meeting duly ended; we left him and returned towards our hotel on the No. 15 trolley bus. This took us all the way to Hwang Ho Lu (or Yellow River Road) for only 10 cents each. The conductor was very kind and asked two Chinese to give up their seats to let us sit down. Feeling slightly embarrassed, we apologised to the two men concerned, and then showed our appreciation by passing money for tickets from other passengers, up to the conductor. The buses were usually too crowded to permit passengers to move easily, whilst the conductors (men or women) rarely pushed through to the passengers. Sometimes the driver used a microphone system to announce names of roads or route stages. Sometimes the conductor just shouts out, "We are coming to XY place; get ready to alight. Please pay for your tickets. Send up your money by another passenger, please".

We were soon back in our hotel, and went immediately to supper, afterwards retired to our room, number 1105 (or room 5 on floor 11), to write up our diaries and some postcards. We then went to bed without even bothering to switch on the TV. It had been an interesting but a tiring day.

Chapter 17

Worship in Red Dragon Country

Sunday, 31st October, dawned about 6am. Our travel alarm clock was not functioning but I awoke early. During the night, Greta had had an attack of cramp in her big toe, a painful thing, but swallowing a salt pill put her right. After we had each had a hot and refreshing bath, in our personal bathroom, we were soon on our way, before breakfast, to the Moore Church for the 7am. worship service. It was not a Holy Communion service (as it would have been in England). This only took place – at least at the Community Church – once a quarter. With so many church members, they ask people to come to Communion 500 at a time, and then another 500 next time, thus avoiding the difficulty of administering so much wine. At the Community Church, the cups and patens (or plates) formerly in use, had been lost, but they now had new ones of their own.

When we arrived, the Moore Church was crowded and some people were standing. At a quick count of the people in different sections of the church building, I reckoned that there were easily over 1,000 people. There was an overflow of 400 plus, making at least 1,400/1,500 altogether – and I could not count those under our side, from the balcony where we were seated. Many were old people and one or two seemed to fall asleep. I saw, with some amusement one lady lean forward to look at the lady in front of her, who was asleep, and then had a cheerful and quiet laugh with her companion. There was a sprinkling of young people in the congregation whilst the choir of twenty three, robed in white surplices and sitting at the back of the 'chancel', or stage, were all young people.

The service was taken in the Shanghai dialect, which is quite difficult for Mandarin speaking people to grasp. It began with the splendid and well-known Wesley hymn, "Love divine, all loves excelling", and sung to the equally famous Welsh tune 'Blaenwern'. Prayers followed, with each short section followed by fervent 'Amens', and there were many sections. The Bible Readings came from Ephesians, Chapter 2, Verses 1-10, which includes that pearl of Scripture, "By grace are you saved, through faith" and Titus, Chapter 3, Verses 1-6, which begins, "In the last days perilous times shall come", and goes on to "…men … shall have a form of godliness but not the power thereof". There followed a hymn unknown to me but very effective : "Today as I walk the road of life". Notices (or as the Scots say so charmingly, the 'Intimations') followed, and afterwards the choir sang a short anthem "Hallelujah. Amen" and sang it well and with fervour. The sermon, delivered most ably by the woman minister, was basically an exposition of the Scripture passages, and forty minutes in length. All listened most attentively. I seem to remember a vesper hymn being sung at the end, after which the pianist played "The Lost Chord".

Some Americans were sitting near to Greta and me, including a black American girl who was a nurse in the United States Medical Delegation. She had slipped away to come to the church service and, whilst knowing no Chinese language at all, was yet obviously happy to be present. We, and others, were evidently sitting in the balconies, in pews reserved for strangers and foreigners. A Chinese lady who could speak good English, looked after us all, duly producing the inevitable Visitors' Book, which we were invited to sign and write where we came from. We met and talked with many people on our way out and were made to feel very welcome; and one of them, an old lady of 72, still active and vivacious, proved to be a friend of a Liverpool Doctor Caradoc Jones, and my home town is Liverpool! As folk say, 'It's a small world'.

We now hastened back through the increasing crowds. As we left the church, we noticed that the long queue at the cinema opposite the church was even longer than when we went in People of all ages were waiting there, but nothing like the 1,500 or more who had crammed the church. Rain had begun to fall, but we reached the hotel without getting really wet. After a quick breakfast of shi-fan (wet rice), a dish of scrambled eggs à la Chinese, two pieces of toast, butter and coffee at 3.71-Yuan (£1.24) we went off to the Community Church, donning our raincoats, and using the No.15 trolley bus from Yellow River Road. On the bus, we met a young

Chinese, about 22 years old, who engaged us in conversation. He was studying languages at the University Department of Foreign Languages, and enjoyed looking after two English foreigners. Discovering where we were going, he said in excellent English, "I also am going to the University Church" – by which he meant the Community Church – and we assumed rightly that he must also be a Christian. He told us a little of his history. "I have been brought up by my grandmother", he said, "and I have been promised a place in a college in the United States. I am waiting for a Visa. I have been a Christian for two years and I hope to study in a Christian seminary there". His name was Hu Hong Qiang.

Arriving at the church, the three of us were directed upstairs to the back gallery reserved for visitors. The church filled up rapidly; the atmosphere was quiet, helped no doubt by the arrangement of the ex-Anglican altar and the two-lighted candles. The Rev. Shen Yi-fan stood up and opened the service with some moving words from Scripture and in the most beautiful Mandarin. The whole familiar service, taken as it was in so reverent a manner, sometimes started tears in my eyes. Was it a sense of the presence of God, or partly nostalgia for days long gone by in the old China scene? I found it difficult to determine.

The large choir, of young people robed in white surplices, sang the familiar and beautiful introit:

> "Lead me, Lord, lead me in Thy righteousness.
> Make Thy way plain before my face.
> For it is Thou, Lord, Thou Lord only, who makest me dwell in safety".

The hymn, sung by the whole congregation, was "Love divine, all loves excelling", (The same hymn we had sung also at Moore Church earlier). The prayers that followed, spoken by Shen Yi-fan in a clear voice, were deeply moving and most real.

The lesson read was taken from St. John's Gospel, Chapter 15; the words of Jesus, "I am the Vine, you are the branches …"

After the next hymn, which I have forgotten, came the sermon, preached by Mrs. Pang En-mai, the evangelist, which lasted 35 minutes. She called it "The Three Trees". ("I speak only of three trees because there is not time to mention more", she added with a touch of humour).

"The first tree is spikenard, which gave all the oil with which Mary Magdalene anointed the Lord's head. She did not use only the oil, she used her hair too! So must we. As Jesus said in reply to the objections of some of the disciples, 'This is a reminder of my coming death and burial', a foreseeing of His death on the cross out of love for us".

Here the preacher kept on speaking of God's love for us, time and again.

"The second tree is the apple tree", she continued. "If we walk through the woods or orchards and get tired, then we can pluck an apple, eat it, and be restored. In addition, the seeds may be planted also. Therefore, we must feed on Jesus, our apple. We need to do this continually in Scripture and prayer.

"The third tree is the Vine and its grapes. We are part of Jesus, the Vine, and his life flows through us to produce fruit. The fruit is the fruit of the Spirit. Without Him, our lives produce only bad fruit like hatred, a disturbed mind and so on. It also figures Jesus' death and resurrection".

Evangelist Mrs. Pang now told two stories to illustrate her theme. The first concerned a Christian woman who was discovered to have bad cancer. She prayed to the Lord, "Lord, I ask you to take care of this cancer". She was quickly put in touch with a cancer hospital and a famous cancer specialist. The big operation which followed proved totally successful. As a consequence, she gave herself more completely to Jesus and His service.

The second concerned a Chinese doctor who had to go to work in the countryside during the Cultural Revolution. In addition to his farm work, he applied his doctor's skill to peasants and to the commune team alike. The Party cadre or leader noticed this and said to him one day, "Why are you so thoughtful and kind to all these people? You must be a Christian".

While the preacher gave her sermon, young Mr. Hu Hong-

Qiang quietly interpreted quite a lot of the sermon for me, although I could understand it quite well. Occasionally, I also gave the American lady sitting next to me, a quick synopsis of what was being said. Later she told me that her husband worked in the University Medical Department.

The sermon was truly a memorable one. After it, the final hymn was sung, the blessing was given from the back of the church and a final four-fold Amen was sung by the choir.

Outside, we spoke to many people, including the Rev. Shen Yi-fan, who invited us to come again if possible. The preacher came to speak to us and also a medical doctor, a Mr. Stephen Wang, who was a teacher as well as a church usher, and Mrs. K. T. Lim, the widow of a Liverpool University graduate and statistician. She was to celebrate her 72nd Birthday the next day. She loved to talk and told us about the present condition of the Chinese Church. Like Mr. Stephen Wang, she also was a church usher or helper, of which the Church had as many as 80. Mrs. Lim arranged the church flowers, which were apparently given by the foreign community. Those on this Sunday had remained from the memorial service for Bishop Shen Tz-gao, who had died the week previously. Mrs. Lim had two daughters, twins, and a third child. She felt that conditions in China were much improved; there was enough food and to spare, and wages were adequate. Some farmers now could even afford to buy washing machines and come regularly into the cities for parties, as we ourselves had noticed in our hotel dining room the previous evening.

Mr. Stephen Wang, the teacher, however, did not feel free to talk about Christianity at his school, whereas a foreigner (like us at Nanning) could do so. When asked about the present situation of the famous Chinese preacher Watchman Nee, he said he had not heard anything nor could they enquire. The doctor had quite a lot to say. He felt the House Churches no longer existed and that recently there had been a scandal about some House Church leaders making money by baptising old people who were uneducated and unable to read. (We had heard about this rumour elsewhere). There were some serious deviations by some people from Gospel truth – such as the man in the USA who had made people commit mass suicide!! (I explained that this man was not in fact a Christian). From others to whom we spoke, we also heard of a recent Youth Conference in Beijing, and described in a report given the previous Sunday in the Community Church itself, when it was also decided to hold another such conference in Shanghai.

There seemed to be plenty of Bibles available, and there was a notice which said that copies of the Scriptures had arrived recently and could be bought on request at the Church Office for cash. It seemed that, of the churches in Shanghai, only the Community Church used Mandarin, whereas the others used Shanghai dialect.

I also noticed that the service which we attended had begun at 10am and had ended at 12.15pm, a matter of two and a quarter hours. Even so, we did not feel it had been excessively long. In England this might have raised some difficulties and protest, although I know of one or two churches even there, which had services of similar length!

After this long talk with our new acquaintances, we returned to our hotel by trolley bus, but found that the dining room was deserted, and lunch time over. However, the staff kindly provided us with our order of two bowls of noodles, one pork and one chicken, together with spinach and completed with some China tea. It tasted delicious; we were hungry, and it cost on 2.70-Yuan (90p). Returning to room 1105, we wrote up our diaries, a letter to John and Anna (number 2 son and his wife), together with some postcards. About 5pm we went down to the reception desk, paid up our hotel bill (two and a half days at 52-Yuan = 130-Yuan, or £43.33), posted our mail and ordered the taxi to take us to the railway station. This cost us only 3-Yuan (£1).

At the station, where we arrived in good time, we met an American consular official wearing a rather attractive Mao jacket. He was quite as tall as our sons (John 6' 1½" and Philip 6' 3"). We admired the jacket, which the wearer said was size 9 and bought in Beijing. Having made a mental note to buy such a jacket for one of our sons, we said goodbye to our American acquaintance and went to the platform to board the Beijing express, which had already arrived a little early at 5.30pm. A train stewardess looked at our tickets and showed us to our seats and sleeping berths in No. 2 coach. This sleeper coach looked very new, and was the best and cleanest we had so far used. A pleasant and slightly rotund Chinese gentleman had one lower bunk and Greta had the other, whilst I had been given one of the two upper bunks. The young and very courteous girl attendant had said that she would try to arrange two lower bunks for us. However, due to the number of passengers getting on at later stations, especial Nanjing, she found it impossible to do so. Then she asked our fellow traveller kindly to move to the next compartment where there was a vacant bunk, whilst she brought in two other men, one a doctor and the other a pharmacologist, instead. This proved to be a happy change, and especially interesting to Greta, who talked with them about medical matters in China today. Our two newcomers had been to some medical conference at Shanghai and were returning to Beijing. The younger man told us that his companion was a well-known surgeon, specialising in abdominal diseases, who was Associate Dean and Professor of Surgery in Tianjin Medical College or Institute. He was studying cardio-vascular drugs and tumour treating drugs, using Chinese materials.

After much interesting conversation, the doctor gave Greta a little brooch with a famous poem inscribed on it, a poem often recited by Chinese children, about a mountain where the leaves in winter fall to the ground like snowflakes in the moonlight. When sick people slept in this place, they were healed. We presumed that the leaves might well have been pine leaves!

For breakfast next morning, after a pleasant enough sleep, we could not get shi-fan (wet rice) as on previous trains, but were given pork meat with noodles and three fried eggs each. This was quite appetising and cost us only 3.40-Yuan (£1.14).

At one end of our coach, there was quite a good and clean foreign-style loo, with a Chinese-style loo at the other end. At the other end there was also a wash place with three bowls set in a metal sink unit, each supplied with hot and cold water taps. Three people could thus wash at the same time: quite a considerable convenience!

In each compartment there was an air-conditioner, operated by a switch, whilst the windows were double-glazed. On the window-table there was the customary thermos flask and four cups on a tray, whilst under the table there was a metal ring holder for the thermos, for use en route. The thermos boiling water was also changed every half-hour by the polite stewardess or steward. Coat hangers were available for jackets. All was beautifully clean and probably new. Fixed to the wall, with an operating switch and volume control, was a radio, over which announcements from the train staff were also made. The bunk seats were very comfortable and indeed soft, and at night could be pulled out to make sleeping easier.

The white bed linen was very clean and nicely laundered, whilst the white lace curtains on the outside window were delicately stitched and pleasantly arranged. Blinds were fitted to the outside and the inside windows looking out on to the corridor.

Thus commenced our journey from the Red Dragon country to its very centre, the Red Dragon's Throne. It was an exciting prospect, and it duly fulfilled its promise.

Chapter 18

City of the Red Dragon's Throne

The Beijing express continued smoothly on its journey through the northern provinces. Just about sunrise, we passed the Tai-Shan mountains, one of China's famous five ranges. About 4,500 feet or 1,500 metres in height, they looked magnificent and sometimes grim against the dawn sky. The train seemed to circle round the great range, the shining engine raced along pouring smoke and fire from its funnel mouth like a snorting dragon. On the tops of the mountain range, temple buildings gleamed faintly in the sun's rays, reminding us of those beautiful mountain top scenes in the TV film the night before.

Fields of winter wheat and great areas of cotton plants filled the landscape, with peasants picking the cotton bolls and collecting them in large carts. The fields were larger than the paddy fields of South China. On the dirt track roads, and sometimes stacked in the fields, were the ubiquitous bicycles, whilst wheelbarrow, occasional trucks, donkey carts, ox-drawn and mule-pulled tucks enlivened the landscape. A metalled tarmac road ran parallel with the rail track, with many new and beautifully decorated bridges where it crossed streams, canals and rivers. At one point, we crossed the Yellow River, still sometimes but less frequently than of old, China's sorrow, at its junction with one or two tributaries. Magpies like very miniature helicopters strayed across the sky. Larger birds, maybe geese, flew into view or waddled in the fields. Bulbuls nestled or sang in the trees, ducks gathered in flocks in large ponds. Sheep and goats were startled by the noise of the racing train. In one place a group of dogs played about among themselves. Greta saw a Pekinese dog.

Before and beyond the Tai-Shan mountains, the countryside was flat and dry. The sun had been shining all morning and no doubt yesterday too. The trees occasionally looked bent in the breeze. Lines of trees formed wind-brakes. Apple trees were prevalent. Avenues of poplars patterned the skyline. Farmhouses were built of stone blocks like Cotswold stone. Brick kilns and piles of stored bricks abounded. A very long water viaduct, and quite low, ran parallel with the rail track. Farmers were ploughing with yokes of oxen, sometimes three, in a team.

In our carriage, the trains radio system broadcast comic interludes and humorous songs, interspersed with semi-classical music, both Chinese and Western, and good songs. At one station, Greta and I alighted from the train to stretch our legs and breathe the clear morning air. It came cold to our nostrils. Platform stalls sold cooked chickens to take away, or were they Peking duck? On returning to the train, I put on my long sleeved sweater.

At 2.30pm we arrived at Beijing main station, to be met by a CITS agent, again a young woman. A taxi took us to the Travel Office, which was in the Gwang-Hwa Hotel, and we paid the usual taxi and service fee at the hotel desk. Our room was number 204.

A large extension was being built to the hotel, and a certain untidiness was apparent. We had heard about this hotel from the American we had met in the Shanghai Station Soft Class waiting room. He and his professor friend had found the hotel to be quite good and comfortable and the charge only 16-Yuan a night. It had seemed too good to be true, but it was so, although we would have classed it second or third rate. We were given just a room. The men's common toilets and shower rooms were next door, including a place for washing clothes and another for washing and shaving in between. Some women folk used the clothes washing facilities in a very matter of fact way, although Greta found the women's toilets and washing facilities on the same floor, but on the other side of the hotel. However, we were grateful for the 16-Yuan charge.

After our arrival and the fixing up of our room, a very polite CITS lady told us details about sleep-train facilities and fares for our next journey to Qingdao on the East coast. It would be 185.40-Yuan for the two of us (£62). There was only one train each day, which left Beijing at 15.21 hours and arrived the next day at 7.59 am. She told us wherc to go, in the City, to send a telegram to our friend Margaret Wake, who was teaching English in the Shantung

University Department of Oceanography in Qingdao.

Having bought some postcards at the hotel shop, which was quite small, we returned to the City Centre – abut 2 miles away – on No.4 trolley bus, which stopped at the end of the hotel road, and found the hotel where the CITS main office was situated. From the bus stop to the hotel, which was near to the station, was rather a long walk. Finding the particular hotel was rather a difficult task, and on finding the CITS office, we were told it had just closed for the day, since it was after 5 pm. Slightly daunted, we set off to find the Telegraph Office, which was near the station. In the gathering dusk, we made it with difficulty to the station. Here, the four lane double highway (or dual carriageway) proved a little difficult to cross against masses of bicycles, taxis, buses, carts, pedicabs and pedestrians speeding first one way and then the other. The traffic lights were very efficient but the masses of people, evidently returning home from work, were in great haste. We made it, however.

Sending off a telegram presented some difficulties. The girl clerks who could understand English seemed rather puzzled. On the appropriate form I had printed out:

> MISS MARGARET WAKE, ENGLISH DEPARTMENT, SHANDONG COLLEGE OF OCEANOGRAPHY, QINGDAO:
> ARRIVING TRAIN NO.239 FROM BEIJING FRIDAY 5TH NOVEMBER 7.59AM.
> GUANGHUA HOTEL, BEIJING. GRETERIC HAGUE.

After much animated discussion amongst themselves, the girl clerks eventually accepted our telegram form and charged us only 1.47-Yuan (50p)! Relieved and pleased, we set off back to our hotel in the dark, returning first to the main dual carriageway, which apparently ran right through the City. We boarded a No. 4 bus, paying only 10 cents each, but could not remember where to alight and the name of the hotel road. The woman conductor told us to get off at the 10 cents stage point, which proved to be the correct one, and we reached the hotel tired but victorious, and with a 'Thank You, Lord' silent prayer echoing through our minds.

Going straight to the hotel dining room, rather empty but for a few foreign (i.e. not Chinese) students, we ordered a dish of sweet-sour pork, a vegetable dish, chicken in sauce and, after we had eaten our way through those, an extra dish of scrambled egg, in mushroom soup and rice.

The first dish was passable, the second quite palatable, the third uneatable, and the fourth never arrived. Therefore, we ate what we could and paid for the first three and regretted even that, as well as the cost which was 5.50-Yuan (£1.93). I said to my wife, "Now I know what Margaret Wake meant about her food in the University Canteen, both at Xian and Qingdao, being rather poor". Greta had just been thinking the same thoughts (we find ourselves often experiencing such silent communications with each other – a sort of mental telepathy!). We also discovered that the hotel was classed as an international hotel, and much frequented by students of many countries.

Returning to our room, we wrote up our diaries and went to bed at 8.30pm – Greta was already asleep before I put my head down on the pillow. At least the bedroom was good. The main fluorescent light was brighter than the lights in our previous hotels, and we each had a desk lamp, and the beds were comfortable.

Next morning, Tuesday 2nd November, we emerged from sleep, made our ablutions in the places provided and arrived in the dining room at 8am. Breakfast was quite appetising, being simply shi-fan, eggs, toast and coffee, all for 3.50-Yuan (£1.17)!

We set out for the City once again and took No.9 bus to the New Bridge Hotel, where I was able to change some travellers' cheques, four of £50 denomination at an exchange rate of 334.66-Yuan per £100, receiving 664.30. Thus armed, we set about finding the Beijing churches. From our address list,, we first looked for the former Bible Society building, which was now a Three Self Church in Deng-Dan-Bei main road number 21. From the minister, the Rev. Shao Shieh-chung (who had a telephone number Beijing 55,5086) we learned that there were 700/800 attending each Sunday at both his church and the other one across the City : that this former Bible Society church now had four ministers attached to it, and the one across the City also had four. Once a month they had a Holy Communion Service and, on a Tuesday evening at 7 pm., there was a Bible Study meeting, whilst at the other church on Wednesday mornings they held a Prayer Meeting at 8.30 am. The chief minister at the other church was named Pastor Yin. Before very long, they were to open a large new church in place of the one at the former Bible Society building, since that was now too small for the numbers who attended. From this church, Pastor Shao told us, the ministers go out into the country to give Holy Communion to the House Churches there, which apparently have no church buildings, and are attached to the City Three Self Church and practice the "Three Self" principles.

The Pastor also told us that part of his house and building is not available for use since it is used by some Government department, for which the church receives a fair rent. This is so with churches elsewhere in China where Government still needs the use of former church buildings. In addition, the Christians practice 'giving', never using collection plates at services, but only boxes at the church door, usually in the vestibule. This method had, in fact, resulted in increased giving. With this money and the rent money, the church was able to repair and redecorate their church buildings and pastors' homes, to buy Bibles and to print their own hymnbooks.

The pastor very kindly presented us with a copy of their hymnbook, in a version which printed the hymns in both Chinese and English. Greta also took a photograph of the pastor and I together in the church upstairs. This room would have accommodated about 300 people, sitting on fold-up stools. There was also an overflow room nearby. The pastor seemed to be a very kindly man indeed, and very open with us. As we were about to leave, he prayed with us.

The other church was the former London Missionary Society's "Morrison Church". It was opened by permission of the Government in 1980. At the Sunday 9.30am service, they have about 500 people, including a young and surpliced choir of 50. For baptisms, they used both "immersion" and "finger" or "forehead" baptism, according to the individual desire of each candidate. Children were allowed to attend the church by unwritten consent, but no official "Yes" had yet been given. The church in Beijing was preparing to open a seminary and was hoping to enrol young men, since many such had asked for enrolment. In Nanking, the seminary gives half the cost of the training of young candidates, 20 years old and upwards, whilst the candidates' local church would give the other half.

An interesting historical incident associated with this Beijing church, is that Mr. Chou En-lai, formerly second in command in the Chinese Communist Government, invited Britain's Red Dean, Dr. Hewlett Johnson, to come to this church to worship some five years previously, i.e. about 1977.

It was our first visit to the Red Dragon's Imperial City, so we decided to explore the ancient monuments and sites. A brisk walk through the City brought us to the Tien-An-Men, or the Gate of Heavenly Peace, and the Gu-gong or Old Palace, and the Museum. We were absolutely astonished by the size and beauty of the place. It took us about one hour to walk through it and to visit the different Throne Rooms of Supreme Harmony, Middle Harmony and Preserving Harmony (once the Examination Hall for First Degree Mandarins under the former emperors), and to enjoy the gardens and the goldfish pools.

Each hall with its surrounding buildings was built in beautifully coloured stone, with great red pillars and lovely soft-coloured walls with green and red and other coloured decorations. The ceilings, too, were attractively decorated.

Leading up to each building were flights of stone steps with decorated balustrades. Going through massive doorways, we were faced with three great thrones, guarded by large and smaller sculpted dragons or lions, occasionally by tortoises in bronze, three feet long at least, and by bronze herons. Outside each building, huge Chinese-style bronze lions stood on guard.

The third of the Throne Rooms was the centre of the Palace of Heavenly Purity, the Hall of Peaceful Unity and the Palace of Feminine Tranquillity, whilst the final gateway was called the Gate of Godly Prowess, outside of which were most attractive gardens of chrysanthemums and varied species of trees.

The Old Imperial Palace

Temple of Heaven

All this was the former Forbidden or Imperial City, but now called the Peoples' Palace Museum, once the personal domain of the Dragon Emperor, and now after much damage in the war years, restored to its pristine splendour by a Communist Government of the people, for the people. It covers an area of 720,000 metres. Within this area there are 9.000 halls and chambers, surrounded by a wall 10 metres high, outside of which is a moat 52 metres wide, with elegant wooden towers at the four corners. Some interiors of the halls reminded us of English cathedrals in their vastness and beauty. The construction of this magnificent City was in the year 1406 AD, in the Ming dynasty, the Emperor Cheng Zu using 300,000 labourers, artisans and guards. It took fifteen years to complete it in the year 1420.

Amazed by all this magnificence and somewhat fatigued by our sightseeing, we found our way out and walked along outside the great moat towards the "Golden Turtle and Jade Rainbow" bridge-causeway across the very large Bei-Hai lake, passing as we did so the white jade Tibetan Dagoba. Whilst living in this Dagoba, the famous Chinese revolutionary writer, Lu Hsun, wrote most of his essays and articles in most pungent language. His bedroom-study there was called "Tiger's Tail".

We continued our way to find the other Christian church, where we met one of the pastors, the Rev. Lee-ke. In the Church Office, he had a photograph album of baptism, including both immersion and forehead touching scenes. One photograph showed thirty-six young baptism candidates, wearing white surplices, presumably donned for the ceremony and borrowed from the choir. There were also some wedding and choir photographs.

During services, said Pastor Lee, the clergy wore black gowns and red stoles or scarves, as in Anglican churches, but there were no candles on the Holy Table. The church had some 400 seats, and this could be increased to 500. This church was re-opened in 1980. Before that there were House Churches in the area.

Leaving Pastor Lee, we looked for a decent restaurant to get a meal, but walking thc very long road into the City again, we could not find one until, turning into the main dual carriageway, we came across the Nationalities Cultural Palace, inside which we found an Islamic Restaurant (no pork!), very clean and spacious, with few customers at that particular time of day. Here we enjoyed a splendid and well cooked meal of slices of beef, an egg and tomato dish, a dish of mixed vegetables of five or six varieties, boiled rice and tea, for the reasonable sum of 7.20-Yuan (£2.60). We were not a little hungry.

Much refreshed and strengthened, we returned to Pastor Lee's Church for the evening Bible Study, at which we met some sixty people, including some young people and a mother with her young child. The service started with a hymn, followed by prayer, and then an exposition of the passage from the First Epistle of Peter, Chapter 1, Verses 2-12: "Whom not having seen, you believe in and worship with unspeakable joy. The prophets spoke about the coming of Jesus – being inspired by the spirit of Jesus – and angels longed to see it". The exposition, delivered in Mandarin, was excellent and lasted one hour and five minutes, and did not seem too long.

Next morning at our hotel, we breakfasted at 7.30 am. Instead of Shi-fan we were given Do-fu (Bean Curd) soup, with eggs, toast, butter and coffee, for 3.50-Yuan (£1.20).

Having remembered the Wednesday morning Prayer Meeting, we sped off to the ex-Bible Society Church on No. 4 bus, only to discover on arrival that it was at the other "ex-Morrison" Church. Following the advice of Pastor Yin, we went by No. 109 bus so far and then another bus to the other church, arriving punctually at 8.30 am. Some 50 people were present. All were praying audibly but quietly, each in his own words. After some 20 minutes of such petitions and praise, (Greta and I joining in quietly in like fashion in Chinese, and I was asking the Lord to pour out his Holy Spirit on this church and its members and its work) the hum of prayer quietened down into silence. Single individuals now began to pray aloud and alone, and I remember one prayer in particular, thanking the Lord that He was utterly trustworthy and utterly loving of the whole wide world, and that His written Word was trustworthy and the food of our souls. Prayers finally ended with the Lord's Prayer said together, and was followed by the hymn "What a friend we have in Jesus", of course in

Chinese. All then rose to their feet and began to leave. It was 10.10 am. Prayers had lasted one and a half-hours. Some young folk were present, and a child. There was no heating in the church and it was quite a cool morning!

When we had first entered the church, it looked to us as if only a dozen people were present, until we realised that there were many more, kneeling at their seats and facing inward. Each person seemed to have a little kneeling mat.

As we emerged from the church building, one of the pastors came by with two large postal parcels, containing ten Bibles, from Shanghai, and just that moment delivered by the postman. They were, we were told, part of a consignment of 1,000 Bibles for Beijing. Each cost 5.50-Yuan (£1.84). "How cheap they are", said the pastor to us, with pleasure in his tone. Greta took a photo of him holding a Bible. When we examined a copy, we found they were printed on excellent, thin but strong white paper, and had Bible maps at the back, and were well bound with hard backs. They were printed in the old version because (we were told) the older people prefer it to the modern translation in the modernised script, which they find difficult to read.

The pastors showed real pleasure in receiving the Bibles, and one of the church members immediately bought a copy. We did not see whether he had to sign his name to purchase a copy. Some Chinese Christians have asserted that this is the case, and is a form of registration meant for government purposes, so that the House Church Christians (who refuse to register their homes) become barred from purchasing the Bibles.

With sincere and gentle farewells, we left the Church and the Christians, and made our way by bus to the Travel Office to collect our railway sleeper tickets for the journey to Quindao. The tickets cost 85.20-Yuan for sleeper facilities, and 40 cents service charge, making a total of 185.50-Yuan (£61.94). It was to be a long journey again!

Because the train was due to leave at 15.21 hours, we had to cancel our plan to visit the Great Wall of China. That journey, by train also, would only get us back to Beijing some four or five minutes before the Qingdao train left Beijing. Our heavy luggage also added to the problem of hastening from one platform to another across the tracks.

Instead, we decided to visit the Imperial Summer Palace some miles outside Beijing, a distance needing two bus journeys, first to Beijing Zoo and the Giant Panda (which we had neither time nor energy to visit) and then an express bus to the Summer Palace. Each journey took 40 minutes or so, yet cost only 15 cents (5p) and the buses were crammed with “the people”.

Jesus comes to his disciples on the sea

Chapter 19

The People's Dragon Children on Holiday

It was a beautiful day at the Summer Palace and warm in the sun. The area includes the huge Kunming Lake, created by a famous Chinese hydrologist in 1291 AD from the distant Jade Spring and the Deity Mountain Spring. There were a great many Chinese visitors and only a few foreigners enjoying the lovely scenery and buildings that day. A great number were rowing on the lake with obvious pleasure and leisurely delight.

We entered the Palace area by the East Palace Gate, and came to the Hall of Benevolence and Longevity, and thence to the Hall of Happiness and Longevity. These halls, as those in the old Forbidden City, were splendid and beautiful, suiting their intriguing names. The halls led to a most beautiful open but covered Promenade, with wonderful decorations in varied colour both on the ceiling and the ceiling supports, whilst hidden loudspeakers transmitted music and announcements!

Our walk around one side of the lake gave us some distant and beautiful vistas of the hall that Dispels the Clouds, and the Tower for Incense for the Buddha which were on the distant shore. Beyond these again stood Longevity Hill, and further still a range of distant mountains rising gradually to an even higher range. Our walk also took us towards the Bridge of the Seventeen Arches, glowing white in the sunshine. On the balustrade of the bridge were many tiny sculptured lion figures – I counted some 106. Time and energy did not permit us to go on further than the bridge round the great lake, which seemed to be nearly two miles long, so we returned to the East Palace Gate and, feeling hungry, went into a restaurant for a meal.

It was a simple business. We ordered our meal at an office and were given tickets which we then took to the cooking counter, receiving our rice and then our three meat and vegetable dishes at different places, cafeteria-wise but much more primitive. We had one plate of pork balls, not unlike scotch eggs, a plate of mixed vegetables, a bowl of soup containing pieces of ginger, and a large bowl of rice. A Chinese visitor, clad in the usual blue jacket and trousers, kindly told us what was available, and found a free table for us (for there were many others eating there). Finally, and courteously, seeing us now sitting and eating, he waved goodbye and left. The meal proved too much for us, we could neither eat all the rice nor finish off the other dishes. It certainly satisfied our hunger for the rest of the day, and upset Greta's stomach as well. I felt a little queasy myself too.

After such a lunch, we went on perhaps a little reluctantly, to walk round the other side of the lake to see the Hall that Dispels the Clouds, and along the beautiful covered Promenade, the Hall for Listening to the Orioles (one of China's most beautiful birds, which has also a lovely song). There were no orioles about as far as we could see, and we pressed on to the Marble Boat, permanently moored of course, and built on Longevity Hill in the Garden where Peace is Cultivated. The decorations on the marble are absolutely exquisite and we could not but continue to marvel at the Chinese delight in, and gift of naming, places with sublime, poetic titles.

After eating a delectable tangerine each, to sweeten the taste of that earlier meal, we turned back towards the bus station. Greta was now feeling most uncomfortable inside and was exceedingly glad to find a ladies' loo. The double bus journey back to Beijing City Centre, and then out to the Guang Hua Hotel took just over an hour, passing through lovely countryside decorated with bamboo, myrtle and other trees. In the City, both trolley and petrol driven buses were crowded to capacity, whilst thousands of cyclists and pedestrians filled the roads and streets.

The main Beijing roads are certainly magnificently wide and straight. A flood of buses speed along the inside bus lanes of the great four lane dual carriageways, cutting in to the side at special bus stations at hair-raising speed. On the main highway, there were islands for passengers at irregular intervals, the wide bicycle lane was outside that again, and on the far outside were footpaths. Trees line these roads, with here and there flower gardens with flowering bushes as hedges.

The whole City is planned on a massive and expensive scale. Old buildings destroyed during recent times have been splendidly restored, and new, huge public buildings, hotels, high-rise living quarters, offices and factories were built at intervals along the spacious highways, yet so that they seem neither to overpower nor threaten, nor be gathered in heaps (as in Hong Kong).

Returning to the hotel in beautiful weather not unlike Kunming's perpetual spring, we felt happy if tired at all we had seen. We could not face supper, but contented ourselves with a glass of what the Dining Room called coffee. In our room, we just lay on our beds and prepared for sleep and our journey the next day to Qindao. We woke up early, had a shower, then the usual breakfast. Wishing to buy a Mao jacket for Philip, we went into the City again but found the shops were not yet open. Calling in at the ex-Bible Society Church, we enquired of the pastor about the Catholic Church. He told us where their church buildings were, and informed us that in Beijing, the Catholics were much more numerous than the Protestant Christians.

Returning to our shopping, we found the shops open and duly bought a Mao jacket for our No.3 son. Padded winter jackets were 60-70-Yuan (£20-23), so we bought a large, size 9, ordinary jacket, which only cost 26.50-Yuan (£8.85), and fitted easily over an ordinary English tweed jacket; plus two "Mao" caps, largest size, one for our honourable son, and one for my humble self.

Going on to the Catholic Church of the Immaculate Conception, we met a church member, who welcomed us in and then called the resident priest. He seemed younger than we had expected, was very welcoming, and asked about Father Joe in our hometown in Hoylake, Wirral, England. He was most interested to hear about the ecumenical Saturday morning Prayer Time for clergy and priests that we had there, and equally so to learn about the ecumenical Thursday evening House Group for clergy and lay people.

In return, he gave us many details of the Catholic churches of Beijing. His church was immense, with a massive painting of Madonna and Child hanging over the east end altar. Between 1,700/

1,800 attended on ordinary Sundays, when there were successive masses from 6am to 10am. At Easter time, 9,000 people had attended the 5 or 6 masses. There was a choir of 100 young people, not robed, and perhaps not exactly what Government officially allowed. There were 10 or more priests attached to the church.

At St. Joseph's, their second church, he continued, 500-600 people attended on Sundays, with 2,000 at the Easter Festival. They were preparing to open a Seminary in Shanghai soon and planned to build one in Beijing too. There were enough Mass books and quite a number of Bibles, although these were not so much in demand as with the Protestants. On entering the Church, we had noticed some memorial preparations, and he told us that a Chinese bishop from West Germany had died in Beijing recently and a Requiem High Mass was to be held at 7pm that night, and there was a memorial coffin in the church for the occasion! They still used the Latin Mass in China, he said, but included some prayers in Chinese, but they had no plans as yet to use the vernacular for their services.

In Beijing as a whole, there were many Catholic Christians, all belonging to the Three Self Patriotic Catholic Church of China, with 7 churches, and a total of perhaps 10 or more priests, mainly old men. They had obviously some problems about the Vatican connection. Like the Protestant churches, they used offertory boxes at the church entrances. Father Shi Yu-Kwan finally added that there was now a drawing together of Chinese Catholics and Protestants (at least ex-Anglicans) in China. With this good news we bade each other a rather moving farewell.

From the Cathedral Church, we took a roundabout bus journey to the Temple of Heaven. Set in a spacious park of many attractive trees, flowering bushes, flower beds and grass-lined avenues all at right angles, with little summer houses at the crossings, the Temple of Heaven itself is supremely beautiful. The dome, perfectly round and tapering up to a shallow pointed spire, is made of deep blue tiles, exquisite in shape and texture. From inside and looking upwards, I was greatly reminded of St. Paul's Cathedral and that great Wren-dome, here not quite so high, but all in beautiful colours, green and blue and Chinese red, and gold, with many inscriptions. The temple contains beautiful bronzes, a huge bell resting on the floor, a series of thrones, the very large centre throne being flanked by two smaller ones on both right and left.

Called the Hall of Prayer for Good Harvests, the Temple of Heaven was built in 1421 and was the most important imperial shrine. The Emperor himself had to go there three times a year to sacrifice on the simple altars, and pray for the gift of Heaven, a good harvest, spending the night in vigil in the Hall of Abstinence to prepare for the ceremony.

From the Temple, we hastened back to our hotel by bus. Collecting our luggage from the reception desk clerk, we called for a taxi to the station. None was available and the hotel staff seemed unconcerned. We settled to go by bus instead. Outside the hotel we spoke to a pedal-rickshaw man who wanted to take us to the station, and then saw a van driver who kindly offered to take us and our luggage to the nearby bus stop. A slight difference arose between the two, with much usual and polite argument, but the van driver won the day and duly delivered us to the bus stop, without charge. Fortunately, or better 'by grace', the first bus was not too crowded and we reached the railway station quickly for only 20 cents.

At the station, having found the Soft Class waiting room, we found ourselves with an hour to spare; and an opportunity to go out and buy some fruit. Most of the fruit had been sold but I was able to buy two pears. These we kept for the journey. The train arrived on time, we found our bunks and settled down to eat our pears. The coach was even more luxurious than on our previous journey, with crocheted white seat-back covers and embroidered pillowcases, all spotlessly clean.

As soon as the train started, at 15.21 hours, the girl train attendant asked whether we wanted a meal at 19.00 hours, at 5, 6 or 7-Yuan. Luckily we chose 5-Yuan! At a station further along the line, a plump and jovial Chinese merchant-trader got in, accompanied by a young man, possibly his employee. They smoked and talked a while, put the older man's luggage bag on a shelf over the doorway, and then the young man disappeared, probably to his own 'hard' bunk compartment. The attendant came to ask about the meal and our new friend ordered simply a bowl of noodles for 30 cents. We had not been given that choice!

With our new friend, we began to talk about age, children (he had three boys and a girl) and ourselves. When we said we were Christians, he smiled and said something about Catholics, so he knew that much! When I asked what he believed, with a broad smile he said, "I believe Marx. I don't believe in the 'spiritual'". I replied "We believe in God, who helps us physically, in our minds and hearts, and fills us with love for others and for Himself".

It was all 'cheerfully' spoken. He smiled his constant big smile. No, he had never been abroad – how could a merchant-trader afford that! Again, he spoke with that jolly laugh and smile – it seemed quite understandable. He was now called to go for his meal, and returned later, just as the attendant called us to our meal.

Our meal, in the dining car, proved to be rather unusual for us. It was almost totally fish – two bright red crayfish (or very large prawns!), a large fish nicely cooked, a dish of vegetables and fish, and noodle soup. Obviously, it was a 'seaside' meal, from the Qindao area. "No beer or other drinks, thank you". And all for 5-Yuan. Sitting near us was an American couple of older vintage, and their young Chinese friend, probably an official interpreter. They enjoyed a similar meal, of the 6 or 6-Yuan variety, which they found as surprising as we did! They mentioned in conversation that they were visiting the College of Oceanography in Qindao, like us.

Returning to our compartment, we found our jovial Chinese friend talking with his young friend. We learned that the young man was 35 years old and we thought to ourselves that he might even be the older man's son. Eventually they both went off with a box of Chinese chess, possibly to the young man's compartment; where they would not disturb us. In the morning, after quite a good sleep, we brushed up and went to breakfast -–three fried eggs, bread and jam at 3.50-Yuan (£1.16).

This was no express train. It sped along smoothly at some 40-50 miles per hour, and called at almost every station. We began to see mountains again and the area seemed much drier than in other places. Our travelling companion, Mr. Hua Wen, said that the area was experiencing a water shortage. One river we crossed seemed to have dried up. The fields seemed hard to plough or dig. Wheat seemed to be the main crop. Gradually, the seacoast came into view. Having washed, and after breakfast at 7.15 am., we watched Qingdao draw near. Soon, small boats of fishermen, then a motorised fishing boat, and more and more boats of varying sizes appeared, as the sea emerged through the morning mist. On the other side of the track, were some very large and many smaller factories. The mist cleared and revealed the Yellow Sea reaching to the horizon, a charming sight, with seagulls about and very like home. I muttered to myself, "O Praise the Lord for the sea and all that therein is".

Patriotic Catholic Church

Students say goodbye

Chapter 20

Green Island of Birds and Mountains

Margaret our friend met us at Qingdao station. Pleasantly excited to welcome us, she escorted us from the train to a college car. Some slight confusion arose with other members of the College of Oceanography. They needed the car to take the two distinguished foreigners whom we had met in the train dining car, Mr. McVicar, president of Oregon University, USA, his wife, and their young Chinese friend, who proved to be their official interpreter. Neither Mr. McVicar nor his wife spoke or understood a word of Chinese. Evidently the interpreter would be paid for either by the University, or, if Mr. McVicar were an invited Guest Speaker, the College, a part of Shandong University, would foot the bill.

When talking with the Oregon University President, he had been surprised that we were travelling alone, without a guide. He had heard that this freedom had only recently been made official by the Chinese Government, on November 1st. He commented, "You must be two of the earliest foreigners to do this!" "We have been doing so since October 12th", we replied. Semi-officially, through the China International Travel Service, it had been possible to do this for at least one or even two years, so long as one could speak the language. Perhaps our being tourists, and not official visitors, also made this easier.

Margaret now swished us off in another car to the College, complaining cheerfully enough at the deviousness of college practices and their apparent intention, which she had already experienced, to be difficult or non-co-operative. They had already shown reluctance to let us all three eat together in the college, where Margaret in fact resided in a small flat. "You will only be given one dish!" they had said. "Very well, we will just eat one dish", she had replied.

Having anticipated difficulties for her to provide breakfast, however, we had eaten a meal on the train. So, after a quick toilette, and a cup of coffee, we at once set out for her classroom to meet her students. All sixteen of them were waiting there and eagerly applauded our arrival. Evidently they were expecting us to give the English lesson, and Margaret cheerfully let us begin, telling us to engage them in conversation. Obviously, as a man, I was expected to start off the session, and I did, saying with a smile, "In England we say 'Ladies First'", and then Greta took over.

She began by giving a simple outline, in her impeccable and clear English, of her life, from her birth in Kunming, Yunnan Province, and her return to China as a young recently qualified medical doctor, stationed in Guilin, GwangXi. She then invited the students, all of whom were already graduated in a number of university disciplines, to introduce themselves in similar vein. Some eight of them did so, in very good English, and with a good command of the language. After the bell, signalling the end of the lesson period, we all stayed in the classroom, and I in turn continued in the same way, beginning with my lowly birth in Liverpool. The mention of the City, world renowned for its football prowess, and known even to the young women as well as the men students, aroused many questions. Greta gave a simple outline of Liverpool's economic status and its unemployment problems. The whole group seemed deeply interested, and Margaret very pleased.

Returning for lunch to Margaret's quarters, we found that the College cook had prepared four lovely dishes and rice – plates of pork, cauliflower, mien-taos (steamed wheat balls), and egg soup. All looked most appetising, and being joined by Margaret's Australian fellow teacher, Carolyn, we sat down to enjoy our meal. Percolated coffee followed, in Carolyn's room. Over coffee, we shared what we had seen and heard of the worship, sermons, Bible studies and Prayer meetings in Beijing and Shanghai. Carolyn, who had confessed to being uninterested in either religion or Christian worship, said little but showed some interest nevertheless, and not least in a passing comment about an Australian missionary friend, Bob Ament, who had worked in Guiyang.

After lunch, we set out to find the local China International Travel Service Office to buy our boat tickets for our next journey, which was to be by sea to Shanghai. The office proved to be in one of the hotels on the coastal road. The Qingdao-Shanghai steamers were quite large, with accommodation for hundreds of passengers. Two berths in a four-berth cabin would cost 51.60-Yuan and Travel Service commission of 7-Yuan; in total 57.60-Yuan (£19.20). The cost of a telegram to Shanghai, booking a hotel, was a further 10-Yuan. They asked for an advance of 60-Yuan.

Having sent off eight postcards to England and bought a local information booklet, we went for a walk by the sea, calling first to register and book in at a different hotel, including a room for Margaret. The College had no extra accommodation to spare for us, and Margaret's flatlet was too small, so she decided to join us and 'live out'. The tide was beginning to come in as we walked towards and along the shore. Out on a promontory jutting into the sea were some Chinese youths fishing with rod and line. To our great delight, and the youths', one of them caught a minnow as we passed. The others crowded round us, trying out some English words with some amusement. Another, who said he owned a cigarette shop away from Qingdao, had had too much to drink and showed it. At the land end of the causeway was a young Chinese painting in oils and Western style local rocks, the sea and the seascape. A number of others were painting too. "Were they students" I asked myself, (or local artists involved in a local industry?" Whatever the answer, some of the paintings were beautiful. Qingdao is set on the Southern coast of the Shandong Peninsula bordering the Yellow Sea and Jiaozhou Bay. With a population of over four million there would no doubt be an excellent market for art paintings, since Chinese generally love paintings whether in traditional or western style. Art seems bred into them. Their writing is nothing if not artistic. Calligraphy, which means 'beautiful writing' is endemic among the Chinese. It is a highly revered and honoured accomplishment. Their cooking methods are artistic, and their food dishes are artistically presented. Their way of eating with ivory chopsticks, on which are beautiful designs and Chinese characters, is artistic. Their porcelain bowls, cups and spoons are artistic; and often decorated with literary aphorisms or scenic views in miniature. The willow pattern is known the world over. However, I grow perhaps too enthusiastic!

Walks by the sea create hunger, and we returned to our hotel for 6pm supper. Rice, four dishes of meat, including fillets of pork, vegetables and soup were on the menu. It was delicious. Returning to Margaret's hotel room for home-made coffee, we talked through the evening until 9pm and then, suitably fatigued, we returned to our own room and after relaxing in a hot bath, soon went to sleep. Up betimes next day at 6.45am, duly refreshed, we took our breakfast with gladness and singleness of heart, as the reader would too, no doubt, on fried eggs, hot toast and butter, strawberry jam and coffee in a pot with extra hot water! Marks of Western rather than Chinese culture, and of American breakfast jam rather than English marmalade!

It was Saturday and we set off for town to visit the local Three Self-Christian Church. In the large Protestant church there was a service in progress. The church janitor said it was a Seventh Day Adventist service, but also available for Christians who had to go to work on Sundays. I counted the congregation – 57, including some young people and at least one small child. The minister-pastor was giving an earnest discourse on Romans 7 (I do not suppose St. Paul in his wildest dreams every imagined this!). The preacher commented, amongst other things, that Confucius had said this and that and the other, but Jesus was the only Saviour who could give us God's Holy Spirit, and we must believe on Him. It would, I imagine, have been tempting Providence, or rather, the Communist authorities, to have said this about Karl Marx and even Mao, rather than Confucius, but perhaps the transposition was mentally and readily made.

We left the church after only 10-15 minutes since the hotel lunch was at noon – but our hearts warmed towards these courageous believers. Seeing the janitor and a gentle woman come from the vestry to greet us and say farewell, we returned the Chinese Bible we had borrowed (it was in the old translation) and introduced ourselves. They were interested to learn that my wife was a doctor and former missionary, and that I was a pastor or "shepherd" (which is the Chinese word). They told us eagerly about their church. The Sunday congregation, they said, was over 1,000. They had two choirs, one with up to forty members, and a more regular women's choir. The next day being Sunday, they were holding their regular morning service at 9am, and then at 2pm a Baptism service for 57 people, followed by Holy Communion. We were welcomed to both. We felt very privileged to be invited to attend both – we had not hitherto attended either.

The buses which would have taken us back to our hotel were all packed out, so we took a bus of another route which went three quarters of the way. However, it was refreshing to walk the rest of the way in brilliant sunshine. Forgive me if I mention the lunch menu! – Plates of roasted pork balls, pork and vegetables, green vegetables with red peppers, beef and vegetables, soup and rice. Fit for a king! Whilst enjoying home-made coffee in our hotel room, Greta and Margaret talked personal matters and I wrote up my diary.

In the afternoon, we visited the former Roman Catholic but now simply Chinese Catholic Three Self Patriotic Cathedral – a huge building of interesting architectural style, with twin towers at one end, topped by pinnacles and built in red-stone or brick. It was German in style and construction. Before the Revolution and the Communist victory, Qindao had been part of the German Concession. Finding our way to the rear of the Cathedral, we met the Chinese man or janitor in charge of the church. "The Holy Father had gone out and has locked up the church", he remarked. "I am sorry that you cannot therefore see the inside of the church". He told us that there were four priests at the church, that some 300/400 people attended the early and only Mass – so many people had to work on Sundays. In the week, at the daily Mass, only ten or more came. At the great festivals, there were crowds of 700/800. They had a large choir. The services were in Latin and there was still no suggestion of using vernacular Chinese – that must and would be decided only by the Diocesan Synod. However, he was aware that in England, Europe and America, the Roman Catholics were now using the vernacular. They were also expecting to open a Seminary in Beijing, as well as at Shanghai, where some 30 priests were in training.

"How long have you been a Christian?" we asked.

"My father and mother were Christians and I was baptised as a Christian soon after I was born", he replied. "I was taught in the school across the road, which was a former church school. Now it is a Government school. We are not allowed to baptise children today before they reach 18 years, but children and young people attend our services. The church has catechumen classes and these last longer, so as to get the meaning of the faith into the minds of the candidates".

"Are there any Catholic House Churches in the countryside?" I asked.

"No, there are not. However, there is a former Lutheran Church now being restored".

Bidding the caretaker farewell, we made our way to the market to buy some bread which Margaret needed, but without avail. However, she bought carrots and bananas instead. At a photography shop, we asked about camera colour film. Only Japanese colour film was for sale at 14-Yuan ($.67), but that seemed too expensive. In Hong Kong colour film cost only £2.50.

Seeing a No.6 bus, we boarded it, and gratefully found some vacant seats. We alighted quite near our hotel. Supper was being served in the dining room and we were given seven dishes of a varied kind, and rice. This proved too much even for us, so we ordered three dishes only plus soup and rice for tomorrow's lunch, and wheat noodles with three meat and vegetable dishes for supper tomorrow. We looked forward with interest to see the result.

Up in our hotel room, Greta and Margaret again talked of many things whilst I wrote a family letter to our son Bill and his family. Then some coffee and afterwards (I am astonished to recall) a banana each. After prayers together, we all retired to bed. I remembered how very friendly people had been in the church and in the streets, and how Greta, entering a shop, had bought a Chinese child's red woollen bonnet with rabbit ears for one of the grandchildren. Of how a young fellow had tried to sell us some old Chinese coins, or to get some money from me, but to no avail.

Sunday dawned and after breakfast we set out for the Protestant church in the City, to attend the Morning Service. It was only 9am but the church was full – quite 900 people. The choir, of older and younger women, numbered 17 and it had a conductor. In addition to hymns, Psalm 32 was read by the minister; and the sermon, based on Paul's letter to the Romans, Chapter 3, Verses 1-31, lasted one hour and six minutes.

He spoke first of what forgiveness means. Job, who was both affluent and righteous, nevertheless suffered greatly. What God does is to help us through the Holy Spirit to bear it, and God's righteousness becomes ours through Jesus. We must recognise that God is righteous when we worship. We must believe and trust in Jesus Christ and not just listen to the words; then God can use us.

From Romans 3, Verses 9-29, but especially 3,20, he went on, we see that Jews and Gentiles have all sinned alike. Jesus, in Mark 2, 17, pointed out that healthy people do not need a physician but only the sick. Paul, a Jew and a Pharisee, thought he was right to kill Christians, but could not see clearly until after his conversion. After that experience, he did a wonderful work for God. Jesus is the Saviour, the One who saves is Jesus. First we must believe, then die, to ourselves and our sins. We are God's children and He is our Father. Jesus rescues and saves us through the Cross. He suffered for us to show us that God loves us, as it says in John's Gospel, Chapter 3, Verse 9.

In the middle of his sermon, the preacher sang a verse of a hymn and some listeners sang it, too. During the prayer that followed the sermon, the congregation responded fervently with 'amen' after each petition. The choir sang an anthem, and sang it well – they did not wear special robes – and at the service end they sang a simple three-fold Amen.

During the long sermon, some young children walked up and down the aisles, whilst some half dozen went out and returned a little later. Quite a number of young people were in the congregation.

After service, we were invited into the vestry to be welcomed and to talk with some of the leaders. A Mr. Wong asked me to write down my impression of the service. I wrote that it seemed full of the presence of the Holy Spirit, that the hymns, the anthem and the sermon were very helpful and interesting; and that I wondered whether, as in the Shanghai churches, there might be more involvement of lay people in reading lessons, leading prayers and in giving testimony.

In the afternoon at the service of Baptism and Holy Communion there was a stillness of expectation. The pianist quietly played two hymn tunes, combining the melodies together beautifully. One of them was the hymn "O happy day that fixed my choice on Thee".

The 57 candidates were assembled in the front rows. A table with a glass bowl of water on it, stood below the platform. Against the back wall stood another table covered with a white cloth which hid trays of small Chinese-style wine cups and plates of thin slices of bread cut into half-inch squares.

The service began with the hymn "O Happy Day", followed by introductory sentences from Matthew 26, Verse 17 (the Great Commission – Go into all the world, preach, baptising); Acts 2, Verse 22 and following (Peter's sermon at Pentecost) and Romans Chapter 1.

There followed an instruction on the meaning of Baptism and Holy Communion, with phrases like "The school of the Holy Spirit", "The water is water and the Holy Spirit baptises". Following a prayer, baptism was administered; one pastor checked each name from a list, another held the bowl of water, a third pronounced the name and added "I baptise you in the name of the Father, the Son and the Holy Spirit", laying his hands on each head and applying water by finger-touch. (This church had no baptistery with a well of water, so candidates could not be immersed). The women and girls were first, then the men, coming forward in rows of twenty. All was very reverently done. Some candidates seemed almost to prostrate themselves.

Holy Communion began with the hymn, "Break Thou the bread of life, dear Lord, to me", followed by the reading of Paul's first epistle to the Corinthians, Chapter 11, in which Paul describes the apostolic way of celebrating the Lord's Supper. A short sermon-instruction followed on the meaning of the bread and wine, and of the Lord's body and blood – "the bread is bread, the wine is wine" – the two elements "representing or manifesting" (Chinese 'Di-biao') the body and blood – and reminding the Christian of Christ's death on the Cross for us. The bread and wine was then consecrated or set apart, using the usual words of Jesus from the Gospel account.

A number of ministers and elders (or assistants) now brought the bread round on plates. It was already broken or cut. Most people waited until all had received and then all ate together. Some, like me, ate the bread immediately. The wine was brought round on trays by another group of men, and each person took a small cup, drank it, and immediately returned it to the tray, although again, a few waited. The celebrant himself used a larger cup of wine and the assistant ministers each received a small cup.

All was simply, quietly, quickly and reverently done. During this 'action', the choir soon followed by the congregation, sang quietly again and again the hymn sung earlier – "Break Thou the bread of life to me". When all was quiet again and movement had ceased, a final hymn was sung, a prayer said and the 'Blessing' given. All then arose and began to move out of the church.

During both the Baptism and the Holy Communion a photographer took photographs. When all had emerged from the church, the baptism candidates assembled outside for further photographs.

This was the first Holy Communion service there for six months, and the one baptism in the year. Margaret, Greta and I, and a Canadian girl from Vancouver who was present, felt deeply privileged to share this special Sunday. Over 600 attended; many children, and possibly older people from outside, occupied the gallery, to watch the ceremonies. Outside the church, a group of men were squatting on the grass playing cards, but I did not see any money used.

Margaret returned with us to the hotel; walking a little more actively than in the morning but still slowly. She obviously tired easily and got short of breath, and commented on the fact too. Physically, she did not appear too fit. She also complained about conditions in the college, about which she manifested a pessimistic attitude, and questioned the wisdom of staying in China if she had not improved by the end of the scholastic year. She was suffering from slight arthritis, which is apparently a family trait. Any effort seemed to drain her strength and she often felt the dampness and coldness of the coastal climate. However a rest on the bed with feet up, and a short sleep, seemed to lead to noticeable improvement and cheerfulness. Although she ate well and heartily, she often seemed hungry.

There seemed to be no doubt that present conditions in China, and perhaps the loneliness of the task, could be greatly blamed for all of this. The Adversary is not loath to harm us in whatever way he can.

Chapter 21

Further Encounters on Green Island

The love of money may be the root of all evil, but the possession of money is a necessity in this world society of the last decades of the twentieth century. Our own hotel, called the Ba-da-kung, meaning Eight Great Valleys, had no facilities for changing travellers' cheques, even if its name was beautiful. For this, I had to go to that same hotel where the Travel Service had its office, and where the Bank of China had a sub-office. Armed as usual and as necessary with my passport, I was able to change two fifty pounds travellers' cheques at a rate of 334.66-Yuan/£100. For some obscure reason, they could not allow me to change £200.

Whilst waiting for the transaction to be completed, I held an interesting discussion with one of the bank clerks and his companion. In a mixture on both sides of Chinese and English – they could not resist the opportunity to practise their English, and my Mandarin was not totally adequate to deal with the ramifications of our conversation – we discussed life in England. The younger man knew about London and Liverpool (football's 'The Greatest'), Cambridge and Edinburgh. He enjoyed describing Edinburgh Castle and Arthur's Seat and, he said, its reflection in the river water below. Both were curious as to my identity, and to my wearing of the badge of No.2 Middle School, Nanning. They suspected that I was perhaps some important person travelling incognito, maybe a Professor.

To surprise them I said, "The Queen of England's son, Charles, Prince of Wales, studied at the same Cambridge University College as did our son". (We had been discussing, and one of them describing, the wars between England and Scotland, Charles I, Charles II and Bonnie Prince Charlie, so I introduced our present Prince Charles as well!). Now they began to believe that I must indeed be some great personage – although I affirmed that I was just an ordinary person but that it was quite possible for our son to go to college with the Queen's son.

The conversation then led, in the curious and inevitable way that conversation seems to take, progressing not logically but laterally, to Queens and Kings in chess. At which they asked me about the meaning of 'chess'. Being at that moment ignorant of the fact that 'chess' etymologically comes from 'Kings', (see the Concise Oxford Dictionary, which, alas, I had not taken with me to China) I had to confess ignorance. However, my traveller's cheque had now been processed, and we had to bid each other a fond and somewhat respectful farewell!

Thus armed with some of the necessities of our common earthly life, I returned to the hotel and enjoyed a supper fit for a king, or at least a prince's acquaintance – mien-soup with pork bits, a plate of chicken pieces, one of celery and meat, and another of shrimps and vegetables, and a kind of biscuit. Adequate and delicious indeed. At another table in the hotel dining room, taking the place of the Chinese girl from Canada and Hong Kong, who had just departed, was a Norwegian, a young Scandinavian with fair hair and very blue eyes. He responded cheerfully to questions about his homeland, and knew Olden where Greta and I had once spent a "chaplain's" holiday.

Returning to our room, we enjoyed some hot cocoa and an apple, intending afterwards to have some Bible study together. Margaret having left her Bible in her own room, I went downstairs to get it for her. In the reception lobby, on my return, I was greeted by an Indian businessman from Bombay, who was (he was glad to tell me) a Hindu. He was travelling in China for Parke Davis, the medical suppliers.

"Kindly have coffee with me and my two companions", he said, invitingly. "Ask your wife and friend also to join us".

Greta and Margaret, being fatigued with our day's activities, declined, and I returned alone to these new friends and spent some twenty minutes talking. "I would like to talk with someone who visited my country in 1943, the year of the great Calcutta famine and the date of my birth", he said with Indian politeness.

I quickly reckoned that he must be 39 years old, but also realised that in reality he just wanted to talk out with me some of his own ideas. Indians of the sub-continent area are so different from Chinese, I thought to myself. Out of courtesy Chinese will refrain from talking too openly about themselves, whilst Indians will talk quite openly and volubly about anything in their hearts or on their minds, and not least religion and religious experiences.

"I have a very high position in Parke Davis," he asserted, "and I have a secretary, a young woman, who is a Roman Catholic. Her brother is also a RC priest. I have asked her to tell me what my employees think about me, but she has refused. I have considered sacking her," he continued. His English was very idiomatic. "I have not done so because she is really an excellent secretary. I think she ought to be willing to do this, and I have asked her brother, the priest, about this, but he has said that he cannot answer the question. What do you think, my dear sir?"

He continued, "This lady secretary is a Roman Catholic and is also thinking of becoming a nun. Is it religion, therefore, or her disposition which makes her refuse? I think she is wrong to refuse".

I answered that it was probably both, but that as a Christian, she would not wish to report on others.

His two companions, also of his nationality, agreed together that he should examine his own conscience regarding his employees.

"Christians believe in the Spirit of God," they said, "who is able to show them what they are like themselves."

"I also believe, as a Hindu, in the Spirit and in God", he asserted.

Here I informed him that I was a Christian pastor or minister or padre in the Church of England, at which his questions changed.

"Why did you become a God-seeker or religious?" he asked.

So, I gave him a brief history of how God had called me from a life of commerce to a life of God-seeking.

"Commerce," he said, going off at a tangent once more, "is, I think, in my case, a very difficult life, but I want to do my best for my employees or the workers under me. It is difficult to speak openly to them because they will fear me as 'the boss'. Nor am I able to walk amongst them and just listen quietly, because I must use a different passageway to and from my office and never go amongst them."

His two companions and I agreed that he ought to examine his own attitudes. I added, "We can only avoid misunderstandings if we love others. Our conscience can guide us. The Spirit can teach us. There is a good Greek Proverb, 'Know yourself'. The Spirit of God helps us to do this and to change, if we perceive that we are wrong."

"My friends won't tell me whether I am wrong or making mistakes." He asserted.

"Then go to your wife," I suggested.

"She won't tell me either", was his reply.

"Maybe your children can do this," I added.

"Yes! Sometimes they ask me why I am so irritable," he admitted.

"My wife helps me," I continued, "and if I am unhappy, she will try to find out why, and help me to become happy again."

"Yes, my wife does that too," he added.

It was time, however, to leave him and his friends and to return to Greta and Margaret, so I thanked him for the coffee and our fellowship, and bade them farewell.

How different indeed are the Indians and the Chinese. The former seem so alive to, and aware of, spiritual things : the latter are reserved and practical. We met at the hotel main door, next day. He was just leaving the hotel and Qingdao. "The Lord be with you", I said with a gentle smile.

"The Spirit be with you," he replied with sincerity.

The Chinese have a saying, "Within the four seas, all men are brothers."

Next morning we awoke to our final day at Qindao. The bill worked out at about 10-Yuan a day for three meals a day for three people, in total 91.50-Yuan (£30.50). Our friend Margaret paid the cost of the hotel accommodation as a gift to us in lieu of not being able to provide accommodation herself in her College rooms.

At the Travel Service office I learned that our boat journey from Qindao to Shanghai would take 25 hours, 3pm to 4pm the next day; whilst the fare would be 25.80-Yuan each, plus 1.50-Yuan booking fee each, a total of 54.60-Yuan (£18.20), plus the usual telegraph fee to Shanghai of 10-Yuan. At a rough guess, the journey would be something like 300 miles.

Margaret and Greta came to meet me at the Travel Office hotel in the college car, and we returned for our morning with the University students again. There were fourteen of these future university teachers of English present and they gave us an enthusiastic welcome.

Greta started off the class lecture by describing what had happened to us over the weekend – our walk around the seaside, and to a park where flowers had been arranged to look like dragons; our visit to the local Christian Church, including the baptism of over 50 people of various ages, followed by the Holy Communion service. The student teachers seemed amazed. All of this, of course, was in English.

In their turn, the students told us, one by one, in English, what they had done over the weekend. Some had gone on walks or watched films on TV, or done some revision of the lessons. One of them had returned to his Qingdao home where his mother still lived; his wife worked in somewhere like Jinan where she also looked after their two children. All the students were able to express themselves very clearly in their second language, and obviously enjoyed doing so.

In the second session, they divided into two groups of seven, with Margaret sitting in, first at one, and then at the other group, and all in the one classroom. With part of my mind, I could hear Greta talking about weddings and about Christmas customs in England, as well as our custom of different rates of pay for different types of work, arising out of questions from the students. When we exchanged groups for a time, she had to deal with problems such as 'Who is the boss of the family? Who looks after the money? What is the relationship with mothers-in-law? What happens to old people in the Old Peoples' Homes?' They also discussed Voluntary Organisations such as 'Help the Aged'. At the break between sessions, the students elected to go on discussing, and Greta took the opportunity to ask their opinions on the recent Chinese Government edict of 'One family, one child'. They all agreed it was good for the nation but bad for the children and for young people and young married couples. One older student found her teenage son difficult and wished he might be sent into the countryside to work there, whilst

Greta told them about Army service and conscription, and about employment and unemployment problems. (Of course, some of this I gleaned later when we had finished the classes.)

In the groups to which I had talked, in my turn, I mentioned the difficulty and the usefulness of thinking in English and dreaming in English (as I found myself sometimes doing so in Chinese). One of them told us, to our amusement, that last night he had dreamed about his English lesson and of being unable to answer the questions!

So we tried a little experiment. I recited in English that well-known poem by Thomas Hood:

> "I remember, I remember, the house where I was born,
> The little window where the sun came creeping in at morn:
> He never came a wink too soon nor brought too long a day ..."

Word by word, clause by clause, sentence by sentence, and then the whole stanza, we recited together the poem. Each student then attempted to recite it alone. It was very interesting to see how quickly they were able to do so. They were now, I suggested, really thinking in English!

Then I invited them in turn to explain the stanza in English and finally to say what they remembered of their own house/home where they were born. One of them remembered how he was born in a temple (the word 'miao' in Chinese), another in a mud cottage, another in a cottage on a hill with trees and birds; another in a brick house; whilst one could not even remember where he was born!

Greta had asked her group about their own weddings. One described how she and her boyfriend had gone to the 'Registrar' taking a photograph and received a 'piece of paper' (no doubt a certificate) and they were then considered to be married, but after a short period, presumable for investigation, and in case of impediment. It only cost them 50 fen or 75 fen (i.e. half a Chinese dollar or three quarters of a dollar, or in sterling, about 16-24p). After receiving the certificate, they visited his family and had a wedding feast. Later, they both visited her family.

Another man student told us that there were some other customs like hanging up a pair of broken chopsticks (over the door?) and having a meal which had to include chestnuts, so wishing the bride the joy of having children. However today, they said, many young people do not want a big feast.

Greta mentioned that in England many young people do not have a church wedding because they are not Christians. She also told them about our No. 3 son who went to a Greek Island to be married. He and his English fiancée were unable to do so, as they were not members of the Greek Orthodox church. Instead they had to journey on to Egypt where they were married in an English Church. This aroused very great interest indeed.

During the break, one of my group wrote in Chinese on the blackboard a spontaneous (?) poem about us all meeting again and when would we meet? So I wrote on the blackboard, in turn, those memorable lines from Shakespeare's 'Macbeth':-

"When shall we three meet again
In thunder, lightning or in rain?
When the hurly-burly's done,
When the battle's lost and won."

They all understood and enjoyed that.

In the second group, I used another two poems in the same way. First, Blake's:-

"Tiger! Tiger! Burning bright
In the forests of the night
What immortal hand or eye
Could frame thy fearful symmetry?"

They had an interesting time with that! When I asked where one finds tigers, someone answered, "In the Zoo!" and why the 'burning bright?': "Both his eyes and his stripes." So also, with the 'forests of the night': "Why 'forests' and 'night'?" "Well, the forests and the night are dark." And 'immortal'? This excited them. Various explanations were forthcoming like '*in*visible', another negative prefix. But 'immortal hand or eye?' One of them dared to add, "God's hand and eye".

What discussion followed! "God? – that is superstition", said one very attractive young girl. "Evolution produces species". "But what or who creates evolution?" "Yes, there are British scientists who believe in God". "But where did the universe come from?" "What was there before the universe existed?" "Science deals only with facts – this is only speculation!"

The questions and discussions waxed furious. Almost without thinking, their questions in English and their answers, tumbled forth spontaneously. Their atheism, or agnosticism, and their intellectualism gave place to inner concern, inner longing to grapple with the ultimate questions of existence.

Going off at a tangent, I began to discuss with them the two films in Chinese shown over the weekend on China's TV, "Red Peony", about the child acrobat in a circus, and "Hu Shan", which we ourselves had seen, both produced in beautiful colour and with real expertise, by employees in a Communist State.

"In each film", I said, "the heroine, at a certain point, cries out, "Shang-di, help me" ('Shang-di' is a Chinese term for God). What do you think of that?" Some thought it was simply an empty saying, meaning nothing.

By this time they were all speaking very freely in English. So I took them to yet another poem, one by George Macdonald, of whom they had almost certainly never heard, and from his 'At the back of the North Wind':

"Where did you come from, baby dear?
Out of everywhere into here.
And where did you get your eyes so blue?
Out of the sky as I came through.
And where did you get that pearly ear?
God spoke, and it came out to hear.
And how did they all just come to be you?
God thought of me, and so I grew."

Again they were intrigued. Here God's 'being' cropped up again. Dr. Dai, the Communist Party Secretary, or representative for the college, seemed specially interested and began to join in the discussion. We began to discuss the nature of man, and I quoted from the contemporary but deceased Chinese Marxist revolutionary writer who had a special monument built in his honour in Beijing – Lu Hsun. "Did Lu Hsun not say that in the natural world, species do not eat their own kind, but yet man eats man."

Mr. Dai replied, "Lu Hsun was only referring to landlords and peasants."

"But," I asked, "what about the Cultural Revolution and the Red Guards?"

Mr. Dai was taken aback. And I continued, "What is the cure for the evil in man? Is it not love?"

However, time had run out. We had to have lunch and then go immediately to the quay to board our boat for Shanghai. Mr. Dai, with a very friendly smile, said that he would make sure that we would get to the boat on time. Indeed, he would send the official college car for us, and come to see us off himself. We were very grateful and the students seemed pleased and when, in a slight excess of mischief, I told the students that in English we had a saying, "Never say die!". They were all highly amused, including the Party Secretary himself, and they eventually interpreted it to mean, "Never give up".

After lunch, at 2pm promptly, Mr. Dai duly appeared with the car, and very regretfully told us that he himself could not accompany us to the quay and the boat, because he had to visit a student teacher, one of Margaret's class, who was ill in hospital. He wished us a very courteous 'farewell' and, with a nice smile, left us to the care of the students.

Almost all the students were there waiting for Greta and Margaret and me, as we got out of the car at the Landing Stage. They loaded us with apples and, with great cheerfulness, escorted us to the ship. Seven of them, even, were allowed through the barrier, past the ticket collectors (who were women), possibly because they all insisted on carrying the various pieces of our hand luggage and our heavy bags. They led us on board and to our proper cabin. Great was our surprise, and I think theirs, that one of the other two sharing the cabin with us was a friend of one of the students!

Certainly the Lord looks after us, and we thanked Him. After the inevitable many handshakes and expressions of '"Farewell", "Come back again" and our sincere replies, "Come to England and visit us one day, if you can" they all finally went ashore with Margaret, waving from the quay and then from the gate, whilst I, through cupped hands, shouted to Margaret a farewell greeting to them, from Romeo and Juliet:

"Parting is such sweet sorrow".

It was too. As we ended another leg of our journey into Red Dragon country, another chapter of our adventures there, a mixture of joy and regret touched our hearts. The great ship on which we were passengers slipped away from the quay, out through the harbour and into the open sea, passing a group of small islands, two junks with sails aloft, numerous fishing boats, a rowing boat with three men fishing by line, and about sixteen liners from many countries and ports like Panama and Canton, with others of imperceptible origin and destination. There were even some naval craft, one flying the Yellow Flag of infectious disease, whilst on the quay now, in the far distance, we could see a great number of naval ratings marching in order into a large marshalling shed.

Loudspeakers in the dining saloon and in the lounges and cabins began gently pouring out a medley of various tunes and songs in Chinese, and even some classical music, like variations on the quick movement from Beethoven's Sonata Pathetique. After inspecting our cabin again, we noticed that it had four bunks, not opposite, as in a railway carriage, but at right angles, whilst there on a desk was the inevitable thermos flask and glasses. There was also a sofa and chair for our enjoyment. Having made our inspection and placed our baggage in the appropriate corners, we set off for the dining room, the time being 1700 hours, the time for supper. Pork liver and vegetables with rice was available, not very palatable but certainly cheap for 80 fen. We would have had the chicken had we seen it in time.

By the time we had finished, Green Island had disappeared into the dusk and the evening mist, and into the past.

Chapter 22

From Green Island to Wide Island
City of the Five Goats

It was good and relaxing to go to bed early, at 7pm, first to read and then to sleep. The night was long but comfortable. At 3am. I woke up and by the light of my bunk lamp, I read some of Basilea Schlink's book *Pollution*. An astonishing work linking up the various aspects of pollution in the world today, and demonstrating the cessation of real life on earth in the next generation, unless something is done on a world scale. Perhaps it is too late. The author saw the process as the fulfilment of scripture prophecies and leading to the return of Christ to the earth. The book presents a very serious world picture. It is eleven years since the book was first published. Greta and I may not live to see it confirmed but it is possible that our three sons may see it. Jesus Himself said, "No-one knows the hour but the Father alone". I find that statement both disturbing and reassuring. However, this did not prevent me from falling asleep again!

At 6am we woke up in time to greet the dawn. Greta had a lower bunk but I had an upper one and climbed down gingerly in the slight swell. Nor did we wish to wake our fellow passengers. Outside on deck, the dawn was nothing spectacular, but it was a simple reminder that God's love is new every morning. Hymns are simple and good teachers. Neither Greta nor I felt like taking breakfast, at least ship's breakfast, so we walked along the deck and ate an apple each instead, with a mental 'thank you' to those lively and thoughtful Qingdao students.

Greta was not feeling too well and had a slight fever in the night. Returning to the cabin, we lay on our bunks again and she went right off to sleep. I picked up a book entitled *The Hour that Changes the World* by an American Christian author named Dick Eastman, published in Michigan USA, printed first in 1979 and already into its seventh printing. The author is part of "Change the World Ministries" in the USA. The book is excellently and yet simply written, and described the power of prayer.

He suggests the division of a daily hour of prayer into twelve separate divisions, commencing and ending with prayer. The book is full of most apposite quotations from a multitude of authors from every part of the world, and contains many telling illustrations. The author had recently been to China, i.e. just before 1979, and described himself walking through a country commune. I wonder whether he had made the boat trip from Qingdao to Shanghai? After reading some chapters, I drifted into sleep.

We woke to changed weather conditions, strong winds, rougher seas and rain during the early part of the day. Occasionally we saw seabirds and, curiously, some pigeons and one tiny bird like a chaffinch, with the chaffinch's looping flight. What were they doing far out to sea? I could not see land, but perhaps we were hugging the coast somewhat. All these birds flew on ahead of the ship, so that they must have been travelling at over 18 knots. We also passed some other ships, which always aroused the interest of the Chinese passengers, with numbers of seagulls near them.

The size of the ship astonished us. There seemed to be over 1,000 passengers on board, including the only two foreigners – us! As more and more ships came into sight, we overtook them all. Marker buoys also began to appear, suggesting sea lanes as we drew nearer land and the entrance to the Shanghai waterway.

Amongst the passengers were some who had birds in cages, budgerigars and other small species. The cages and occupants aroused considerable interest amongst the people now gathering on deck; and so did the Nanjing 2nd Middle School teachers badges which we wore on our lapels. Some passengers asked us about them. Amongst these were a handsome young Chinese couple who engaged us in conversation. Then there was a young doctor (27 years of age, so he said) who worked in Qingdao and was having a short holiday in Shanghai. When he saw me looking at the cigarette he was smoking, he confessed that he did not smoke in the hospital.

"Many doctors in England have now given up smoking", I commented, "because of its harmful effects", at which he threw his cigarette into the sea. In talking, mostly in Chinese, he also included one or two English words and phrases, like "ship" and "boat". "What is the difference?" he asked, "are boats smaller and ships bigger? That's a buoy", he said, as one slipped by.

Another man who spoke some English was a sailor who had visited the USA, Canada, Australia and other countries.

Our ship did not dock or berth at Shanghai until 5.30 pm., over an hour late according to schedule. No doubt the night's and the morning's rougher weather had delayed her. However, the CITS agent was there at the ship to welcome us and take us to our hotel. This was the well-known Peace Hotel – "Yes," he said, "just at present this is the cheapest." The taxi had been waiting about an hour. The travel agent told us that the taxi fare was 6-Yuan (£3), a telegram to Canton would be 10-Yuan and the train fare would be about 360-Yuan (£120).

Having found our hotel room, No. 3316, and depositing our bags there, we went down to the dining room for supper of fried pork noodles, chicken noodles and Chinese tea, at 5.60-Yuan (£1.87). Reasonable and very satisfying, for we had not eaten much on the ship. Feeling replenished and fortified, we went across the main road to another sector of the Peace Hotel, where we looked around the attractive hotel shop, bought a Kodak colour film for 6.50-Yuan (£2.17) and a bar of milk chocolate to munch.

Returning to our room, we rested and watched the colour TV. The film or play on one channel was not very interesting, so we turned over to the channel showing a Chinese opera. This was most intriguing. The costumes and head-dresses were beautiful; the costumes had very noticeable long white sleeves, which were elegantly waved about. There were no masks but the sets and background scenes were lovely. The narrative text was set to music and to fit the music. To help viewers to understand, screen captions were added.

Eventually, we switched off the television and went off to sleep. Greta had a feverish spell during the night, with accompanying extraordinary dreams, including a car accident and an English friend, Mrs. Joan Kemp, who kept getting lost or going missing. After taking a Disprin-type pill, she went to sleep and awoke later feeling a little better but not absolutely well. However, a hot bath at 6.30 am., followed by breakfast at 7.20am (wet rice, omelettes, toast, butter, jam and coffee at 6.20-Yuan (£2.07)) improved her situation.

Paying our bill for one night (44-Yuan (£15)) and cheaper than what a young Chinese traveller, also from the ship, had to pay – we went with the CITS agent to the Travel Office. It was in the building across the road (the other half of the Peace Hotel) and we arranged by telegram our hovercraft journey from Guangzhou to Hong Kong, for Sunday at 2pm, five days later. However, on asking the cost of a certain "cheaper" Guangzhou hotel, we were told that it would probably cost 65-Yuan a night (£22)!

Calling a taxi to take us to the station, we went into the ticket office to buy our train tickets and two soft class sleepers (for 336-Yuan) plus the usual handling charges. Having given our young Travel Guide 20-Yuan to sweeten our parting, and for all his trouble last night, we boarded the train, found our bunks, as the train left at 9.15 am. Shanghai to Canton was a journey of 1180 kilometres or some 600 miles, so we settled down for a long ride and to see what new encounters the Lord was preparing for us. They were to prove most interesting and exciting.

Our two fellow passengers were a Mr. Tam, a young businessman from Hong Kong, 27 years of age, unmarried, selling machinery in China. The second, was an older man, 61 years of age, father of four children, and one grandchild, and employed in the Canton Government Planning Department. His name was Mr. Kim. These two, who had not met previously, discovered that they each came from the same village area near Guangzhou. Mr. Tam was able to converse in Mandarin, Cantonese and English, whilst Mr. Kim had only Mandarin and Cantonese, whilst we could converse in English and Mandarin, with a smattering of Cantonese. In consequence, we had amusing conversations in three languages. Some old friends and fellow villagers of Mr. Kim also kept appearing to say hello.

Eventually, a young Chinese girl joined us, and we welcomed her to share our lower bunk seat. It transpired that she was on her honeymoon. She shared with us the fact that in China today, those getting married get a permit from the Government to travel anywhere they please, of course, so long as they can afford to pay the fares. She and her husband, alas I forgot to note their name, being so interested in her story, had already travelled to places like Hangzhou, Shanghai, Beijing and Nanning. "You must have spent a lot of money," I remarked.

"Yes, we have done", she replied, and went on to tell us that she and her husband lived in her home because both her parents had died and she was bringing up her two younger sisters; this was proving quite a responsibility. She had a job as a statistician in Canton; he worked in Hong Kong.

It came out in her conversation that she had been attracted by seeing Greta and me sitting together so happily after thirty-four years of married life. With considerable openness, she asked about how we had met and become engaged, and many other personal questions, and did so with an entertaining and genuine glee.

"I hope my husband and I will be as happy for as long as you have been" she said with an attractive smile.

This gave us an opportunity to talk a little about peace of mind and contentment in life coming from our belief in God and in Jesus Christ.

"My husband is a Christian," she confessed, "but I am not yet one".

She went on to describe her wedding. They met either in her home or a hotel (I forget which), the guests having received invitations, and then had the wedding feast. They seem to have registered the marriage and had been given their honeymoon permit to travel. On her finger she showed us her wedding ring with a stone set in it. Although she looked about 18 years old, she was in fact 27, but she asserted that she had not waited simply in order to obey the Government's marriage-age rule, but rather because she had chosen to do so! This she said with considerable emphasis.

She was a very vivacious girl and often had the other two men in the compartment laughing and listening quite interestedly. Without displaying any unease, she sat with us for quite a long time.

"The men in my compartment sent me out!" she confessed

with a smile (because they wished to play chess or cards or something of the kind, I believe). So she found us. Like the others in our compartment, she spoke Mandarin, Cantonese and English, which all added to our colourful discussions. Feeling a certain sensitiveness towards her, neither Greta nor I asked about her feelings regarding the Government edict of 'one home - one child'. It seemed hardly the right time to mention it!

About 7.30pm all those in our coach were called to the dining car for supper. Not having had any lunch, and Greta feeling better, we were both hungry and enjoyed a bowl of chicken noodles each, and an extra dish of pork. Soon after 6pm we all four took to our bunks, and having read two or three chapters of *The Hour that Changed the World*, I spent a time in meditation prayer and went off to sleep without trouble, even after our stimulating afternoon.

The next day was Thursday and, as the Chinese would say, the 'double-eleventh', but also to us Armistice or Remembrance Day. Not that I thought about this, for having wakened about dawn, we witnessed the sun's rising, and the mountain and earth's mist disperse, and saw the beautiful Xiang-jiang (or Xiang River) somewhere between Changsha and Henyang. Our older fellow passenger, Mr. Kim, the Communist cadre, burst into song and then told me to describe the dawn in my diary! It was very reassuring and pleasing to observe such poetic feeling manifest itself in him.

We were briefly interrupted by the train steward who came in to give tickets for breakfast. Evidently he thought that bread, milk and eggs would be enough, but I persuaded him to give us the ticket for noodles as well.

There were, I reckoned, about 1,000 people on the train, for there were fourteen coaches (pulled by one diesel engine). Although in the soft class sleeper coaches, we were not too crowded, in the 'hard' or second class, the passengers would be very crowded indeed, as we had found on our earlier journey from Nanning when, accidentally, we had travelled hard class and in a non-sleeper coach. The train service obviously tried, or were prepared, to feed all the passengers. For the 'soft' class there was a restaurant car, which, outside meal-times, seemed to be available to any passengers to sit there, and for the majority there seemed to be boxes of food available on trolleys. Some passengers, probably to save money, brought or had bought their own food, for there was plenty of food to bc bought at the stations.

At some of the larger stations, especially as we drew nearer to Canton, which is in the warm South as compared with the colder North, there were rows of taps, with cold water, over long troughs, where people could wash their hands and faces. In our particular soft class sleeper coach, there was at one entrance a Western-style loo, and at the other end, a Chinese type, plus a water basin. These were locked on arrival at a station.

To us, one interesting custom or fact was how people came in and sat down in our compartment and began public conversation. After breakfast, and for a couple of hours, some young Hong Kong and Guangzhou Christians joined us, presuming probably and correctly as it happened, that Westerners like ourselves would be Christians. Maybe the honeymoon girl had passed on the information. In their free and lively conversation, they included, without any apparent embarrassment or suspicion, our older fellow traveller, who openly said that he was a Communist Party member and was employed in the Canton City Planning Department. The same was true of our younger companion, who also spoke freely about his travelling job, selling machinery including magnesium bars, and his Buddhist beliefs. The Christians had no hesitation in declaring their faith and in questioning (one might say 'evangelising') our companions, so we soon had an open discussion on Christianity and the Chinese Christian Church. Two of the young men explained that they were evangelists from Hong Kong, belonging to the Evangelical and Church Alliance, whilst a young girl or woman with them told us that she was a Pentecostal Christian of the Assemblies of God Church.

The group explained, with great enthusiasm and again without any hesitation, that they had been up to the Beijing area and had held evening meetings in the hills, in a large open space, to which came between 100/200 people. A number of these had become believers, including a married couple. They told us that in Hebei Province there were many House Churches, and that amongst the

Christians there was still felt to be some danger in, say, registering at a town church or in buying a Bible there.

The girl who was a member of the Assemblies of God Church, and who said she was 30 years old – but looked much younger – had been sitting in the corridor of the coach and outside our compartment earlier in the morning. Noticing her reading a book, I asked what it was and she showed me a copy of the New Testament plus The Psalms, in Chinese. I had also heard her singing quietly to herself, and the song proved to be the 23rd Psalm set to a new and irregular melody, which was pleasing. (I recalled the meeting in Hangzhou where the leader of the service had taught such a new Psalm 23 setting to the 800 congregation. However, I was unable to remember it if were the same.)

Whilst our two travelling companions went for lunch to the dining car, Greta and I remained in our compartment, eating some bread and egg sandwiches which we had saved from breakfast. As we were about to settle down for a brief rest, an appeal was broadcast over the train's loudspeaker, asking for any doctor to come and attend to a young man who had become ill. Greta immediately went along the train corridor and, three coaches along, found a man passenger in an epileptic fit. One of the young Hong Kong men, who was named Francis (after Francis Xavier) had accompanied Greta. Because the sick man was very big and heavy and lying on a top bunk, Francis was of great help. My wife tried the sick man's pulse at both wrists and neck. He had already lost consciousness, but examination of his eyes proved him still to be alive. Providentially, the train now stopped at a station, and when the patient was recovered sufficiently to speak, he agreed to being taken to the hospital at that particular place. With great difficulty, first in examining the man and secondly in lifting him down from the top bunk, Francis and my wife eventually manoeuvred the patient to the carriage door, where a train attendant helped to get him off to hospital. The man was now walking.

Because the train had stopped at a station, the interconnecting doors between coaches had been locked, thus naturally preventing the crowds of curious onlookers from gathering and hindering the operation. At the same time, Greta and Francis were unable to return by the train corridor but had to return by getting down and up from one coach to another via the platform.

In our compartment, another discussion now arose with Francis, who had begun to tell us something of his personal history. He was divorced from his wife who, along with his two daughters, were Roman Catholics. One of the daughters, apparently, was named Panacea! Although I did not ask the reason for this, it would have been most interesting to have learned the answer! Francis told us that he worked in a watch factory and sold watches. I could not resist telling him the story of William Paley, a famous Cambridge scholar and lecturer, who in writing about the origins of the universe, likened it to finding a watch. Both, he suggested, needed a designer to explain the fact of their existence. In each case, the designer was outside the realm of the object, be it universe or watch. It was impossible, therefore, to examine the designer by scientific method, to measure him or discover him. He could only reveal himself to us directly. Francis grew quite thoughtful about this. One of our evangelist friends also arrived again and had much discussion with Francis and also Buddhist Mr. Tam, who had been listening with interest.

Altogether, it had been a very evangelistic day. In spite of some inadequacies of language, we could only pray that some seeds sown might one day produce spiritual fruit. The further fact that our young Christian friends were only too ready to talk openly in front of our older companion, who was both a Government employee and a self-declared Communist Party Member, made us reflect upon the greater freedom of speech there is in China today.

Buddhist Mr. Tam's interest had also been aroused by the Christian Evangelist. They both carried on a real discussion about Buddhism and went on to questions from Mr. Tam about the reason for existence of both Protestant and Roman Catholics. Leading to the need of the Protestant reformers to oppose and reject the old faith and replace it with the new restored beliefs based on the original biblical revelation.

Eventually, the two young men left our compartment, as did my wife, whilst I was left alone with dear old Mr. Communist Kim. We began to talk together. As I remarked that we might never meet again, he became most affectionate, saying that Communists and Christians were in fact, co-operating in Jong Shan area in Guangzhou. He seemed quite moved by our farewells.

As the train now moved further into Gwangdong Province, the scenery grew increasingly spectacular and beautiful. The mountains rose higher and higher, the rivers more plentiful. For a change, the higher mountains were not unlike the Scottish Mountains at home. There were also many different kinds of craft on the rivers, which flowed through rugged gorges with occasional rapids and weirs. Small sampans were being poled up the current but many larger boats were engine-propeller driven. This, alas, meant a lack of the old picturesque sails. Occasionally a large passenger boat appeared, and some very long rafts of bamboo lengths tied together. There were also clusters of houseboats in considerable numbers. As we looked at this panoramic scene, Mr. Kim spoke up:

"You saw and photographed the sunrise this morning. Now you must watch and photograph the sunset. The sunset is always more beautiful".

"In England," I replied, "we are living by the seashore, and our house faces West and across the sea. The sunsets there are very beautiful too."

As we exchanged addresses, Mr. Tam returned to the compartment and did the same. Mr. Kim expressed the hope that he might be permitted one day to visit his sister (or was it his daughter?), who lived in Hawaii, and go on to England. Mr. Tam was his imperturbable self, just waiting to return to his flat in Hong Kong.

Guangzhou Station was crowded. We walked from the platform to find the Travel Service agent waiting for us, and after a longish walk, he led us to the CITS taxi-van. Our first move was to pick up our tickets for the Sunday boat journey to Hong Kong in three days' time. The Travel Service Office was still open. Our tickets cost us 60-Yuan (£20) plus the usual extras for service, taxi and arranging the tickets purchase – another 20-Yuan. The agent said he had fixed up for us a "cheaper" hotel – like Liu Hwa – which would only cost 36-Yuan (£12) per day instead of the 76-Yuan the Shanghai office had said. The taxi-van took us there and the agent left us to fix up the room ourselves at the hotel reception, and this we did.

Chapter 23

Gwangzhou or Canton
City of the Five Goats and Dr. Sun Yat Sen

Gwangzhou means the Wide Delta; it is "like a carpet of stony and muddy islands woven through with threads of channels and backwaters and drying brooks" – "it is not a port – it is thousands of ports. Where ever you look there is a quay and some boat or other, moored or afloat". So reads *The Face of Ancient China*, a lovely picture-dialogue volume, written by 'the authors'.

To me it was the Wales of China, part of the great land of China, but where everyone spoke Cantonese, much to our own and their confusion. Our knowledge of the Cantonese language is small, and we had spent over a month speaking only Mandarin. However, the hotel staff, the shopkeepers, and the man in the street proudly prefer to speak their own language dialect, rather than Mandarin. Cantonese really has no written form. The people here write the National Language, the written form of Mandarin, but speak their own patois. In churches, for example, while using the National Language translation of the Bible, the pastor will simply translate mentally and immediately; and, without effort, out from his mouth comes Cantonese. Compared with the beautifully rich tones of Mandarin, Cantonese is staccato, sharp, and abrasive, almost like a machine gun's sharp stutter. I think of the Cantonese people again as the 'cockneys' of China, quick-witted, small in stature, of rapid speech, westernised, exceedingly clever merchants who, being sea-bound on their southern-eastern coast, have ventured abroad into foreign kingdoms perhaps more than their other fellow countrymen.

Be all that as it may, we were duly able to fix up our hotel room, number 1356. It was a large hotel. A female porter quickly took up our luggage on a trolley. Through a series of steps and ramps she pushed trolley and luggage until she had found the building, the lift, the floor and the door keys (at the floor reception) of our room, and had opened the door to let us occupy the place and settle in. She then left us to our own devices.

Leaving our luggage safely in our locked room, we returned the same way and tried to find the dining room. It was a huge hotel, much larger than any we had found in the other cities we had visited, and absolutely throbbing with Cantonese vigour, excitement and chatter. Eventually we found by trial and error, what was probably the cafeteria. We ordered as best we could from a numbered Chinese menu, a meal of pork and vegetables, duck and bamboo shoots, and rice. It was more than adequate and cost only 6.40-Yuan (£2.14), included tea – green tea, a la Chinese, and was very refreshing.

The noise, the hubbub, chatter and the crowds in this cafeteria was unbelievable. Having enjoyed and finished our repast, we enquired about breakfast. Using a mixture of Mandarin, Cantonese and English, we found that we could have shi-fan (wet rice), plain omelette, bread, butter and jam, but no coffee at the restaurant. Coffee and extras can be had at the Coffee Room but not before 9 am.

Leaving the matter there, we toured the hotel, looked in at the shop, enjoyed noting the prices and examining some lovely scrolls, and then went up to bed. After enjoying a hot bath in our private bathroom, I set to work on my diary whilst Greta wrote some postcards. At 11 pm., we called it a day (or should one say a 'night'?) went to bed, read our Bibles, and had our prayer-time as usual, and were soon asleep, with thankfulness in our hearts for the day, the journey, new friends (who had helped us to find the churches in every city) and for our safe arrival.

Next morning, Friday, we were up at 7am and had a bath. Then out to find the proper dining room, which we discovered at last on the second floor (what in England one calls the first floor, with typical English illogicality), and we had to approach it through last night's cafeteria. Coffee was available here, as well as omelette, toast, butter and marmalade (none of your 'jam') and it cost us 6.70-Yuan (£2.23). Not bad really.

Returning to our room, we wrote letters and postcards until about 11 am. I also made a quick estimate of money needed for the last lap of our China journey:

The hotel bill would probably be 2½ x 36-Yuan	90.00-Yuan
Gifts to take home, say	150.00-Yuan
Taxi to the boat quay, say	4.00-Yuan
Meals still to take, say 5 x 6-Yuan	30.00-Yuan
Fruit to eat during our wanderings	2.00-Yuan
Laundry and buses, say	6.00-Yuan
Total	282.00-Yuan
	(£94.20)

So I thought I would sell £150 worth of Travellers' Cheques to be on the safe side in case of emergencies:

At 330.17-Yuan/£100	491.50-Yuan
Plus money/cash in hand	72.90-Yuan
Total	564.40-Yuan

Looking back over our previous Travellers' Cheques sales, I found that to be some	£950.00
Therefore, total cash sterling not used so far	+ £150.00
	£1,100.00

Going out into the town, we found the Telegraph Office and wrote out a telegram to send to Joyce Bennett in Hong Kong. The girl clerk in the office seemed to have some problems with the form, insisting eventually on reversing the order of the words in the English address. Presumably she thought it ought to be written according to Chinese address custom, where one begins with the country, followed by the town, then by the road name and so on, up to the person's name which comes last of all. Since the telegram was being sent to a destination outside China, it also cost more, much more in fact than our telegram from Beijing to Xingdao, although the distance between the latter two cities must be five times greater than from Guangzhou to Hong Kong. We now went out to find the churches. At least one of the Canton churches, the East Hill or Dong-Shan Church had a Saturday evening service at 7pm, for Seventh

Day Adventist Christians and for other Christians who work on Sundays but are free on Saturdays. They then have a Sunday service at noon! Only small numbers attend the Saturday service, but we were told that 1,000 people attend the Sunday service. There is a Sunday choir of forty members, all of whom wear white surplices, and most of whom are young people. Five clergy, including some who are retired, are attached to this church, and the minister is the Rev. Leung Lai-tong.

Baptism is administered by immersion, since the church has a deep baptistery under the platform. Holy Communion or the Lord's Supper is administered once every two months. At Christmas time and at Easter, about 3,000 attend the services. At this church, we saw plenty of Bibles, printed in the old version at Shanghai, in 1980. It included maps.

At our hotel, we met a very interesting and warm-hearted Christian named Mrs. Rae Freckleton, from Earlwood in Australia, who knew an old friend of ours, Archbishop Marcus Loane. Her husband was a Church of Christ Minister, very ecumenical in outlook and probably charismatic in Christian practice. We also met a Dr. Ian and Mrs. Fran Hutchinson from 43, Virginia Way, Abingdon, England.

At Zion Church, which we also found and visited on the other side of the City, there was a Sunday morning 12-noon service of 800 people. With 400 in the evening, most of whom were young people. On Wednesdays they held an evening Bible Study and Prayer Meeting. A young Christian of 19 years of age was employed by this church to keep the place clean and tidy. His father had been a preacher who had graduated from Nanjing Theological College, and his grandfather was a Christian, as was his mother.

In a cupboard in the church, we were shown a large number of Bibles in the new Shanghai printed edition, which cost 5.60-Yuan (£1.87) a copy, together with new hymnbooks printed in the new Chinese script.

The young man told us that recently there had been a Youth Conference at which 50 young people had been present.

At their morning service, they had a choir of 60 older women;

and at the evening service a choir of 40 young people. Last year, he said, 10 men had been ordained, presumably in the whole of China, and in the Three Self-Patriotic Christian (Protestant) Church.

The next church we found and visited was the South River Church. The minister himself was away at a conference, but we were told by another official that they, too, had a regular service at noon each Sunday at which 300 believers attended whilst their choir, including many young people, numbered about 40. On Thursdays, at 7.30pm there was a Bible Study and Prayer Service. There was no Youth Group as such, but many young people attended the Sunday services. They also had over 80 copies of the 1980 Shanghai printed Bible stored in a cupboard, and many soft-back hymn books containing perhaps 150 hymns and printed locally. As with the other churches. Holy Communion was celebrated on the first Sunday, every second month. There were 10 ordained ministers in the whole Canton area; each of the three churches had three (I did not ascertain what happened to number 10). The attendance at the great festivals of Easter and Christmas was much greater than the average weekly congregation. The actual church building itself was the smallest of the Canton churches we visited and very simple in its construction and layout.

Each of these three churches printed a complete outline of the Sunday service, giving details of lessons, hymns and anthems, including introits and vespers, and the names of those leading prayers, reading lessons and preaching. On the obverse side were printed also details of the coming week's activities and notices. These "outlines" were properly printed and not merely duplicated.

Having visited the Protestant churches in Guangzhou, Greta and I went to the Chinese Catholic Church of the Sacred Heart. In Cantonese, the name reads as follows: The Shek-Shap Heavenly Lord Church. We were very gladly welcomed by a lady worker, who might have been the housekeeper equivalent of an English Roman Catholic Presbytery. There was also a young woman acting rather the role of the church secretary. They called one of the priests who I gathered was the Rector. Whilst Greta held a long conversation with the lady worker, I talked to the priest. He asked us to convey his greetings to our own local Roman Catholic priest in Hoylake, one of my own friends. The story was much the same as at the other Roman Catholic churches we had visited.

Father Lin, the Rector, was 69 years of age, as I was myself. We shook hands on that! He had spent 41 years here as priest and had been trained at the Aberdeen Seminary in Hong Kong. He was, of course, of Chinese race. As in the other Catholic churches in China, they used the Latin Mass. As a Chinese Catholic Church, they were not allowed by Government to have any contact with the Pope. On Sundays, some 400 attended Mass, and at the main service a choir led the singing, but was not robed except at Great Festivals. Many young people attended the services and recently they had held a Youth Conference in which many of their young people were involved. There were few, if any, baptisms, since none were allowed by Government edict under 17 years of age, with the exception of young children of foreign nationality persons (perhaps meaning embassy staff persons and other foreign officials).

Around the church, there were a number of buildings formerly owned by the church. Since 1979 or 1980, the Government had allowed the church to receive rent for the use of these buildings. This money helped to support the work of the church and its ministry. The buildings included a former church primary and secondary school, which were now closed. These buildings had now been sold and the proceeds were available to help the work of the church.

One of the problems of this particular church was that the priests were now all advanced in years and the supply of younger priests was very uncertain. From other cities, we had heard that there was hope of seminaries being opened to train new men.

As we left the church, we noticed that it was surrounded by beautiful gardens, kept up by the church members, and we saw many lovely flowers blooming even this late in the year in the middle of November.

At supper in the hotel that evening, we met Mrs. Rae Freckleton from Australia again. Her pastor husband had in fact recently died, and at his funeral,, she told us, there were people from all the denominations present, from Pentecostal to Anglican. Listening to his wife, one could easily guess that both he and she had experienced the Pentecostal or charismatic power of the Holy Spirit.

After supper, Mrs. Freckleton came with us back to our room, where she had a long talk with my wife, and occasionally me, about how and where to contact the churches in China. She took notes on the addresses in Canton of the different churches in the hope of being able to visit them before she flew to Beijing the following day. We also gave her directions about churches in Beijing and in Guilin, which she planned to visit.

In conversation, she told us how she had earlier felt the Holy Spirit's call to visit Turkey and China, and now she was obeying that call. We were invited to visit her in Australia, whilst we invited her to visit us in England. Travelling with her was a young American girl, who had been helping in one of the churches in Hong Kong, who had also spent some time in Israel, and who now planned to visit China, with yet another girl friend. They all had Pentecostal connections, and their experience of and faith in the indwelling Holy Spirit undoubtedly drew them together in a common bond and across the bounds of their denominations.

With a hug and a kiss, Mrs. R. F. eventually bade us a fervent farewell. Her favourite word was "beautiful" – which she said meant for her "God's activity is beautiful to see".

That evening I began to run a slight fever and I had a dry throat. I did not have a very good night and another slight wave of fever came upon me. Otherwise, I felt right enough if rather languid and heavy. As for Greta, she had a touch of cramp but otherwise slept well.

Breakfast next morning, Saturday 13th November, consisted of the usual shi-fan, omelette, toast, butter, marmalade and coffee. It tasted good, so I guessed I was better! It cost us 7.40-Yuan (£2.47). During breakfast, we admired the rice bowls we were using. On enquiry, the waitress said we could buy them from the hotel. This proved to be possible and we purchased 10 bowls and 10 Chinese spoons in similar design, for 20-Yuan (£6.67). We intended to use them as presents on our return home. For safer travel, the waitress kindly wrapped them up carefully and put them in a cardboard box.

Leaving the hotel to walk into the City sight-seeing and to look for other gifts, we felt the weather to be warmer than the last two days, but still quite pleasant. It can get hot and sticky in Canton even in mid-November. Strolling through a lovely park, we were attracted by pleasant pools and streams, decorative bridges, and colourful flowering shrubs, and a variety of flowers and trees. There were some chrysanthemums being trained by tying the stems to thin bamboo sticks and spreading them out from the centre in a kind of chimney sweep's brush. There were many potted bushes and the whole was covered with birds.

There were also many parties of children, with their teachers, each carrying their water bottles at their waists and possibly filled with tea. Many youngsters were rowing on the lake, thoroughly enjoying themselves. The boats were of different shapes, one being like a great swan. Our path led through bamboo woods or plantations, and low hills. Eventually we heard what sounded like a railway train rushing along, but on investigation, it proved to be a figure-of-eight roller coaster and other fair merry-go-rounds. Nearby, we came across a full-sized football stadium, shaped like an amphitheatre, with rising stone seats on all sides, not quite as large as the Liverpool Football Ground. There was a large clock, with the face marked for 45 minutes, obviously for players and spectators alike, 45 minutes being the normal time for each half of a match in England and, I imagine, world-wide. England could with profit copy the idea, I think.

Emerging from the beauty of the Park, we came to one of the main City streets, where we tried to find a music shop, which I had noticed yesterday from the bus. This shop we duly found and, near to it, one that sold Chinese musical instruments, where we bought a Chinese two-stringed fiddle and bow for 32.96-Yuan (£11.00). This fiddle we earmarked for our No. 2 son at home.

However, what about No.1 son? Eventually, we found for him a charcoal-cooking stove, normally used on the dining table, called a "hor-gor" or fire cooking pot. In a trough round the central chimney (which contained smouldering charcoal), the cook or housewife would put water and add chopped-up meat and vegetables. These are served up piping hot, more fresh meat and vegetables being added as required. The whole thing looked very 'posh' ("port out, starboard home", as on the old China passenger liners!) and cost just over 15-Yuan or £5. Finally, for our three daughters-in-law, we found three lovely damask tablecloths, with beautiful Chinese designs, and in varied colours of material. Each cost 23-Yuan (£7.70) and, in my wife's eyes, very reasonable at that. All the presents, of course, were of real Chinese manufacture and so doubly attractive as gifts.

Somewhat weary after walking in the heat through the traffic and the crowds, we returned by trolley bus to the hotel. After an iced Coca-Cola and orange drink to cool us down, we went to the hotel dining room for a bowl of noodles and pork each, somewhat expensive at 7.40-Yuan (£2.47), but delicious. As we were due to leave Canton tomorrow, Sunday, soon after midday, I paid the hotel bill, 3 days at 36-Yuan, posted various letters and postcards, had supper (not very good – a dish of steamed rice and chicken, one of pork, and Chinese tea) all for 5.50-Yuan (£1.83) – and so to bed, and slept well.

Next morning we were up betimes, had a bath (very necessary in that humid climate) and packed up all our gifts. They were many and a little bulky, but Greta found space for all of them in our two larger cases, except for the food bowls which, in their cardboard box, went safely into her red knapsack, whilst the hor-gor (normally Romanised by 'hwo-gwo') and the fiddle were in their own separate boxes.

After breakfast, we posted more letters, leaving the appropriate cash with the postal clerk for him to add the stamps – he was most obliging. Feeling the need to buy fruit for the journey, we went out on to the street, but had to be content with three oranges, not having enough loose change for more. The shopkeepers in the street market seemed unwilling or unable to change my 10-Yuan foreigner's money (or travellers' cheques) into the local currency. This was just as well, for I would probably have lost any local money left over as we passed through the Chinese Guangzhou customs.

On returning to the hotel, we lay on our beds to read and rest until departure time. Greta actually went off to sleep. Then at 11.15am we assembled our luggage and took it downstairs to Reception, where we showed our receipted bill, surrendered our keys, and took back our passports.

En route to the quay and the boat, we decided to call at Dong Shan Church to share in some ten minutes of their Sunday morning service. However, our taxi driver knew all the short back ways to the church and we arrived 17 minutes before service time. The taxi driver agreed to wait for us and we went into the church, which was only just beginning to fill up.

As we sat down in a pew, Greta found herself sitting beside a Chinese woman, who proved to be both a Christian and a doctor of Chinese traditional medicine. She was trained in the Guangzhou Institute of the discipline for three years, and had been a qualified doctor for twenty-five years. Her parents had also been Christians, and as she, their daughter, attended their church, she eventually decided it was the only answer to all life's problems and made a personal decision to commit herself to God and to Jesus as Lord and Saviour.

In the meantime, I had seen another foreigner sitting nearby and I went over to make his acquaintance. This was equally as interesting a meeting. He was, he said, an American, and an attorney in President Reagan's office in the White House. He said, in his typical drawl:

"I pray daily for the President, who himself really is a Christian, and I also pray daily for Chairman Yu Hua-bang of the Chinese Republic."

Obviously, he himself had an interest in China, but I did not have the time or the opportunity to ask about that. With him were two Chinese Americans and another Chinese, possibly a pastor, from Hong Kong. The latter, hearing that formerly I myself had been a pastor-missionary in the former Chinese Episcopal Church or 'Sheng Kung Hui', asked me if I knew a Hong Kong pastor called Lee. It may have been one of my acquaintances, but Lee as a name is common, or more so, in Hong Kong or China, than Smith is in England, and I could not identify the man.

About 11.55am, and as the church was rapidly filling up, we reluctantly took our leave of these new companions and the church officials, to the sound of the church bell ringing, and of recorded music being played over the loudspeaker system.

The church itself was large. It had a long Holy Table set against the back wall of the chancel, or rather sanctuary, since the choir sat elsewhere, and on the table was a large cross with lovely flowers, nicely arranged on either side. There must be hundreds of thousands of Christian churches so arranged all over the world! The church also had a balcony, almost as large as the ground floor auditorium, in which many people were now sitting. There would almost certainly be over 1,000 people when the service began, but we had no time to discover this. Our taxi and taxi-driver were waiting.

The driver, who had a friend with him, drove his machine at great speed across the City towards the quay some few miles away. Both of them spoke in Mandarin and conversation began.

"We are friends and we both come from Qingdao", they said, and in answer to our questions added, "No, we have never attended a Christian service in the church there, we have little opportunity".

The driver's friend asked us, "In order to join the Christian Church, or to attend, would we have to undergo special training, as we would if we wished to become Buddhists?"

We answered, "Anyone can attend a church service, but to join the church, special preparation would be necessary."

"In that case" said the driver, "we may attend one day".

It was useful, and to them interesting, that we had just come from Qingdao, and we were able to tell them about our visit to Qingdao, and of the two services we had attended, with 900 people at 11am, and the baptism of 50-plus people before 600 people on the Sunday afternoon. They both showed some interest. I imagine that in the early days of the Christian Church, in the apostolic period and long after, in some such ways was the Gospel gossiped about on the roads of Palestine and all the way, through present Turkey, Macedonia, Greece and Italy to Rome.

Now our taxi journey ended, as well as our conversation, at the Hong Kong Steamers Quay. With a "Goodbye" and 10.80-Yuan (£3.60), we took our farewell of the two men, not a little relieved that it only cost so much, for it had been a long drive and driver had had to wait nearly 20-25 minutes outside the church. The Customs

Officials gave us no trouble at all, with no enquiries about gifts, and only asking for Greta's larger case to be opened for inspection. This was very cursory; they saw the clothes and gave us permission to move through. Nor did they ask for receipts of purchases, but simply asked about our Chinese money. The special foreigners' money, they said, must be changed at a Bank of China. As for local Chinese currency, "You may keep that", they said.

The Customs Officials were really quite courteous and friendly, and even asked us if we had enjoyed our visit to China. They looked pleased to our answer of "Yes". These formalities took five minutes, which left us with two hours to spare until the Hong Kong steamer departed at 2.25 pm.

In the meantime, we discovered that we were to travel on a catamaran hovercraft, and we waited patiently to experience yet another form of China travel. Quite a large number of passengers had begun to assemble. Most were quiet and orderly, but a group of American (US) forces personnel were rather noisy and loudly talkative, but not rowdy. They were none the better for intoxicating liquor that they seemed to be drinking. A pity really. They were not very good "ambassadors" (in St. Paul's sense) of their country, their culture and their religion.

The catamaran was called the Liuhua Lake, Liuhua being also the name of our Canton Hotel, as well as of a well-known lake in the area. Obviously quite newly built, it was very spic and span indeed. In the large saloon, right at the bows, it looked like a large modern jumbo plane, having four sections of seats separated by two wide passageways, i.e. 3 seats/3 seats, passage; 3 seats. The seats were all inclined backwards for better resting or sleeping, with a headrest at the top like a modern car seat. The upholstery was both comfortable and attractive, there was plenty of leg-room, and the whole deck was carpeted.

Within this lounge or saloon, there was a counter for buying food and drinks, including fizzy orange in cans as well as tea and coffee. As far as we noticed, there were no alcoholic drinks. The two toilets were good, adequate and clean. At the rear of the lounge were two doors, either side, opening out on to a small rear bridge or platform, open to the weather yet warm, since hot air ducts came up and out and over at that point. We went out to stand and walk the few paces there, three or four times, looking astern at the turbulent wake of the ship and towards receding China. It was pleasant. About a dozen people could gather on this platform, the hardier ones! The remaining passengers rested in their comfortable inclined seats. There were 150 seats, according to my counting, and only three were vacant.

Next to me sat a young Chinese businessman, very modern in dress and appearance, resembling one of our better-dressed businessmen in England. With him were his wife and two children. I was amused to see, first the boy and then the girl, brush their father's hair. We struck up a long conversation. He said he was not a Christian, but his children (and possibly his wife – I forget) were being taught the Christian faith and were attending church. He believed that China was better now than it was earlier, but not as ordered or as good as Taiwan. In China, he went on, there was not yet real freedom. When I told him of our visit to China, about the vigorous churches there and of our earlier work as missionaries in Guilin and other places, he was very interested.

Greta in the meantime had contacted an American businessman who had been with General Stilwell during the war. He had been over the Hump (i.e. the Himalayas) like me. When I told him of our early experiences in Guilin, and in particular of the choir of thirteen American Colonels who attended our English language service there, he was exceedingly surprised. He had also known the Friends' Ambulance Unit, in which, during the Sino-Japanese War, Greta's brother had worked.

Only too soon, we had arrived near our destination and began to travel through all the picturesque scenery of the lovely Hong Kong harbour. Lan Tau Island duly came into view; we sped past it, but not before we had noticed the large power station at shore level – once a rocky beach – and many large buildings. We could also see the 3,500 feet peak where we used to spend our August holiday, away from the very hot and sticky climate of Kowloon and Hong Kong. Quite a procession of ships were coming from and going into the harbour, one of them another hovercraft going at great speed out towards the approaches to Canton (Guangzhou).

As we drew nearer and nearer to the City of Victoria and the tip of the Kowloon peninsula, so the darkness of evening came down upon us. All the lights of the colony began to sparkle, glow and spread, until the wonderful fairyland of Hong Kong at night became a reality.

Our venture into Red Dragon country had finally come to an end. It was still Sunday November 14th, 1982.

Chapter 24

Return to Fragrant Harbour and Nine Dragons Country

Faithful, energetic, the Rev. Honourable Joyce Bennett OBE had been waiting for us at the ship's berth for over an hour, due to some delay in our arrival. Her little Mini Austin car soon transported us back to her flat in St. Catherine's School in Ngau Tau Kok. Some of that evening was spent in giving Joyce some account of our adventures. We were glad to be back, and we were each one stone lighter in weight.

The next day, Monday, Greta spent the morning washing clothes, and I worked out our accounts for the journey. It was good just to relax and reflect. However, in the afternoon, Headmistress Joyce, asked us to take some English Oral examinations with some of her pupils.

The girls, between 14 and 15 years of age, showed good ability in the hearing and speaking and understanding of English. I heard the *Old Ladies of Mumbling Hill* poem, many, many times, until I was almost mumbling myself. Some of them had also read, amongst other books, *The Tale of Two Cities* and *Fairy Stories*. Quite a number of them, in giving brief biographies of themselves, said they were Christians. Although they all looked spotless in their school uniforms, some were living with their families in one-room homes, with the families being sometimes between five and eight in number. As an exercise in remembering and speaking English, I taught some of them Thomas Hood's poem, "I remember, I remember,, the house where I was born". It was shades of China proper again. These young girls learned it almost as quickly as those Chinese graduates in Qingdao.

One girl told me that her brother was in the University, and she hoped to qualify to go there also. She wished to read Economics. Although she was in the Bookkeeping Typing stream in the school academic system, she really showed some artistic talent or knowledge and eventually hoped to become an artist or study architecture.

The next day we journeyed into Kowloon city centre and checked up on our account in Barclays International Bank and withdrew the remaining credit balance from our joint account, which was some £122. From there, we walked to St. Andrew's Church Centre and visited the Christian Bookshop on the second floor. This was run as a kind of inter-varsity bookshop that dealt specially with students. We were able to buy books as presents for Joyce and for our now distant friend Margaret in Qingdao and for other friends. Christmas cards, however, were scarce and unsuitable, both at the shop and in the Lutheran Bookshop nearby.

A visit to the Vicar of St. Andrew's and his wife and family produced a very acceptable cup of tea. On the previous Sunday, the preacher had been an ex-Overseas Missionary Fellowship member (formerly known as the China Inland Mission). He had recently visited the Kunming area, including the House Churches there, where he found a rising suspicion that the Chinese Government would again try to oppress the Christian Church there within two years. The Vicar, or it may have been the Preacher, felt that their information came from the grass roots level, whereas the Hong Kong folk like Joyce, operating in Hong Kong Government circles, did not really know what was going on. There was some suspicion, also, at the grass roots that the Chinese Government might well take over the Colony about that time too. The suspicion was 17 years too early!

It was inevitable that we should turn to discussing the problem of Freddie Wong and others like him as Priscilla Tze, who want the old wine in old bottles in church worship, or to pour the new modern wine into the old bottles if that were possible. Ken Coleman, the Vicar, and his wife said they really loved Freddie but were irritated by his way of always waiting until the discussion or the meeting was nearly over and then to give his own point of view – usually anti-progress. Some people, they said, felt it was time Freddie retired from the Church Council. We put in a good word for both Freddie and Priscilla.

Next morning after breakfast, we went into Kowloon again to buy some more presents for home. At the China Products Emporium, there was nothing suitable and everything was too dear. At the Hong

Kong Welfare Lutheran shop we were more successful and bought two dolls for our two granddaughters and a miniature brass gong with an engraved happiness character for our friends Bob and Edna, who were living in and looking after our Hoylake house.

For lunch, we had been invited to the Kowloon Cricket Club by Freddie and were able to have a long talk with him about his family, his wife and himself. He certainly showed real Christian conviction and seemed to respond to our urging that he should try to help St. Andrew's in positive rather than negative ways. "I still say my prayers", he told us, "and I sometimes read my bible. I keep the old Family Bible. I do not like all the present emphasis in St. Andrew's on external missions, (i.e. giving to groups outside the church when the church itself is in debt), although I do acknowledge that Jesus Himself told His disciples to go into all the world and preach the Gospel." The problems of this Western Chinese Church, involving both groups and Eurasians as well, seemed so different from the Christian Church in China. Truly, it was a different world, and we found ourselves preferring the China pattern and the China spirituality on the whole.

There was no doubt, however, about Freddie's sincerity, and we urged him to help Mr. Coleman. Freddie again told us about the Roman Catholic Christian who, when Freddie was young had seen him, his brother and sister playing out on Sundays. The neighbour had then himself taken them to St. Andrew's Church seeing that they did not know where the Anglican Church was. We hoped he would try to do the same for others.

Returning to St. Andrew's, we met the Rev. Denham Crary, that old colleague of mine, a Eurasian by birth, who had deliberately married a Chinese girl, presumable choosing to identify with the Chinese race, and perhaps Chinese culture, rather than western. He looked and sounded very much the same as 25 years ago. In his cheerful, carefree or independent way, he was still very critical of 'that bunch' who went to the Bishop's weekly breakfast for clergy. He was not impressed at all by our account of the hundreds, even thousands, who attended the churches in China, and who readily accepted hour-long sermons!

"What's the use of that?" he exclaimed. "Just sitting there and listening. Why don't they all return to their House Churches, and, if there are not enough ordained men, let laymen take services and celebrate Holy Communion? The return to church buildings", he continued, "is always a financial burden, and is a backward step".

His mind was as vigorous as ever it had been, and listening to him now, I recalled those brilliant sermons he had preached long ago, in language (whether English or Chinese) which showed a kind of natural understanding of prevalent philosophical and theological and religious ideas, whilst seeing through them to the real truth.

When we began to speak about prayer, he said, "My wife and I never have prayers together at home. What we have to do and try to do is to be Christ to others, and to say to others not 'Do what I say' but 'follow me'"! At first I thought he said or meant "Follow Christ", but in fact, he affirmed that he said and meant "Follow Denham Crary, or follow Eric Hague!" "Christ has no hands but our hands", he quoted, asserting that God could not act at all without us.

However, our time was up and we had to say a very sincere farewell. As we went away, I asked myself, "Was Denham just being Devil's Advocate, perhaps, and mischievously trying to provoke us?" But he was not really speaking tongue in cheek when he criticised the Pope.

"Let him free his peoples from the 'no birth control' attitude and let him accept other Christians and other churches". No half measures suited Denham.

"And what do you think about China and Hong Kong?" he asked us.

I replied, "I feel it would be better if Hong Kong came into China now, but this is more difficult for Mrs. Thatcher and the British Government to say this."

"No," he urged, "Hong Kong should remain just where it is – a capitalistic society, where people could get a good livelihood and life. That is much better than being like drab China. There is no such thing as more equality. Take two boys. One is intellectually dull; the other may be intellectually brilliant. They could not possibly remain 'equal'."

He did not think much of my suggestion – 'equal before the law and before God'.

"What do you think about pacifism?" he asked me.

I said, "Theoretically, it is a Christian concept, in a personal and individual way. However, Christians and others have also to care for social and international justice. We should support Paul's teachings that we should obey Government and those whom God allowed to be over us."

Denham added, "I could not accept pacifism. The country and society gave us protection and we should value, and fight for, what it has given us."

It was a challenging discussion, perhaps disturbing too. Somehow we sensed that Denham was a little in danger of becoming anti-social and anti-fellow clergy, and that, instead of ignoring them and criticising, almost despising them, he should try to share himself and his convictions with them. As for God being helpless without us, was he not in danger of forgetting that God is finally in control of the universe, and in control of world events and world history, and it is not man. God could act and did act, through people or upon people even without their knowing – e.g. Cyrus, or St. Paul at his conversion on the Damascus Road. It is not that God cannot act without us, but that He prefers, if possible, to enlist our co-operation. "Work out what God works in", as St. Paul put it. God did not need us to create the world and the universe, not to keep it in being, nor to bring it to an end. He can and may – no will! – do that without us and in spite of our opinions or desires, and even when He permits our stupid actions to result in the world's destruction, say through the nuclear bombs.

Denham may not, I think, hold to the Bible as the inspired word of revelation of God's will and purpose for mankind. However regretfully, and mutually, we said "Goodbye, and God bless you". Then off we went to meet Priscilla Tse.

Priscilla used to be my church secretary. As arranged, she met us at the YMCA car park at 5pm, both she and her large air-conditioned car were at our disposal! So we went back to the church bookshop to get more books. Then, because of the complicated one-way street system, we made another long detour to the post office to post our letters to No. 1 son in England with details of our home journey. This accomplished, she took us out to her flat in Shatin, on a little hilltop in the New Territories. So efficient was the air conditioning that she opened the car window to let in some warm air since we felt a little cold.

Priscilla now gave us a lovely meal, cooked by her old amah who had been in the family since she was born. Her flat was beautifully decorated with wall scrolls, and with exquisite Chinese carved Blackwood chairs. There were two bathrooms with toilets, two bedrooms, a well-furnished kitchen, and everything most artistically arranged and with air conditioning to boot.

With quiet candour, she told us of her so-called 'love affair' after her marriage had broken down. "Now," she said "I really see it was wrong for me as a Christian, and I am faithfully seeking the Lord personally for forgiveness and true repentance, through my church, St. Andrew's."

Deeply glad and somewhat humbled, we left her and returned home on the Kowloon Shatin railway. This seemed even better than the Mass Transit Railway that served the inner city. The seats were wider apart and were made of very comfortable upholstery. We were soon at Kwun Tong Station, but had to wait in the road outside quite a long time until the proper bus came along. We arrived back at Joyce's school and flat about 9.45pm.

Next morning, Joyce took us in her Mini to the Cathedral weekly celebration of Holy Communion and clergy breakfast. We were welcomed back with hearty clapping by the clergy. The Holy Communion service was taken by a woman priest, with an Englishman priest assisting her. It seemed perfectly natural to all concerned. At breakfast, we sat by the new Dean, the American, the Very Rev. Dr. Paul Caspar, whom we had met on our earlier arrival in the Colony from England.

We had an interesting conversation with the Dean about Denham Crary.

"He is certainly one of the best preachers I have ever heard," I said. "In his forceful presentation of the Christian faith, he reminds me of Reinhold Nieburgh of thirty years ago".

After the breakfast, Greta and I visited a "Welfare Handicrafts" shop in the huge Landmark building and bought another gift for home. We then found another old friend, Mr. James Lam, in the ancient printing firm 'Ye Olde Printerie' in Duddell Street. In spite of his 72 years, he looked fairly well, if perhaps a little stiff in the back. We had a long and moving talk with him.

At the end he said: "I continue to keep my faith in Jesus, read my Bible occasionally and say my prayers".

He also knew Freddie Wong, originally through Freddie's and his own connections with the Hong Kong Morning Post Newspaper, and they had become very good friends. So, he had arranged for us all to have lunch together at the Peking Restaurant, perhaps one of Hong Kong's most prestigious restaurants, and thither we now made our way. The restaurant was beautifully decorated with red as the predominant colour, whilst the girl waitresses and attendants wore beautiful red 'cheung-saams' (the Chinese long gown). Not only did we enjoy the most delicious meal in a most leisurely manner, but all of us spent quite a refreshing and nostalgic time recalling the old days.

In the evening, Greta had been invited to visit the United Christian Hospital in Kowloon, to see two old friends – Dr. Ted and Mrs. Patterson. I was invited too, and the doctor enjoyed showing us first round his large hospital. It was very clean and seemed to work most efficiently. The ratio of medics, nurses and staff to patients was about 2:1, rather less than in England. He told us that they had a resident or visiting chaplain, internal broadcast radio services, church visitors who tour the wards, and facilities for baptism. A great proportion of the patients would not, of course, be Christians, but they were able to hear the Christian message over the radio and through ward services.

After our tiring walk around the hospital, we were more than ready to return to the doctor's quarters and to enjoy a very appetising supper.

During the meal, we recalled many memories of former days and in particular our No.3 son's amazing recovery from measles, as a small babe.

Dr. Patterson told us that he hoped to remain at the hospital until the new building was added to the old one when, possibly, he would retire. In our inspection journey round the hospital, I was interested to notice the doctor's excellent command of the Chinese language. As a modern Christian puts it:

"His word is Love, Love's his word
That's the message that I heard.
Take his hand, we are glory bound."

Jesus Christ is alive today

Chapter 25

More Close Encounters and Chasing the Sun Home

Our next interesting encounter took place the next day. We had been asked to visit and take letters from England to the Rev. Murray Rogers and his wife, friends of our good friend, Bishop Kenneth Cragg. They were now living in Shatin, having moved there, and led by the Spirit, from India. They lived in a Christian Buddhist centre called Dao Feng Shan, where Buddhist priests were welcomed to study the Christian faith. Here, Murray Rogers and his wife, Mary, with two other adults, Heather and Rosemarie, formed a community called the St. Francis Community. This is not linked with either the Anglican or the Roman Catholic Franciscans. Their community house was called St. Francis House. It was very simple in set up, almost primitive to us more sophisticated missionaries.

Murray Rogers told us that while he and his wife were CMS (Church Missionary Society) missionaries in India, they were attracted by the ashram idea. Eventually they willingly surrendered their reliance on western money, and on 'doing things' or work, and began to concentrate on their search for God experience. In 1957 the Indian Prime Minister, Mrs. Gandhi, made it difficult, even impossible, for normal missionaries, intent on making Christian disciples, to be granted visas. However, Murray and his wife (and presumably others) were looked upon as genuine God-seekers, like the Hindu religious men, and they were allowed to remain in India.

We could not but compare this with the China situation, where religion in the Chinese Communist Party's eyes, is deemed to be "superstition". More recently, since 1979/1980, the Chinese Christians have been granted a limited freedom to worship God in their churches.

Our last Sunday in the Colony was, appropriately enough, "Stir-up Sunday" because of the prayer used in all Anglican Churches all over the world, which reads:

"Stir up, O Lord, the wills of thy faithful people that they plenteously bringing forth the fruit of good works, may of thee be plenteously rewarded. Through Jesus Christ our Lord. Amen".

The day at St. Barnabas Church in Kwan Tong, where Joyce Bennett assisted, was celebrated with a special service followed by a confirmation of seven candidates, four young men, two girls and a one-legged boy, 12 years of age, crippled with cancer.

The church was crowded to the doors and the Rt. Rev. Peter Kwong took the Confirmation and preached. Following the service, they held the Anniversary Meal.

After the celebrations were over, we returned to our friend Joyce's flat for tea and supper and to prepare for our journey home to England.

Tuesday 22nd November, our departure day, duly dawned and we spent it quietly. A taxi arrived at 6.15pm and off we sped to the Kai-Tak Airport, where Joyce arrived at the same time in her little mini.

At this point, the British Airways baggage clerk, a young woman, came up and asked for our tickets and we were quickly led through the formalities.

We had two seats next to a porthole window, but since the return flight to England was almost wholly at night (as we chased the sun, so to speak) this was not especially important. At 9.10pm or 21.10 hours, we had lift off.

The flight journey was without much incident. Meals were always appetising and attractively brought and presented on trays – always more than enough and very palatable. As we crossed over Kunming in Southwest China, where my wife had been born, the plane met strong headwinds and there was some turbulence.

At Abu Dhabi the plane was delayed by an engine fault. Apparently, from information received, one of the engines in reversing on arrival, got stuck and had to be rewound back into position.

We caught up with the dawn in Rome, but although we stopped at the airport to stock up with food, the passengers were not allowed to leave the plane. However, through out porthole window we saw a little of the beauties of the great City.